Effective Therapy
for
College Students

Alternatives to
Traditional Counseling

Eugenia Hanfmann

Effective Therapy
for
College Students

 Jossey-Bass Publishers
San Francisco • Washington • London • 1978

EFFECTIVE THERAPY FOR COLLEGE STUDENTS
Alternatives to Traditional Counseling
by Eugenia Hanfmann

Copyright © 1978 by: Jossey-Bass, Inc., Publishers
433 California Street
San Francisco, California 94104
&
Jossey-Bass Limited
28 Banner Street
London EC1Y 8QE

Library of Congress Catalogue Card Number LC 78-1147

International Standard Book Number ISBN 0-87589-371-6

Manufactured in the United States of America

JACKET DESIGN BY WILLI BAUM

FIRST EDITION

Code 7814

A joint publication in
The Jossey-Bass Series
in Social and Behavioral Science
& in Higher Education

A Joint publication in
The Jossey-Bass Series
in Social and Behavioral Science
& in Higher Education

To my mother,
Katherine A. Hanfmann

Preface

This book has roots in my total professional experience—that of an academic who turned clinician while keeping her holistic and cognitive theoretical orientation. More specifically, however, it is the product of the decades I have devoted to psychological work with college students. In 1952 I joined the faculty of Brandeis University and was charged by Abraham Maslow with starting and directing a student counseling service, one that would emphasize health rather than illness. Since then my main concern—as counselor, administrator, and teacher—has been to provide college students with effective psychological assistance in their normal developmental tasks and in the resolution of emotional problems of all degrees of severity. In *Effective Therapy for College Students* I record what I have learned—greatly helped by students' feedback—about the promise and the problems of this badly neglected area of mental health work. I hope that this presentation will stimulate others to tackle the many problems that must be solved if the promise of timely psychological work with young people is ever to be fulfilled. A larger percent of emotionally mature people among the educated is a boon not to be minimized, one well worth an investment of time, thought, and money.

The bulk of the book is devoted to the conduct of various courses of counseling. In discussing the factors that further or hinder progress at different stages, I have used numerous examples—some brief, some detailed. The issues relevant to the beginning and the end stages of counseling are dealt with separately in Chapters Four, Twelve, and Thirteen. To describe with sufficient concreteness what happens during counseling, I have ordered the periods of counseling into different typical courses; in Chapters Five–Eleven each of these courses is discussed in detail. These groups are not mutually exclusive classes but impressionistic types which in part overlap or shade into each other; they yield, nevertheless, an adequate framework for the discussions of what takes place in counseling and what comes out of it. The cases used to exemplify these patterns have been selected from those I have known well, most of them my own. All or almost all of these students were seen at the time when the service was able to provide clients with the equivalent of up to one school year of weekly sessions.

The most important division of the courses of counseling is into productive ones (Chapters Five–Eight) and unproductive ones (Chapters Nine–Eleven), those that were of value for the client and those that had no value, or even produced negative effects. By incorporating this all-important aspect into my "classification" of counseling courses, I have tried to avoid the artificial distinction between "process" and "outcome." It is impossible to formulate simply and unequivocally what to do and what not to do in the course of counseling, but it pays to consider the complex events of the counseling period in conjunction with what ultimately gives them meaning: the value the student derives from their totality. I prefer the terms *productive* and *unproductive* to the more commonly used dichotomy of therapeutic successes and failures, or of positive and negative outcomes, which seem to connote static states, conditions that are absolute and final; when one talks about changes being wrought by counseling, such connotations are useless or misleading.

It is unprofitable, for example, to think of any "successful outcome" as equivalent to the final resolution of the client's personal difficulties, as his reaching a state with which he will be permanently satisfied. Even an adult person who has undergone "successful therapy" may change his attitudes in the future, or the conditions of his life may change; he may find himself facing new problems and may decide to seek help for their optimal resolution. The young people with whom we deal in counseling, unless hopelessly stuck in a neurotic blind alley, are still in the process of changing, maturing, finding, and forming themselves. Although counseling during this period can be extremely valuable, it is not guaranteed to see them through to the achievement of psychological maturity, even if the counselor and the student should be able—as they rarely are—to give unlimited time to the task. The terms I chose have a wide application: We can term "productive" all courses showing movement in the desired direction, regardless of just where the client started and how long a stretch he has traveled.

In choosing illustrative examples of productive and unproductive courses, I consulted the counselor's (usually my own) evaluation of outcomes, recorded in a written summary and in a rating (good progress, some progress, no progress), and compared it, whenever feasible, with the student's own evaluation, either recorded in a questionnaire or communicated to the counselor orally in one of the last sessions or in a follow-up visit. Most of the longer illustrative cases are those of students counseled many years ago. I have abstained from presenting the personal material one would view as confidential (it was usually irrelevant to my purposes) and have omitted or changed the external detail that might make these people recognizable to those who know them. I am grateful to the few clients in whose case neither precaution could be fully observed for giving me their permission to publish this material.

Chapters Four–Thirteen will be of interest primarily to college counselors, both beginners and experienced mental health workers, but also to therapists working with young people in other settings and to all those interested in the problems of short-term treatment. Much of the discussion bears also on the theory of therapy as such and, secondarily, on the issue of the training of therapists. In particular I have attempted to demonstrate the productiveness of the conceptions of therapy held by two original thinkers and effective practitioners, Andras Angyal and Hellmuth Kaiser, whose ideas have not had the impact on clinical work which I believe they should have had.

The second focus of the study is the relationship of the counseling center to the total college environment of which it is a part. My purpose in discussing this topic is to provide a background for identifying the policies and the administrative arrangements that are likely to maximize a counseling service's effectiveness and to promote the cause of mental health on the campus. The chapters touching on these issues (Chapters One, Two, and Three) should be of interest primarily to directors of counseling and of mental health centers and to the college administrators charged with organizing student services. The fact that I have not given as much space to environmental-organizational issues as to those of counseling proper reflects my own professional identification and should not be taken to mean that these issues are of minor importance for the design of effective and timely psychological work in our schools.

This report of college counseling is directed toward professional audiences, but it may also prove illuminating to anyone interested in the problems of young people or curious about what goes on in counseling or therapy sessions. I have kept technical language to a minimum; I find that in dealing with common human experience the use of jargon serves only too often to obscure facts and to confuse issues.

I owe a debt of gratitude to the many colleagues, at Brandeis University and elsewhere, who shared in my work of the last decades or furthered it in other ways—in particular, to Richard M. Jones and Ricardo Morant. But most of all I am grateful to my student-clients; they were my main teachers. In writing this book I benefited from the advice and encouragement of several competent consultants: Alexander J. Morin and Joseph D. Matarazzo gave theirs at an early stage, Meryl Cohen throughout. Assistance essential for preparing the book was given also by the late Gertrude Vakar and by Nina Babaian, Huldah Tracy, and Shirley Roderick. Daniel Yankelovich, as chairman of the Cambridge Center for Research in the Behavioral Sciences, helped to finance the analysis of the student questionnaire data that I carried out during a leave of absence from Brandeis. I thank the Schenkman Publishing Company, Inc., Cambridge, Massachusetts, for permission to quote and paraphrase many passages from our report on the early years of the Brandeis University Counseling Center, *Psychological Counseling in a Small College* (Hanfmann, Jones, Baker, and Kovar, 1963), and to the Viking Press, New York City, for permission to quote from Andras Angyal's *Neurosis and Treatment: A Holistic Theory* (1965; reprinted 1973).

Watertown, Massachusetts   EUGENIA HANFMANN
January 1978

Contents

The Author

EUGENIA HANFMANN, professor emerita of psychology and currently consultant to the Psychological Counseling Center at Brandeis University, is engaged in private psychotherapy practice and in supervising therapists in training. She grew up in Russia and was awarded the Ph.D. degree in psychology by the University of Jena, Germany, in 1927. In 1930 she came to the United States to be research assistant to Kurt Koffka, a prominent German psychologist and a member of the Gestalt school of psychology, who at the time was research professor at Smith College. Subsequently, Hanfmann conducted research, taught, and did clinical work at the Worcester State Hospital (1932–1939), Mount Holyoke College (1939–1946), Harvard University (in the Department of Social Relations and at the Russian Research Center, 1946–1954), and Brandeis University, where she founded and directed the Psychological Counseling Center.

In addition to numerous journal articles and monographs, Hanfmann has published (with coauthors) *Conceptual Thinking in Schizophrenia* (1942), *Psychological Counseling in a Small College* (1963), and *Six Russian Men: Lives in Turmoil* (1976). She contributed to *Assessment of Men* (1948) by the Assessment Staff of the Office of Strategic Services, edited the translation from Russian of Lev Vygotsky's *Thought and Language* (1962), and prepared for publication (with R. M. Jones) Andras Angyal's posthumous work, *Neurosis and Treatment: A Holistic Theory* (1965).

Eugenia Hanfmann resides in the Boston area. She is a member of the Appalachian Mountain Club and enjoys camping, swimming, and hiking, as well as rereading the Russian classics.

Effective Therapy for College Students

for

College Students

Alternatives to
Traditional Counseling

1

The Promise of College Counseling: A Personal Perspective

When more than twenty-five years ago I started on the job of student counseling, I felt some degree of confidence. I had been reasonably successful as a clinician in other settings and had done some therapeutic work with neurotic adults. But when, before long, some of my clients began showing unmistakable, even striking, improvement in sessions and in their daily lives, I was greatly surprised; my expectations of therapy had not been that certain or that high after all. Nor was I alone in my joy at seeing how fast and how far many counseled students were able to move. A young colleague, for example, who had professed a firm belief in psychotherapy to start with, was overwhelmed by this demonstration that it really worked; he promptly entered therapy himself. No less impressive was the

1

amazement expressed by some students about their changes in outlook—changes so far-reaching that these students now regarded
counseling as the most important enterprise of their lives.

As the years continued to bring many successes, I kept wondering why college students are generally so responsive to counseling. Is their ability to gain insight and to change rooted in some
characteristics of their developmental stage that have been over-
looked or underemphasized by our current theories? Is the college
situation as such—where knowledge and understanding are emphasized, where separation from the family is necessitated, and a
community of age-equals offered—an environment uniquely favorable to the guided pursuit of self-knowledge? Have the counselors,
in responding to the implicit demands of the clients and their situations, changed their original conceptions of what is proper in therapy
and introduced effective variations into their dealings with students?
I for one often found myself doing just that.

During the early years, I did not have much chance to
pursue these issues systematically. In addition to counseling and
teaching, I had to work out policies and administrative arrangements needed to make the center an autonomous, student-centered
service, fully accepted by students as their own. This was not easy,
since the school administrators naturally expected us—my colleagues
and me—to serve them in their dealings with students at least as
much as to serve students directly. Old-timers among them pointed
to other schools, some of them respected models, where mental
health personnel would evaluate students upon the administration's
request and where the confidentiality of the clients' communications
was not defined very clearly or observed very strictly. But I also
could point to at least one small college, where several attempts to
start a modern counseling service had ended in failure precisely
because of the administration's involvement; and at Brandeis I had
plenty of evidence from the start that effective safeguards of confidentiality and autonomy from administration's demands were pre-
conditions for obtaining the students' trust.

We were ultimately successful in obtaining conditions optimally favorable to our work because, first and foremost, the competent service rendered to students by a devoted core staff was
genuinely appreciated by the many who benefited; within two or

three years the center acquired a very good reputation among students and those who were in close touch with them and with their problems. This development would hardly have come about, however, if simultaneously we had not been acquiring better safeguards of confidentiality and more staff, since—even with capable counselors—favorable campus opinion cannot flourish if too few students come and are not given enough time when they do come. Again, to persuade an administration to grant the conditions necessary for a successful counseling program, the person in charge must have some sources of prestige and support, both inside and outside the school. In our case this condition was amply fulfilled. The center's original sponsor effectively backed our demands for autonomy and defended the service's nonmedical orientation against criticisms by members of the medical profession. Moreover, the school was young, its formal structure minimal and plastic; it had as yet no developed bureaucracy and no set traditions to place insurmountable obstacles in the path of novel enterprises, so that problems could be brought up and settled in face-to-face meetings with key people. My own position with the faculty of the school was a favorable one; being acceptable as a scholar and a colleague, I was forgiven for being a clinician. A teacher might rail against psychoanalysis yet would not try to dissuade his students from seeing me. I also had the influential support of a visiting committee composed of distinguished local psychiatrists who were interested in education. By convincing the administration that our requests were professionally sound, they helped to overcome the school's initial resistance against certain safeguards of confidentiality. Finally, the dean of students was greatly concerned about student welfare and fully understood and appreciated our work. He realized that to keep up the quality of the center's work two conditions had to be fulfilled: first, a large proportion of the staff had to be permanent or at least not subject to quick turnover; second, the total staff had to grow proportionately to the growth of the student body. During the years when the university grew steadily but slowly, he saw to it that our budget enabled us to maintain high staff-student ratios without having recourse to the work of trainees, who usually leave just when they start being useful. I, on my part, managed the resources carefully. In calculating the amount of staff time needed for a given year, I based my estimate on the periods of average demand on the service rather than the seasonal "highs." As a result, all counselors were fully occupied most of the time; at times some of them contributed extra hours, with or without extra pay. The dean made funds available to meet the peak demands; if our own staff resources were insufficient, I called in some well-recommended outsiders to take the overflow for a moderate hourly fee.

To determine and to maintain the staff-student ratio needed for efficacy seemed to me to be merely common sense at the time, as indeed it was and still is. I found out only later that the situation at Brandeis was a happy exception; even before the present financial crisis hit the schools, very few college mental health services formulated and defended this principle, to say nothing of being able to implement it. As a result, few schools have been equipped to maintain the high counselor-student ratios that are required if a counseling center is to become and to remain an effective community service, not just a source of help for a select few.

By the end of the first decade of the center's existence, all crucial issues had been resolved, and reasonable arrangements acceptable to all concerned had been worked out. From the start, we had had a de facto connection with the department of psychology, which at that time had a strong clinical section; this tie was formalized when the counseling center was transferred from the jurisdiction of an administrative dean (dean of students) to that of the academic dean (dean of the faculty). Since the dean of the faculty is not concerned with individual students or disciplinary matters, the center after the transfer was under less pressure for questionable cooperation with the school authorities, or at least the pressures were not coming from our administrative superiors. All subsequent deans honored our promise to the students that counseling sessions would be kept confidential and agreed that no staff member would be required to participate in any committees, or any administrative decisions, dealing with individual students. Concerned administrators and faculty members learned when and how to mention counseling to troubled students, leaving it up to them to act on the hint. They also learned how to obtain consultation about problem students without asking whether these students had been seen at the center. This full acceptance by the school of the center's policies and practices enabled us to assure the students that the content of their communications, and even the fact of their having been counseled, would not be divulged to anyone outside the center's staff.

In addition to allowing us greater freedom from administrative pressures, the center's administrative connection with the department of psychology strengthened our link with education and simplified the task of staffing the service, a task that presented some special problems. The rewarding work and the congenial, high-morale atmosphere of the center were great attractions to clinical psychologists, as was the long summer vacation; yet the pay was moderate, the work itself was not especially varied, and there was no possibility of promotion. Under these conditions, people who wanted to work at the center half time proved to be a good bet: mothers of families, graduate students who had finished their clinical training and were struggling with their Ph.D. theses, young Ph.D.s who had part-time jobs elsewhere. Such people often spent several years at the center, and many became in effect permanent staff, but their contracts had to be renewed each year and they missed having a closer connection with the school as a whole. With the center's transfer into the academic jurisdiction it became possible to provide such a connection for some. The dean of the faculty helped to work out arrangements that enabled us to attract highly qualified clinical psychologists; if fully acceptable to the department, they could be provided with a teaching position carrying full academic status. In this way the center acquired the services of some gifted counselors who were also excellent teachers and researchers; being highly regarded by students, they were effective spokesmen for the center. They also helped to extend the scope of the mental health work on campus by experimenting with novel approaches. One of them added group work to our program; another successfully implemented in his classroom teaching Lawrence Kubie's idea (1954) that true assimilative learning requires the participation of the preconscious (Jones, 1966, 1968). These counselor-teachers greatly contributed to the students' growing understanding that "psych counseling" is not simply a method to spot and treat maladjustments but is a special part of the total educational enterprise, from which most students, no matter how "well adjusted" or "mature," can benefit.

The center's relationship to the school's health office presented some problems during the initial years, partly because its director strongly agreed with the American Medical Association that the best place for a mental health service was in his department, partly because the physicians were concerned that the psychologists might fail to notice and identify the medical (physical) problems of their counselees. We had to agree to send for a medical checkup all students who decided after the initial trial period to continue counseling: an arrangement both cumbersome and ineffective. The center's own psychiatric consultant, selected for his established effectiveness as therapist and teacher, provided supervision to the junior staff members and consultation on difficult cases to others; but he spent no time on campus and did not see students himself. The physicians' misgivings were eventually met when a part-time psychiatrist was added to the staff of the health office; since he was neither a member nor the boss of the center's staff, our collaboration was problem-centered and unproblematic. The psychiatrist, in functioning as a liaison between the health office and the center, worked out effective streamlined methods of insuring proper attention to the medical aspects of the students' problems. He also established policies and practices for working with a small but important minority: those students who became seriously disturbed, requiring consultations with school authorities and families and in some cases hospitalization. Both he and his successor participated in our staff meetings and became our valued collaborators and colleagues; they were also instrumental in making the college infirmary a useful temporary refuge for the acutely upset students. Thus, our dual system worked smoothly.

As the organizational problems were being resolved and our staff grew, more and more students utilized the service. The absolute number of students seen during the school years almost tripled during the first decade; their percentage doubled (from 8 percent to 16 percent) and continued to grow. The average length of the counseling period also grew steadily. During the period when the ratio of full-time counselors to students in school was at its highest (1:350), more than 20 percent of the students in school were seen at the center yearly; the average length of the counseling period, which had been four sessions to start with, rose to eleven sessions.

We were able to guarantee a school year of weekly sessions, about thirty, to "all those who need it and can use it"; more than one-fourth of the students who came were seen for more than fifteen sessions. The large majority of those who came—from 80 percent to 90 percent in different years—were self-referred, often with the encouragement of friends. The service's visibility and reputation were reliably good. A questionnaire returned by 40 percent of the graduating class in 1966 indicated that 90 percent of the respondents had learned about the center's existence in their freshman year; most of them had heard exclusively or predominantly positive things about the service. These data and the accompanying student comments confirmed our impression that students had indeed accepted the service as theirs to use, as a natural part of the college scene. The following description reflects changes in the students' perception of the center that took place in the course of a few years.

> At first there seemed to be an air of mystery surrounding the center; I had assumed that you really had to have a big psychic disorder to go, and I even attached some sort of stigma to the whole idea. During the last few years I have heard not terribly much more about the center, but the conversation seems to have changed in character; psych counseling seems to be accepted as a useful service—even at times the "cool" thing to do. I was surprised at the number of my friends who had been there at least once.

Students were not the only ones to change their attitude toward counseling; the attitudes of the counselors were also undergoing changes. Given the clinicians' training and experience, their initial focus was on the clients' unconscious dynamics. A counselor might abstain from asking for fantasies and dreams but would view the student's report of his daily doings and problems primarily as material for uncovering his personal pattern or for facilitating expression of feelings. It was not our job, some counselors felt, to concern ourselves with the client's normal realistic problems as such; that kind of guidance was available from other campus advisers. Yet the "normal problems" were often urgent, and some students had to make vital decisions before their personal dynamics could be fully elucidated. The counselors soon found themselves engaging in realistic problem solving with some students, while following others in their self-explorations as far and as deep as they seemed prepared to go. Our growing willingness and ability to meet our clients' diverse needs and demands must have been a factor in the students' growing acceptance of the service. They felt that they could approach us without having to worry about their problems being too small or too big for the center.

Another important shift of attitude took place during these years. We started perceiving therapeutic opportunities in the features of college life which, to start with, we had viewed merely as obstructions. School vacations, terminations forced by academic failure, and gossip about the center among the students could all be dealt with in a productive way. We also learned to pay close attention to the people and the circumstances that are highly significant for the student because of their relevance to the developmental tasks of adolescence. The student's current interactions with parents, school authorities, and other students can function not only as material for pinpointing his problems and immaturities, his dependence or his resentments, but also as reorienting experiences. When well prepared, these experiences can make a strong impact and aid the young person in establishing himself as an adult, no longer merely the child of his parents. Having left home for a residential college, a student often gains new perspectives on the issues and the people left behind; after these have been discussed in counseling, most students start using their visits home for reappraisals and reorientation. The outcomes vary. Sometimes a fresh look at the interactions of the members of his family, including himself, enables the student to discover and to oppose an entanglement fostered by neurotic parents, who may bribe the adolescent to remain dependent, or stir up and exploit his guilt feelings. In other cases, when the student takes active steps to test his assumptions about his parents, he finds them surprisingly human and more understanding than he had given them credit for being. When he takes courage to face them with his secret grievances, or to ask them, at termination of counseling, to finance his therapy outside the school, these actions may lead to increased strife, but some parents will respond to the student's new frankness in kind, and a chain reaction of emotional growth will result. To give one example for many: A student imagined that her brilliant father would never believe that she had problems. After she had explored her own disappointment in herself, she timidly told him that she had been seeing a counselor. She was amazed to learn that he was aware of her problems but had felt hesitant to discuss them and was pleased with the initiative she had taken in seeking help.

Positive or negative, these novel interactions are vital, full-bodied experiences for the student, very different from mere unchecked fantasies about his family or from pale intellectual insights; and they often result in conviction and action. A young person who for a long time has been stuck in some blind alley may quickly change his pattern of behavior once an alternative has been brought home to him through some vital new experience. The source of such experiences is not limited to interactions with parents, the actors in the original interpersonal drama. Teachers and other school authorities have an intrinsic appeal for students as persons on whom old attitudes and skills can be tested and with whom new ones can be tried out. All counselors eventually came across instances of the dynamic leverage of these "here-and-now" interactions and of their reeducative value. One girl, for instance, could not participate in class discussions and was also afraid to seek individual conferences with her teachers. Although the counselor, in working with her, was able to trace her covert expectations of ridicule and rejection—expectations also manifested in her attitude toward the counselor—to childhood experiences, the girl still made no visible therapeutic gains. Then one day, in the midst of an academic crisis, a conference with one of her teachers—carefully planned in the counseling session—brought the unrealistic nature of her expectations so clearly into focus that she began to face seriously for the first time her own self-defeating tendencies.

The shift of attitude does not always benefit the student's academic performance as it did in this case. When mobilized for an important personality change—for instance, for discarding his conformity or overdocility—the student may have to sacrifice some aspect of his current academic success. This may also arouse a conflict within the counselor, who shares some of the values of the academic community. In a service aiming to further the student's total personal development, however, the ultimate criterion of therapeutic success cannot be identical with any segmental one, such as good grades. Fortunately for the counselor, he is not the one who has to make the choice.

Incidentally, if one wishes to keep the counselor-student relationship free of all adventitious conflicts, one will avoid assigning a student to a counselor who is currently also his teacher: "We have learned through making exceptions to this procedure that . . . the counseling has unpredictable effects on the course work. One student was unable to complete written assignments for the first six weeks of a semester due to misplaced resistance. . . . Even when the course work is not directly impaired, the necessity of assigning grades to clients creates a sticky problem. A 'B', for example, comes unconsciously to mean not only that one *was* a 'B' student in Psychology 15a, say, but that one *is* a grade 'B' *person*. This problem is best solved by avoiding it" (Hanfmann and others, 1963, p. 80). This policy creates no difficulties if the staff is large or if only a few staff members are teachers; students who want them for counselors can arrange to take their courses at another time.

As mentioned, a student's peers also play a role in the process of counseling. This role is particularly noticeable when the student population is small and a large proportion comes for counseling. In this case it pays to check on the new applicant's friends in counseling, so as to avoid the complications that often arise when two close friends—or rivals or enemies—find themselves sharing a therapist. When this happens unavoidably, one does of course try to improvise ways to deal with the difficulties productively. The following case is that of a student who actively sought out the "overlap" situation.

A senior girl, in applying for counseling with a particular staff member, concealed the identity of her fiancé, whom this counselor had formerly seen and advised to seek treatment. She presented her engagement as unproblematic and concentrated on her feelings toward her family; gradually she became more accepting of them and was able to introduce her fiancé and obtain her parents' consent to an early marriage. After that her productions in sessions became vague and repetitive, and the counselor's comments precipitated an inner conflict about stopping or moving ahead. This conflict was solved as if by a deus ex machina, when at a student party the counselor became aware of the fiancé's identity. The girl then confessed her panic about her impending marriage to a man who—as both she and the counselor knew—was not ready for a real commitment. She accepted a referral to a private therapist, with whom she could continue after graduation, while her fiancé also made plans for therapy. Marriage was postponed and took place a year later.

This girl's conscious reason for concealment was the fear that if the truth were known she would be assigned to a different counselor, but this very determination to work with one who knew her boy friend probably sprang from her conflict about her marriage plans. Since she knew that chances of being "found out" were high, and practically invited discovery on the given occasion, it seems likely that she had wished for just this outcome, whereby her misgivings came to light without her having been guilty of any disloyalty to the boy.

The most important consequence of our clients' belonging to an interacting closed community is the high degree of communication among them. Unlike most people seen individually in outpatient clinics or in therapists' private offices, students can and do share their experiences of counseling, at least up to a point, and this results in the formation of campus opinion both about the service as such and about individual counselors. This publicity can cause trouble when some unfortunate incident occurs or some unfavorable rumors travel around; once the service has earned a reputation for competence and integrity, however, the advantages of communication among clients greatly outweigh any temporary disadvantages. Even before the advent of group therapy, many counseled students succeeded in confirming and enlarging their insights by sharing them with friends. Students also commonly apply for counseling with a staff member who did well with a friend. If this wish is honored, the student can start on this novel project with some confidence: It has worked with others, so it can work with him. "Several friends," one student told me, "have mentioned that they were considering going to counseling; they seemed quite reassured and interested that I had found counseling helpful." The counseled students who are satisfied with the experience and its outcome become not only effective referral agents but also a great help in emergencies; many disturbed or suicidal students have reached the center through the active and ingenious efforts of friends.

To return to the staff members' conduct of counseling: Although we were aware that our proceedings were changing, I doubt whether any of us realized at the time that some of our innovations implied also a changing conception of what is effective in therapy. Psychoanalysis had been the most important influence in almost all the counselors' backgrounds; we used its terminology in our discussions, assumed that insight is *the* curative agent, and spoke of transference without attempting to identify the different roots of the client's attitudes toward the counselor. Yet, from the vantage point of my present thinking about therapy, I see that the experience of working with students not only had made me more optimistic but was imperceptibly changing my other assumptions as well. In realizing how important for the outcome was the impact of vital reorienting experiences arising out of contemporary interactions with significant people, and in seeking to facilitate them, I was, in fact, departing from several traditional conceptions, including those of the nature and use of "transference." Yet, if asked at that time to define the therapist's proper role, I would still have invoked the benevolently impassive observer—part screen on which to project fantasies, part provider of insights or reflector of feelings. Probably that is why I was blind at the time to the obvious fact that the student's interaction with the counselor is potentially as promising a source of reorienting experiences as any. Such obtuseness is particularly striking because, as far back as the 1940s, I had been much impressed by what Alexander and French had to say in *Psychoanalytic Therapy* (1946) about the importance of corrective experiences in and out of sessions. Actually, my behavior in sessions no longer conformed to my definitions, but I did not put two and two together until much later. To borrow the formulation from one incredulous student reporting striking changes in his behavior, my self-concept lagged behind my performance.

All in all, the developments during the first decade of counseling at Brandeis created an effective pattern of mutual adaptation between the school environment and the counseling process. To my mind, these developments also confirm the proposition that the college years present a unique opportunity for effective psychological work. Our experience indicates that—given capable and open-minded staff, effective safeguards of confidentiality, and an adequate salary budget—this work can be carried out on a scale large enough to have an impact on the future fates of a large number of graduates. (If the student participation in counseling could be maintained at the high level we reached in the peak years, a large proportion of each graduating class, possibly 50–60 percent, would have had some contact with the center.) Only 10–20 percent of the students we counseled yearly showed a degree of disturbance rated by us as severe enough, perhaps, to bring them sooner or later to a psychiatrist's attention. Most of our work was done with students who did not consider their problems extraordinary and whose suffering was not intense at the time, though for many of them neurotic development was clearly in the cards. These students, who often used counseling to great advantage, would not have sought professional help if it had not been made easily available and socially acceptable. If such conditions could be duplicated on a large scale, college counseling could have a function transcending by far the goals of the academic institutions it is supposed to subserve. By aiding emotional maturation when it is still an ongoing process, and by reducing the incidence of the "character neuroses" responsible for so much misery and inefficiency in our culture, it might raise the level of mental health of an influential sector of our adult population.

The second decade of my work at Brandeis was very different from the first decade, when relative stability and continuity had marked the development of both the school and the counseling service. For one thing, the student body was permitted to grow more rapidly than before, and the characteristics of a small pioneering school were gradually lost. Given the faculty's research orientation, the amount of student-faculty contact diminished drastically, greatly increasing the importance of the counseling service for the students. One student, in writing to his counselor, gave an articulate description of this situation: "Personal attention is a luxury unavailable to the average student. To the registrar I am a transcript photostat, to my adviser I am a cream-colored Final Study card; to most professors I am a scrawling hand and an occasionally open mouth. . . .

The center provides what is much needed: it sponsors a humanization of the education process." Another expressed the same feeling succinctly: "Counseling is one of the few things at Brandeis that remembers that students are people." As the 1960s rolled on, more and more students turned to the service for the express purpose of establishing contact with an adult "who knows you are there and cares what happens to you." Yet we were less and less confident of being able to fulfill these needs, of being allowed to increase the counseling staff so as to keep pace with the fast-growing student body. In the late 1960s and early 1970s the financial pressures at Brandeis, as at many other private schools, became severe, necessitating increasingly stringent economy measures.

Moreover, the student ferment of the 1960s did not bypass Brandeis. Student attitudes were changing, as were sexual mores; under student pressure, rules regulating campus conduct were liberalized. Drugs became a problem which stayed with us for several years. There was a period of political activism; in one episode black students, who for the first time were being admitted in larger numbers, supported their demands by taking over a school building. The crisis was resolved without violence, but it shook up and polarized the college community. Other groups that felt discriminated against—women, homosexuals—were also becoming vocal. The students' new values, stressing freedom and spontaneity, found reflection in their attitude toward therapy. The prestige of psychoanalysis was waning. Students were eager to explore new techniques, some of which were being taught on campus, formally or informally. Group work of different types became available outside the center. At the center itself the younger staff members, having received some training in new approaches, were eager to apply them and to proselytize.

These developments presented the center with new tasks and new challenges. Old issues, such as confidentiality, had to be rethought in the light of new problems, such as the use and sale of drugs. One had to find a course that would avoid the pitfalls of countenancing something illegal and possibly harmful, on the one hand, and of alienating students by being or sounding moralistic, on the other. The counselors, particularly the older ones, had to come to terms with the students' changed attitudes and behavior and to make up their own minds about various issues that their clients regarded as crucial. Some staff members drastically changed their views on what was to be considered "normal" for today's students. Other counselors, including myself, did not need to reconsider the basic assumptions underlying their work, since, in their conception of emotional disturbance, deviation from established societal norms had never played a major part. All of us, however, felt called upon to find ways to respond usefully to the students' new beliefs and demands, learning to separate the wheat from the chaff. Obviously, the content of an ideology does not unequivocally determine its function for a given person or at a given time. Self-expression, an increase in one's individual autonomy and power, is as basic a human need as the need to love and belong; yet, like yesterday's dominant ideology of commitment to persons and tasks, the ideology of spontaneity and freedom can either be a genuinely integrative force in one's life or it can be subverted to serve neurotic purposes—in this case, often that of noncommitment.

The one event of the second decade that had the greatest impact on the fate of the counseling center was the change of its administrative connection and its leadership. In 1965 President Sachar transferred the counseling center to the university's health office and appointed as director a local analyst who was well regarded in the community. He in turn added two half-time psychiatrists to the staff of the center; the amount of psychiatrists' time used by the school increased at least fourfold. The reason given for this move was the need to take care of the severely or acutely disturbed students, whose absolute number was growing steadily with the growth of the student body though their proportion among our clients remained constant. The president made no criticism of the center; in fact, he acknowledged its reputation for excellence and our ability to attract and counsel large numbers of students. The change, then, was not intended to abridge or modify our work but merely to add to it a new dimension, that of extensive psychiatric care.

This matter having been settled, the main concern of the old staff was to safeguard the conditions which we believed had been responsible for making the service uniquely effective with students. Fortunately, our new colleagues were men of good will, personally congenial and respected by the staff, who fully appreciated the personal distress their arrival had caused some of us, if not our less personal reasons for alarm. Their experience of college mental health work had been acquired in the typical setting of a minimal facility, where the psychiatrist could usually do no more than evaluate the student's case and try to refer him elsewhere for help. They were impressed with the scope of our operation and eager to preserve the positive image of the center, which might be threatened by change; it was already rumored among the students that psychiatrists were being brought in because they were more willing than the old staff had been to do the administration's bidding. These apprehensions were quickly allayed; the old and the new staff were in full agreement on confidentiality and even worked out together some new safeguards of it. What proved difficult for our new colleagues to accept was the absence of formal intake interviews, intake conferences, and psychological tests. The latter we had discarded when some early experimentation convinced all of us that talking to a student for an hour was as a rule much more informative than giving him or her tests and was a much better introduction to counseling. Unless the student requested a particular counselor, he was assigned to one of those whose schedule of free hours fitted his. This counselor would continue working with him, unless either he or the student found some reason for a transfer to another staff member. Whenever problematic situations arose in the course of counseling, it was up to the counselor to seek help from his colleagues, individually or in staff meetings. These flexible and informal arrangements took a minimum of the staff's time, and they placed no barriers in the path of the student approaching the center: no waiting lists, no evaluation or testing sessions, no questionnaires to fill out, no waiting for the staff's decision and for an assignment to a counselor—in brief, no routines to slow things down and to make the client feel like an object rather than an agent of the enterprise he was embarking on. The obvious advantages of easy access to the center and the weight of the old staff's opinion made the new director accept our policies (although growing waiting lists soon made evaluation sessions necessary for identifying those whose problems were urgent). We were thus able to preserve our essential policies and most of our practices.

The change of leadership resulted nevertheless in some serious disadvantages for our work, apart from the temporary tensions and conflicts which usually accompany changes arbitrarily imposed from outside. Accustomed to older clientele in their private practice and not having had our years of experience with students, the newcomers did not share the optimism of the old staff about what one could hope to achieve in a relatively short time. The students, unavoidably, sensed this. I remember one student who, in refusing further contact with one of the new staff members, stated positively: "Dr. X does not expect much of me." He did not know that Dr. X had in fact predicted in a staff conference that within three years this student would commit suicide, a prediction which proved false. Ironically, this diagnostic pessimism worked to the greatest disadvantage of precisely those who were supposed to benefit most from the strengthening of the psychiatric sector—the seriously disturbed. Recognizing the presence of pathology and assuming a need for long-term treatment, the psychiatrists tried to refer such students quickly to private practitioners or to outpatient clinics, disregarding their lack of preparedness. More often than not, this hasty attempt miscarried; it merely frightened the student badly and caused him and his friends to keep away from the center, with such comments as "We are too sick for them" or "When he heard my symptoms, he dropped me like a hot potato." Some of these students found their way to clinicians in the psychology department and did well with them. None of this helped the center's reputation. Quite some time passed before our psychiatric colleagues became better attuned to the students' expectations and to the opportunities inherent in the college environment. They learned, as we had before them, that one cannot force referrals but, instead, can devise ways of working with, or at least keeping in touch with, disturbed students; one can mobilize many supports available to them on campus while working toward an effective referral.

The greatest long-term damage caused by the reorganization was its contribution to the loss of staff time available for counseling—a commodity without which the best policies and the most competent counselors are of little avail. In part this effect was direct and foreseen. Having highly paid psychiatrists do the work previously done by psychologists led to a spectacular increase in the center's budget without a commensurate increase in the time available for students. Obviously, the change to an expensive medical model was only one of the causes of the center's financial troubles. Our budget was bound to be examined and trimmed when in the mid 1970s the school embarked on a course of stringent economy, but we might have been considerably ahead if we had not had forced upon us at a most inopportune moment an extravagant organizational pattern conspicuous in a small school even in times of affluence (a pattern which could not and did not survive the years of the school's financial crisis). My successor also cut down the staff time available to students by defining full-time work as thirty hours a week instead of forty and by allocating much more time to supervision and to various other meetings. My own policy had been to keep the obligatory supervision to a minimum, limiting it to the newcomer's first year at the center; the task was assigned to the center's consultant, an outsider who did not himself treat students and who had nothing to do with hiring and firing staff or recommending salary raises. I adopted these policies mainly because I wanted to save time for working with students, but I also wanted to avoid authoritarian entanglements, to leave the new counselor the initiative in asking a colleague of his or her choice for additional help, and to prevent supervision (a poor term to my mind) from becoming routinized. In addition, I felt that the new counselor's best teachers were his clients; when asked by novices for help, I would try to provide it, but I would also try to direct them to this source. My successor, who felt he should know all that was going on, had standing individual appointments with all counselors and also introduced weekly meetings in groups. These meetings, devoted to group supervision or group consultation, met the staff's need to share experiences with colleagues and were obviously a useful innovation. Other types of meetings, however, did not seem to me to justify the time spent. Listening to some mildly interesting talk by a visiting lecturer, I could not help figuring how many students could have been seen by the staff during that hour and gotten off the waiting lists.

As a result of these changes of routine, even less time was actually available for counseling than would be indicated by the changing staff-student ratios (in which, to assure comparability, we continued to count forty weekly hours as equivalent to one full-time counselor). This ratio sank from 1:400 in 1962 to 1:800 in 1972. Deterred by the long waiting and by rumors of rush and in-attention, the students stayed away from the service. The proportion of those applying for counseling kept decreasing: 20 percent in 1962; 14 percent in 1972. The reputation of the center on campus took a plunge. Those who did apply and waited their turn could not be given as much time as before; the maximum time offered was reduced from thirty to twenty-five sessions, then to twenty, then to fifteen; the actual average number of sessions per student sank from ten in 1962 to seven in 1972. Complaints about premature termination multiplied. One did what one could to remedy the situation. Trainees from psychiatric and counseling programs were brought in, and group therapy work was expanded. In the hands of those who were proficient at it, group work proved quite effective, though it seemed to many that for good results it had to be com-bined with at least a minimum of individual work. Since I observed the developments of these years closely and reviewed the pertinent statistics, I can say with assurance that the loss of time available for counseling is a snowballing factor leading to a deterioration, not just a quantitative reduction, of counseling work in a college. This factor more than any other has contributed to the loss of our service's previously high potential for developing and maintaining an effective comprehensive mental health program on campus. I shall return to this issue in the second chapter.

Distressing as most of these developments were, eventually I was able to make some use of them for formulating my own thoughts about counseling. First, freedom from administrative work, if not from related worries, gave me time to review the material I had accumulated over the years—material pertinent both to the running of the service and to the counseling process as such. Second, the developments of these years resulted in a wider range of phenomena confronting me in both of these areas. We now had psychiatrists on the staff whose psychoanalytic approach to therapy had not been modified by years of college work; we also had young staff members and interns, some of whom were advocating, discussing, and trying out novel approaches. Reports by students and letters from former counselees were telling of clear-cut therapeutic successes achieved through methods other than the traditional: Synanon games, Gestalt therapy exercises, psychomotor techniques. Overall, there was richer, more varied material on therapeutic interventions to be compared and contrasted; in the often heated staff discussions of our differences, the assumptions underlying them became more apparent. Were it not for the experiment unwittingly initiated by the president and perpetuated by the financial squeeze, I would never have become so explicitly aware of the specific effects of a variety of factors on the students and on their interaction with the counselors—factors such as the staff's attitudes, the length of waiting lists, the selection and rejection of clients, and the consequences of haste in deciding on "disposition" and in making referrals. Finally, my wish to correct at least some of our shortcomings became one more motive for writing this book.

Some developments of the second decade furthered my informal research enterprise in a more direct fashion than those described above. First of all, I took steps to insure a more systematic student feedback, instead of assuming that such feedback would reach us on matters of importance to the campus. I was becoming impressed by the acuity of the comments that students made to their counselors in sessions or in post counseling letters or, occasionally, to the director when requesting a change of counselor. I found this feedback so useful, in clarifying to myself and to others some of the reasons for our successes and failures, that I decided to try to obtain it on a larger scale. After some experimentation, I worked out a simple questionnaire which, since 1966, has been mailed routinely to all students counseled during the given school year. They are asked to indicate to what degree counseling has been helpful, or not helpful, and to comment on their "experience in counseling, both its positive and negative aspects." The students are not required to sign the questionnaire, but the majority do.

I have not attempted to use the questionnaires accumulated over the years as material for systematic research—partly because of lack of means, partly because the value of such a study would be limited by the fact that the questionnaires are rarely returned by more than 50 percent of the students to whom they are sent. We did compile the statistics of evaluations of outcomes each year for whatever information or comfort they could give us. For example, during the years when our reputation on campus was at its lowest, it was reassuring to know that, of those respondents who did get counseled, the usual 75–80 percent felt that they had benefited. We also occasionally culled from the students' free comments those that we hoped might serve a useful purpose in dealing with the administrators—those, for instance, praising the service as a source of personal concern otherwise missing on campus, or those complaining about the waiting lists and the deterioration of counseling caused by lack of time and the resulting hurry. The questionnaire's primary function, however, has been to educate the counselors. The name of the counselor who has seen the given student is filled in before the blanks are sent out, so that all replies, signed or unsigned, can be delivered to the right address. Ordinarily the counselor is the only one who reads the comments of his counselees, though he is free to show them to others. When it comes to pinpointing those aspects of the counselor's performance, whether good or bad, that he himself is not fully aware of, this source of information is second to none; some counselors have been able to make very productive use of it (Bader, 1974). These questionnaire comments have often provided a very useful complement to my own record of the course of counseling and sometimes made it appear in a different light.

Last I want to mention some developments in the theoretical underpinning of the counseling work done at the center. During my second decade at Brandeis, I and some of my colleagues made more and more active and productive use of guidelines to therapy formulated by Andras Angyal, the center's first psychiatric consultant. In 1941 Angyal—who had both psychological and medical training—published *Foundations for a Science of Personality*, a work viewed today as an original early version of systems theory and of the humanistic conception of the nature of man. After many years of therapeutic work with neurotics, Angyal had developed a comprehensive theory of neurosis and therapy—a theory that incorporated many insights of psychoanalysis but reordered them, together with Angyal's own keen clinical observations, within the holistic conceptual framework he had previously developed. Richard Jones and I learned of Angyal's theory of treatment in the seminars he gave at Harvard in the early 1950s and were greatly impressed by it; subsequently, I asked him to supervise the work of our new counselors and to provide occasional consultations to others. At that time Angyal was working on the manuscript of his second book, but it was far from completed when he died in 1960; to Jones and to me fell the task of organizing his material for publication as a book, entitled *Neurosis and Treatment: A Holistic Theory* (1965).

I had been familiar for some time with Angyal's theories and practices, but in working on his manuscripts I realized that my understanding of them had been shallow. Angyal's system is deceptively simple; many of its theoretical and practical implications do not become obvious at first glance. But when I started thinking them through, I quickly discovered that his formulations were congruent with what I had learned, in a rather inarticulate way, in my years of working with students. Since my preclinical days I have shared the Gestaltists' view that every item of our personal world receives its meaning from its context; and I have never completely trusted any advice "always" to do this or "never" to do that—in therapy as elsewhere. Yet this holistic tenet did not become a vital factor in my conduct of therapy until my counselees, in obstinately failing to confirm my most plausible predictions, provided me with exceptions to all therapeutic rules I had ever heard of. Angyal's holistic concepts, freshly thought through, accommodated much of what I had learned earlier and provided me with flexible guidelines to be implemented differently in different circumstances. After *Neurosis and Treatment* had been enthusiastically received by students in courses, I started, experimentally, bringing the book to the attention of some counselees. Many a student's thinking was stimulated by this reading, and progress speeded up as a result. Student after student expressed his astonishment at Angyal's insight into his "unique" individual problem, or his gratification at having had a book written about himself.

The convergence of my own counseling experience with the tenets of Angyal's holistic theory resulted in several interrelated shifts in my conduct of therapy. I began to place emphasis on elucidating the pattern of general trends as they shape the person's life *now,* rather than on their early origins; on *vital emotional experiences* rather than detached insights; on the *real, not the transferred,* aspects of the client-therapist relationship; on letting the neurotic patient experience fully his predicament, *the bankruptcy of his ways,* rather than viewing his condition in a detached fashion; and a particularly strong emphasis on discovering and developing the person's *healthy patterns,* formed by all that was right in his early and later life and distorted or suppressed by the neurotic developments. According to Angyal's theory of "universal ambiguity," health and neurosis are present in *everyone* as two mutually exclusive ways of organizing experience and action. One organization is governed by realistic confidence; the other, by pessimism and doubt, a residue of traumatic experiences. The goal of therapy is to ensure a secure dominance of the system of health. Accordingly, the therapeutic task has two aspects: that of uncovering and demolishing neurosis and that of uncovering and fostering health; to be fully effective, these tasks must be performed in conjunction with one another.

Angyal's system is best learned from his own presentation. Here I want only to mention briefly some advantages of using his concepts in therapeutic work, both in thinking about therapy and in practicing it. Within the holistic frame of reference, a place can be assigned to a great many therapeutic factors which, seen superficially, seem to be disconnected or even mutually exclusive. At a time when new approaches to therapy proliferate, the possibility of ordering them and clarifying their interrelationship is a real boon; it dispels and counteracts confusion. What is more, Angyal's basic concepts facilitate the conversation between clients and therapists, not only that between therapists. General as these concepts are, they are lucidly elaborated and are congruent with the commonsense concepts of "naive psychology" (Heider, 1958). Being readily grasped and confirmed by clients (who do not feel mystified by them), Angyal's descriptions of neurotic patterns and of typical courses of treatment provide excellent leverage for therapeutically effective dialogues. Finally, the concepts used by Angyal are acceptable to the patient not only because they are close to his experience but also because they do not disparage this experience or the patient himself. Angyal views neurotic trends as twisted, ineffective methods of pursuing the common human goals of mastery and participation; such methods are based on unformulated false beliefs generalized from early traumatic experiences. Thus, Angyal squarely replaces all concepts connoting some basic ill or deficit in the person with the concept of an understandable error. By doing this, he avoids the very real danger of undermining the neurotic's tenuous self-respect and of confirming his secret belief that he has some basic flaw, possibly inborn but anyway unalterable. In looking back to the beginning of counseling, one of my counselees wrote a year later:

> I remember presenting to you a biological theory, self-concocted, to account for my predicament. I now see it as a good metaphor for the way I saw my situation at that time, expressing an assessment of my basic self as worthless, and also expressing the futility I felt after five or six unsuccessful attempts with therapy; it was beyond anything I could possibly do.

Unlike the idea of a basic flaw, Angyal's concepts have a double reference: to the error or the distortion that is proving so damaging to the person, and to what one gradually infers about his nonneurotic personality makeup, his individual patterns of health suppressed by neurosis. As shown by the student comments that follow, such concepts are well adapted to the performance of the double therapeutic task: "Counseling has helped me to understand and differentiate health and neurosis; it reduced my fear that I was *all* sick." "In my earlier psychotherapy I had come to define myself through my problems and weaknesses, my illness. Now I see myself in my strengths—and also in my difficulties, which now seem surmountable."

Angyal was not the only thinker whose ideas had a great impact on my later work. Hellmuth Kaiser's description of his odyssey in his book *Effective Psychotherapy* (1965) was also an eye-opener to me. I find it impossible to give the reader an idea of the content of this unusual book, written in the form of a fictionalized autobiography. It is sufficient to say that some of the discoveries Kaiser made in the course of his unremitting search for effectiveness in his work helped me to make my interaction with my counselees a much more useful therapeutic tool than it had been before. Still, I believe that my work has improved in the past decade mainly because I have learned how to implement Angyal's idea of the dual therapeutic task. Interventions aimed at undermining neurosis must be complemented and balanced by those aimed at uncovering and furthering the healthy self behind the neurosis. Then and only then will the client see that the "undermining" interventions are actually also serving the healthy self, and he will be appreciative rather than resentful. An articulate reaction to the "demolition" and "reconstruction" aspects of the total period of counseling was given by a student with whom I tried to compress a great deal into the available short time, though with some apprehension about moving too fast.

Counseling has involved therapeutic interventions which often had violent consequences. For this I was most grateful. It would have been easy to resist and fall back upon neurotic patterns of behavior I had become habituated to in the past years if the therapy had been less intense: I would have tried to turn the sessions into a shallow word game. The sharp pointed summaries of what I was like shocked me into wanting to pursue the process, painful as it often was. The clear explanations of what was happening in the sessions made me feel not so much a victim of outside manipulation as a willing and understanding partner in the process. The silences forced me to confront myself honestly though desperately, which was a novel experience for me. But something else was more important than all this: it was the encouragement that I received from X and the sense that there was some hope in it all that helped me to pull through.

Most of the themes touched upon in this chapter will be elaborated upon in the rest of the book. The experiences at Brandeis will be placed in a wider framework through comparison with reports from other schools and will be discussed in the light of some selected theoretical approaches pertinent not only to the therapy of adolescents but to adolescence as such and to therapy as such. I hope that the discussion of the topics pertaining to the nature and organization of the mental health work in colleges will supply the advocates of this work with arguments in favor of its radical extension and with some pointers about effective ways of carrying out this task.

The material used in discussing the course of counseling comes largely from my own counseling contacts with students. I did not attempt to reread the detailed session notes I kept on nearly one thousand students whom I have seen over the years, but I did examine samples of them from different periods as well as hundreds of summaries that I wrote at the completion of counseling. To a small extent I have also used the experiences of some of my colleagues at the center, recorded in their case summaries or communicated to me in staff conferences or supervisory consultations; I am grateful to them for their contribution. Lastly, I have used the highly informative material of student questionnaire comments. In addition to all those returned to me personally since the questionnaire was introduced in 1966, I had access to about four hundred questionnaires returned to other staff members during four consecutive years. I attempted to extract and to order the information they contained, and I have used them as illustrative material. Most of my points are illustrated only by quotations from student comments or by brief vignettes, but I do present some longer cases to illustrate various courses of counseling. I rarely attach diagnoses to cases and do not usually earmark the suggested approaches for use with this or that type or degree of disturbance; the fluid pictures presented by most students seen on campus make diagnostic labels even less informative than they are with older people. The omission of diagnoses is not meant to deny the existence of some typical patterns of disturbed functioning, the knowledge of which can be quite useful to the counselor. In fact, some of the cases included were deliberately chosen to exemplify Angyal's holistic formulations of the two dimensions of neurosis, that of "vicarious living" (hysteric) and that of "noncommitment" (obsessive-compulsive). His detailed descriptions of these patterns are readily confirmed by many clients, young and old, and provide them with effective therapeutic leverage. But Angyal views these two patterns as two dimensions present in varying degrees in all instances of neurosis, not as mutually exclusive diagnostic categories.

How effective can a book on therapy be as a teaching device? Nothing a would-be teacher can provide is a substitute for the beginner's own grappling with the problems at hand; it alone can result in genuine discoveries and in efficacy based on conviction. As Carl Rogers has put it, people cannot be taught; they can only learn. What another can do to be of use to the learner, whether a student or a client, is to try to stimulate this person's own functioning: his perceiving, feeling, imagining, thinking, experimenting. For doing this, a writer has fewer means at his disposal than one who can speak face to face. In trying to indicate the rationale of the approaches I described, or the experiences on which they were based, I did not limit myself to a schematic formulation of the gist of these personal discoveries. Believing that the reader gets more actively involved in the ideas discussed if he can follow their actual emergence and development, I chose to use a personal account of my work in student counseling as an introduction to this book, nor shall I exclude personal reference and personal anecdote from the chapters that follow. Apart from its communicative value, the personal framework serves another useful purpose in reminding the reader that the viewpoints presented are those of a particular person, formulated on the basis of a particular set of experiences. Persuasive as these experiences have been, their scope is necessarily limited. The guidelines that have resulted from the work of ordering and clarifying my accumulated observations are not absolutes. No guidelines can be; to forget that is to misuse them. More often than not, there are several valid ways for a counselor to act in a given situation. Keeping this in mind, I have tried to guard against dogmatism, though not always perhaps against statements that sound dogmatic. I hope that in this informal personal synthesis of a range of observations and ideas the readers may find items that intrigue them, or confirm their experience, or challenge their beliefs, or contribute in some other ways to their own journeys of discovery.

2

Counseling in American Colleges

In outlining, in the preceding chapter, the basic issues of student counseling, I have drawn on my own experience, acquired largely at one particular school. The course taken by the counseling service of that school, though not unique, was far from typical. One critic of our program—while hailing it as "a symbol of an ideal," "an expression of what can be done with therapeutic services on a small campus under optimal conditions"—considered the Brandeis center so atypical that it was "likely to guide the development of few budding counseling centers" (Warnath, 1964, p. 400). A review of the pertinent literature yields no reliable estimate of the incidence of personal-problems counseling in American colleges, but it does provide some support for this statement of our atypicality; there are certainly not many college centers that provide competent quasi-therapeutic services to a substantial percentage of the student body.

28

Varieties of Counseling and Testing

Most large schools maintain organized counseling facilities that may include "personal-adjustment counseling," but these facilities usually provide mainly specialized or topical counseling. According to one estimate, in the mid 1960s 70 percent of college counseling centers viewed educational and vocational guidance as their main function; and a great deal of testing and some remedial educational work were done in the service of these goals. Very few centers, apparently, are devoted primarily to providing help with emotional problems (beyond dealing with emergencies and referrals), and the centers that do provide such help generally work with small numbers of students. The authors of the most comprehensive and informative questionnaire survey of college counseling centers (Oetting, Ivey, and Weigel, 1970), in listing various existing "models" that such centers can follow, do include "the psychotherapy model" and briefly discuss its disadvantages: the restricted range of services, the high cost of the trained staff, and the small number of students who can be seen when extensive time commitment is necessary; they obviously do not view this model as viable. Nor could I find evidence in the literature that the growth (if any) of college mental health facilities has kept pace with the emergence of new schools during the 1960s, when the college-age population was on the increase. In the late 1960s, in giving a workshop on college counseling, I was surprised by the number of participants who came to learn not how to run or improve a counseling service but how to start one. I also got requests for information from groups of students who were struggling to obtain from their colleges an adequate source of psychological help and wished to get from me some verbal ammunition to use in this fight; some of these colleges were established, well-known schools. The 1973 Glasscote-Fishman study of mental health on the campus was sponsored by the Joint Information Service of the American Psychiatric Association and the National Association for Mental Health for the express purpose of stimulating interest in creating mental health services in the many schools, old and new, that were doing almost nothing to meet the students' needs in this area. If one considers the devastating effect that the recent financial slump has had on student services in numerous schools, one can safely assume that effective mental health work in schools, far from advancing, is in a state of retreat. This situation makes it even more imperative to keep in mind the long-range promise of psychological work with college students and the conditions that are necessary and sufficient to make this work bear fruit. In this and the next chapter, I shall use the data from my own experience and from that of other college settings to try to identify the factors that help and hinder the delivery of effective psychological assistance to maturing students—call this work what you will: counseling, therapy, prevention, or education.

Let us look first at the kind of counseling that is prevalent in our schools. The critic quoted at the beginning of this chapter may have expressed the feeling of many college counselors when he denounced the staff of the Brandeis center for doing no educational-vocational counseling, for advocating "therapy for all," and for seeming to imply "that anything less than their brand of therapy is not adequate counseling for college students" (Warnath, 1964, p. 400). This sentiment is understandable, and it deserves an answer. My experience with "personal-problems" counseling (which might also be called "holistic" or "developmental") has indeed convinced me that the extended awareness and the reorientation it tends to bring about can propel the late adolescent toward emotional, social, and intellectual maturity. To acknowledge this, however, is not to consider inferior and useless all counseling that focuses on circumscribed issues; they may be vital for the person, as academic issues are for the student. But if the two kinds of counseling are to live under the same roof, to be governed by the same set of policies, the academic-vocational one should be organized and conducted so as to be compatible with the "psychotherapy model." In particular, the counseling discussions and the test results must not be revealed to the administration or the faculty. According to Oetting, Ivey, and Weigel (1970), a service following exclusively the "academic affairs" model may obtain a high degree of faculty and administration support, but it obtains this support at a cost. Because it gets easily involved in evaluating students and contributing to administrative decisions about them, students are not likely to use a service of this kind for any confidential discussions, particularly those that may lead to the discovery of emotional factors within the study problems. To do therapeutic or quasi-therapeutic work, any office of "study counsel," must, unequivocally, provide counsel *to* the student, not to others *about* the student.

Testing has its place in educational-vocational counseling, but if it is to be potentially valuable to college-age subjects it must be handled with care. Otherwise, it may turn out to be positively "antitherapeutic," encouraging passivity and exaggerated faith in experts or, alternatively, providing students with a basis for an equally uncritical revolt against testers as manipulators or "secret persuaders." Students deserve to be given a realistic account of tests that might be appropriate—an account that covers the rationale of the operations involved and evaluates the evidence for their validity and their limitations; it is better to lean over backward than to make any exaggerated or uncritical claims. The student can be then invited to choose those of the tests described that seem to him most pertinent and acceptable. Similarly, the interpretation of the test results in relation to the student's problem should shun dogmatism and stress tentativeness; testing can be useful only if it is embedded in competent counseling.

This emphasis on counseling is shared by many of those who work in student guidance, both in colleges and in other types of schools. In their book on counseling, Boy and Pine (1968), proponents of the client-centered approach, advocate extended use of competent counseling to replace routine testing at all levels of schooling. In some school systems such a reform would be practically a revolution; to achieve it, as Stewart and Warnath (1965) point out, one needs a source of power to exercise political pressure. Guidance work in colleges, however, may be already moving in this direction—at least in those influential college centers sympathetically described by Oetting and his associates under the heading of "traditional model." The directors of these centers, located in large schools, fought early and successfully for the privilege of keeping counseling confidential. They are said to run strong professional counseling programs, which provide both educational-vocational counseling and short-term treatment of emotional problems, regarding the two as overlapping areas. They unambiguously view service to students as their centers' primary function; they use a flexible, eclectic approach to counseling; and they strive for a continual improvement of the staff's skill.

The "traditional" centers usually have a well-developed testing service; however, they do not view its use as a "test-and-tell" process but as a means of approaching the student's personal problem, with the focus on fostering his or her ability to make academic and vocational decisions. Conducted in this way, educational-vocational testing and counseling should indeed be very useful to many students, particularly in large schools with heterogeneous populations, either as a supplement to personal-problems counseling or in its own right. It may be all that many students need; or it may be all that some students can take at the time, though they actually need more. Work inhibition is a ubiquitous neurotic symptom—for many students, men in particular, a symptom that is easiest to talk about. Consequently, educational counseling often brings in those students who would not consider asking for help with more widely conceived personal problems. Should the participation of attitudinal factors become clear, or at least plausible, to student and counselor, the counselor who already knows the student can continue working with him within this enlarged frame of reference, or he can refer him to another. If no holistic personal counseling is attempted to supplement or replace the topical one, the student should at least take along with him two crucial insights: that factors other than basic ability codetermine his and everyone's performance and that, when all is said and done, the decisions and choices are his; he is the one to find out what he wants and how to go about getting it. Only if these conditions are fulfilled will the student be able to assimilate the evidence provided by the discussions and the tests, be it encouraging or sobering, and add it to his growing fund of effective self-knowledge, which serves to delineate his identity.

Referrals can also be made in the opposite direction, from personal counselors to topical counselors. At Brandeis, with its highly selected student body, I rarely met with students whose ability was insufficient for the work required. The students themselves, with the exception perhaps of some panicky freshmen, usually considered it at least probable that their difficulty was of emotional origin. However, if an occasional student, uncertain of his ability and his vocational goals, persisted in his wish to be "tested and told," refusing to think and talk about the issue first, I would refer him to some good testing service, inviting him to come back to discuss the results. If the test findings did help him to reformulate or solve his problem, well and good. If the "objective evidence" proved irrelevant to his doubts or his wishes, the student then might decide to grapple, in counseling, with the elusive subjective realities.

The testing I have discussed so far is part of educational-vocational guidance; though predominant in most schools, this is not the only kind that one encounters. Along with intelligence, achievement, and aptitude tests, many university centers give personality tests, the results of which are assumed to be relevant to personal-problems counseling. These are mostly standardized paper-and-pencil tests, but well-staffed services often include projective tests such as the Rorschach and the Thematic Apperception Test. These are rarely given routinely, but they may be given frequently in psychiatrically oriented settings whose staffs have come to rely on these techniques as a help in arriving at diagnoses or as sources of information on matters that the patient himself is unwilling or unable to disclose. Projective testing is the domain of clinical psychologists; it has been useful in delineating their specific contribution to the work of psychiatric settings on and off campus and has furthered interprofessional harmony. Yet, valuable as projective techniques may be in personality research and assessment, their wide use in clinical work is not justified if usefulness to the client is the criterion. The elaborate formulations of personality dynamics based on projective test data may give staff members the comforting feeling that they understand the patient "in depth," but there their usefulness usually ends; the results of these tests rarely determine the disposition or treatment of a case. Since college centers are not obligated to report their work loads in terms of psychiatric diagnoses, they lack even this reason for administering the time-consuming, hard-to-interpret projective tests.

When I came to Brandeis, I agreed to take part in a modest program of psychological testing previously started by the school. To the group Rorschach they were giving to each entering class, I added a sentence-completion test especially designed for this age group, a semiprojective test that I had found useful in a variety of contexts. The administration hoped that the tests could produce a list of students who were likely to become disturbed and thus were presumably to be watched or handled in a special way. I doubted, however, both the validity of such prognoses and the wisdom of informing the graduate students serving as dormitory counselors that some of their charges had "suicidal indices" on the Rorschach; I felt that keeping the center's doors open was a more effective preventive measure. (And, indeed, a suicide did not take place on campus until the center developed waiting lists.) For spotting the potentially disturbed among the few hundred new students, an inordinate amount of time would be used in working on records—time which was more profitably spent in talking to the students themselves. For one freshman class we did attempt to identify potentially disturbed students, by quick impressionistic Rorschach evidence, and to check against this list the names of those who subsequently applied for counseling. The correlation between the two lists was negligible—probably because most of the students seeking "psych counseling" proved to be not at all "abnormal" whereas some of the most disturbed ones stayed away, as we learned from their friends. (Also, while Rorschach has the reputation of effectively spotting pathology, it is also known to do the job almost too well.) Whatever the reason, the experiment helped to confirm our growing conviction that our tests were of no use to the school. To the counselors the test data were sometimes helpful. In one instance the sentence-completion test provided the means of opening up with a student the concealed issue of his recent suicidal attempts. I had been informed of them, in confidence, by the student's friend and found them clearly spelled out in his test responses. Occasionally, test data provided us with additional insights in some difficult cases or could be used for a stimulating discussion with the student himself. Also, a few hesitant students could use an inquiry about their test results as a covert mode of approach to the center. Yet these occasions for making use of the test data were infrequent from the start and became increasingly rare as the counselors acquired experience with the students' problems and ways. When the student personnel office decided to discontinue the freshman testing program, of which the psychological tests were a part, the center did not object.

The overuse of personality testing may stem from the high valuation we place on knowledge of the client's psychodynamics, reflecting the view of insight as the main therapeutic agent. Yet most psychotherapists now agree that there is more to effective therapy than insight, particularly the therapist's insight. There is a place in the training of clinicians for practice in deducing personal dynamics from a wide range of data, but one can hardly justify the use of this exercise in a clinic by referring to the agency's teaching function. By investing our limited time in diagnostic procedures which in no way benefit the clients, we contribute to waste and pretense. We actually model attitudes that make poor therapists: putting the client's need second to some needs of our own, relying on someone else to do the job of understanding our clients. Only those clinical settings that unambiguously give priority to delivering effective service to clients are fit places for training clinicians to deliver effective service.

I strongly suspect that a great deal of useless routine testing is being done in colleges as well as in grade and high schools. I doubt that any mandated testing can be useful; certainly an uncritical use of test results makes the counseling based on them worse than useless. Fortunately, we are witnessing today the emergence of promising new approaches to the established educational and vocational fields of counseling that treat the client as an agent, not as an object of assessment and guidance. Furthermore, in some schools the traditional areas of counseling are being supplemented by many other kinds of specialized counseling. The sex-information service developed at Yale is apparently an unqualified success; it is credited with an almost complete elimination of abortions. Some of the other schools studied by Glasscote and Fishman (1973) have special facilities for counseling graduate students, black students, foreign students, and married couples; for drug counseling and abortion counseling; and in one large school, for groups of engaged, widowed, blind, and overweight. The subdivision of counseling settings according to the type of client, or client situation, enables the counselor to amass a great deal of pertinent background knowledge, which greatly facilitates counseling. Even in small schools, in the absence of specialized facilities, one can try to match student and counselor. Graduate students usually do well with counselors who share their

academic frame of reference, the foreign born do well with counselors from the same or a similar culture, and most black students
prefer a black counselor. Just as the common cultural background
facilitates communication, so does the focus on a common problem,
vital for all participants. In witnessing demonstrations of problem-
centered group consultation, I was greatly impressed by the active
and productive interchange developing between the participants,
even though they did not know each other and were being observed
by a large audience. A similar approach can be useful for students;
that is, group sessions for freshmen in their first months or weeks, for
students with similar ideological concerns or similar factors in their
past, for those considering a year abroad, for transfer students, for
seniors with similar plans—or similar absence of plans. Some of
these group sessions have been tried at Brandeis.

Communication between people who are in the same boat is
put to even better use when students are trained—or have trained
themselves—to counsel other students or at least to give them pertinent information on academic matters, sex, and drugs. The success
of such projects depends on many factors. One of them is the
student-leader's own ability to facilitate and organize discussion;
another is the possibility of consulting with experienced and competent people, not necessarily professionals. To guard against over-
professionalism it is well to remind ourselves that some very effective
programs for treating difficult conditions have been developed not
by professionals but by laymen who themselves "have been there":
Alcoholics Anonymous for alcoholism, Synanon for drugs (Yablonsky, 1967). The informal counseling that is provided to students—
only too rarely nowadays—by concerned faculty members is also
not to be underestimated. To train self-selected teachers to be better
counselors is a promising enterprise. The features that make counseling effective are to a great extent the same, whether it is professional
or informal, holistic or specialized. Many of the skills and attitudes
required are the same, even if they must be implemented differently,
depending on the problems dealt with and the client population.
In a sense, college counseling as a whole is also a specialized area.
It requires, besides counseling competence and mastery of methods,
an empirical knowledge of college students and their world: its
social structure, living conditions, intellectual concerns; it helps to

be familiar with the books students read and discuss, with the ideological controversies that currently engage them. The better the counselor is oriented to the students' world, the more aware of its concerns, pressures, and opportunities, the better his chance to be of use to its inhabitants. For this reason counselors who are members of the college community have an advantage over those who are not. Other conditions being equal, arrangements for student counseling made by some schools with outside agencies are likely to be less effective.

Some Determinants of Success

What determines the initial acceptance by the school of a counseling or mental health service, and what determines the direction of its development? Many characteristics of the school as a whole, of course, will come into play: its conservative or "innovative" orientation, an impersonal or paternalistic atmosphere, its location with respect to various mental health resources, the degree to which faculty and students share in the widespread and deepseated cultural prejudice that accepting help of any kind is a sign of weakness and leads to unhealthy dependence. These general trends, however, shape the events only insofar as they affect the choices made by those who initiate plans or are charged with making decisions. These people will also have their own ideas and may have their own axes to grind. A dean of students, for example, may find it difficult to renounce control of some of the students' activities, even if it is merely control by knowing what is going on, or thinking one does. If he enjoys counseling students himself, he may oppose the advent of a professional counseling service, as a rival, or he may welcome it, hoping to learn from his new colleagues; he may even get some specialized training himself and change his job for that of a counselor. When the plan is under consideration, a great deal depends on the sources to whom the administrator turns for information and advice. Will he limit himself to discussion with the people at his school who have initiated the plan, or will he write to schools comparable in size and orientation to find out what they are doing? Will he invite some other expert advice or listen to his knowledgeable friends?

The decision eventually arrived at will to some extent predetermine the direction of the service's development by the three interrelated choices it will have to incorporate: the administrative connection for the new service, its professional sponsorship, and the person charged with directing it. Will the service be placed under an administrative or an academic dean? Will it be connected with a medical school or with a department of psychology of one or another theoretical orientation? Will it be run and staffed by psychiatrists, social workers, clinical psychologists, or counseling psychologists, or by some combination of these? Some of the trends resulting from these choices are obvious; some have been exemplified by my story of the developments at Brandeis; more material on them can be obtained from the literature. Some administrative connections are more favorable than others for obtaining and keeping autonomy and the right of privileged communication, and different professional directors and staffs may emphasize different activities: psychiatrists qua physicians may stress diagnosis and "triage," counseling psychologists may focus on academic and vocational testing and/or counseling, clinical psychologists may hold on to projectives. None of these professional overemphases is mandatory, however; the less the members of the different professions feel threatened by each other, the easier it should be for them to coordinate their efforts.

The characteristics of the student body and the attitudes of the faculty will also influence the new service's fate, facilitating or hindering its development or skewing it in a certain direction. At Brandeis the acceptance of "psych counseling" in the 1950s was made easier because students were well informed about therapy, partly through the popularity of the psychology department with its strong clinical and humanistic sectors. Other influential teachers, however, were strongly opposed to analysis and therefore had a counterbalancing effect on students. Mostly they abstained from advising students against coming to the center, but I remember quite a few counseling sessions spent discussing Professor X's or Y's views on the validity of psychoanalytic concepts and such. New counseling services in traditional schools are also subject to pressures from the administrators to prove their value by doing something for them, even if the basic arrangements have been agreed on from the

start and the director has been given carte blanche for the rest. The
director, however, is not helpless in the face of these forces. Most
of us feel their impact; very few have been so lucky as to receive a
carte blanche that was really a blank. But we *can* struggle, negotiate,
and reach agreements with people in positions of power. Many
services in both small and large schools have won the fight for
privileged communication and for a measure of autonomy that is
necessary for their work. In their comprehensive survey, Oetting,
Ivey, and Weigel (1970) found that—although the sum total of
counseling operations varied greatly from school to school, no two
programs being exactly alike—the nature of each program reflected
the views of the director on the goals and tasks of college counseling, and these views did not always coincide with the views of the
school administrators.

This impressive finding serves, I believe, to qualify a statement made repeatedly by Oetting and his associates; namely, that
the counseling offered in institutions should subserve the institutional, in this case the educational, goals. This statement deserves
close attention, precisely because it appears plausible in both of its
aspects, the normative and the pragmatic: that counseling offered
and paid for by institutions should serve the legitimate goals of these
institutions and that, if shaped and presented as such, the counseling service will find acceptance and support. The truth is that bona
fide counseling, or bona fide therapy, can do its task and fulfill its
promise only if it centers on the goals of individual persons, whether
found in institutions or elsewhere. If one loses sight of this fact, the
above formulation can easily lead to confusions; aiming to serve the
institution, the counselor serves the administration uncritically and
thereby undermines his own ability to serve his rightful clients,
whose good functioning is necessary to implement the school's goals.
Oetting, Ivey, and Weigel do not themselves share in this confusion.
They and I could agree, I believe, that students should have an opportunity to focus on academic and vocational matters in counseling; I hope they could also agree with me that these young people's
central task, in and out of school, is development toward maturity.
If our schools are nearsighted enough to disclaim responsibility for
fostering all but one aspect of maturation, and this at a time when
so many families renounce the task of socializing adolescents, we

would be failing both the students and society at large by limiting ourselves to serving the schools' present narrowly defined educational goals. Widely conceived counseling work with college adolescents, who will soon themselves be an influential part of the adult social environment, has the widest possible bearing not only on their personal fate but also perhaps on the school environments of the future.

It is realistic to assume that the bulk of today's students at traditionally run schools will get only as much skilled help toward their emotional maturation as is provided by the schools' counseling facilities. These facilities have to be paid for. The most crucial and the most difficult job of a counseling service's director is to persuade someone to pay for them, and to pay in the most generous way possible. That is why, I believe, the surveys conducted in the 1960s usually focused their inquiries on items like the staff's educational level, academic status, and case load; the information collected probably determined the amount of money one could realistically demand from the school. The need to demonstrate the value of the service to those who have a voice in the distribution of funds doubtless accounts also for a variety of activities that counseling services engage in, some of which lie outside the staff's competence and take their time away from the work they know how to do. In an attempt to counteract this trend, Oetting, Ivey, and Weigel suggest that the college counselor should simply put his efforts into doing good counseling in all situations that permit it.

To insure personal counseling to large numbers, one must view its function in the educational, not in the medical, context; even if it admits that college age is a period of great stress, no school administration in its right mind will agree to employ one psychiatrist for each 350–400 students. However, if one grants the counseling service the status of a special educational unit comparable to the other departments, one which 20–30 percent of the students may elect to have instruction in, these ratios are nothing out of the ordinary; they are, in fact, quite moderate.

Another important issue is the demonstration of the novel service's effectiveness; for this purpose, student feedback of the kind we obtained in questionnaires can be useful, even in the absence of the desirable complete returns. Concrete examples are often more self-evident and convincing than figures of doubtful origin. Also, if asked for statistical proof of its value, a counseling service might well remind the traditional departments that for them also the only evidence of educational success is the students' evaluations of their teachers and courses, plus perhaps the later outstanding achievements of some of those students who have gone on to graduate schools. A counselor of a well-established counseling service could also call on some of his "graduates" years later to communicate to him—and through him to others—their views on the long-range effects of an early period of counseling. For some students the problems that brought them into counseling are all but forgotten after being resolved, but some others are well aware of the importance which the period of college counseling—with or without a continuation outside—has had for their lives. Work with college students presents many opportunities for this kind of informal follow-up; if the amount and the quality of time the student spent with the counselor was sufficient to create a personal bond, he or she may keep in touch by occasional letters or visits, much as some do with their teachers. In talking to people whose support for the service one is seeking, one might expect to find a sympathetic hearing from those who can translate the general descriptions of young people's and their parents' plight into examples close to home; we might do well, therefore, to provide a wide range of concrete illustrations when we talk about adolescent problems of today and their mature resolutions. We can also preselect our examples and formulations for different audiences. Psychologists or others interested in stages of intellectual growth might respond to the descriptions of emotional and social maturing given in terms applicable to intellectual development, or borrowed from that area. Even if the teachers in question would not spend time comparing the methods they use in their classes with those used in counseling, they might learn to value the counseling approach if they were shown how it contributes to keeping students in school and to making them into the kinds of students who are rewarding to teach. We might also emphasize the connections between intellectual and emotional-social maturation by citing the holistic concepts of developmentalists such as Piaget. Concepts of this kind can also connect skilled counseling with other areas of endeavor prominent in a given school—for example, training of teachers or community workers. Take the case of theological colleges, or of schools with religious orientation, which tend to identify personal with religious counseling; one might assume that a professional counseling service would not have much chance in such schools. The example of Brigham Young University shows, however, that under certain conditions the two approaches can coexist and even collaborate closely. Along with many others, Angyal, who was interested in the comparative study of religions, has pointed out that many of the religious and psychiatric tenets are identical and translatable from one language into another. His book on neurosis has been used intensively in the program of training of pastoral counselors sponsored by the American Foundation of Religion and Psychiatry.

In conclusion, I would like to elaborate here on a hunch that small colleges present especially good opportunities for developing programs that provide personal counseling to students on a large scale. This hunch is based on the assumption that a person advocating such a program, if he gains his colleagues' support, might have a stronger impact in a small than in a large school. Some statistical data on college counseling are also relevant here. First, many of the small colleges have not yet acquired a counseling service; in a favorable situation, the person who gets in on the ground floor of a new development will have a good chance to influence it. Second, the surveys show that those small colleges that *have* introduced formal counseling services into their structure make better provisions for them than do large schools with their large budgets. Oetting's survey showed that, in schools with enrollment under 1,000, 58 percent of the graduating students had been counseled during their years in college; in schools with enrollments of 1,000 to 5,000, 34 percent had been counseled; in larger schools the percent went down to 25. Although some of the figures cited are only estimates, they come from a sufficiently large number of schools to have some validity. This is further confirmed by the finding of a later survey (Lamb, Sutter, and Parrish, 1969) that schools with enrollment under 5,000—and only these schools—have been able to maintain the ratio of one counselor to fewer than 1,000 students. The difference, then, between the amount of time already available and the amount of time needed for developing counseling on a large scale is less in small schools than in large ones. Third, since presumably the student population of small schools is relatively homogeneous and faculty members possibly more accessible to students than in large schools, there is less need for a counseling service to get involved in testing and in academic advising. Should the staff—even if it is a one-man staff—resist the pressure for administrative and other undesirable work and put all time available into counseling proper, its work might make a real difference to a large proportion of students, large enough perhaps to assure the support of this work by the future alumni.

The Factor of Time

Once a student counseling service has been established, the fate of the school's mental health work will depend primarily on the factor of *time*. The amount of time available for working with students obviously determines the amount of work that can be done. Less obviously, it determines the quality of the work and the direction in which the counseling or the mental health program will develop. I shall take up the quantitative aspect first. A rough indicator of the amount of counseling help available to students in a school is the staff-student ratio. At Brandeis, to work with 20 percent of the student body for an average of eleven sessions (a maximum of thirty), we had to have an equivalent of one full-time (forty hours) counselor for each 350–400 students. Oetting, Ivey, and Weigel (1970) speak of a recommended ratio of one counselor for 500–1,000 students. Counting the personnel of both mental health and counseling services, four out of six model programs studied by Glasscote and Fishman (1973) fulfill this requirement. The proportion must be considerably smaller among other schools, particularly the large ones. For example, according to Clark (1966), the mean ratio for thirty-six schools with an enrollment over 10,000 is one counselor to 3,000 students. If one considers that a large proportion of a staff's time is likely to be employed in educational-vocational guidance, such ratios are proof that personal-problems counseling is badly neglected. The statistics of most surveys lump together counseling of different kinds; whenever separate data are available, however, they show that mental health counseling involves a much smaller percentage of students than does counseling of other kinds, although the periods of mental health counseling are on the average longer. The Congdon-Lothrop (1961) survey of school facilities in the early 1960s, the period that yielded the Brandeis data reported above, shows that offices providing personal-problems counseling exclusively saw yearly only 2.5 percent of the students, six sessions being the median number of interviews per student. Offices that provided some (undetermined) amount of such counseling along with the educational-vocational one saw yearly about 10 percent of the student body, four being the median number of interviews.

This is a discouraging situation, and it is not astonishing that much discouragement is expressed and reported by the directors of counseling centers. In 1969 nearly three-fourths of the 131 directors who responded to Lamb's questionnaire indicated that they did not have enough staff to meet adequately the needs of their students. As demands and pressures mount, one tries to meet them with emergency measures. One increases the counselors' case load beyond the customary twenty to thirty appointments a week; one cuts down the length of sessions to thirty minutes or less; one pressures students who want individual counseling to enter groups; one develops waiting lists or else, to avoid them, introduces periods when students can be seen right away, without an appointment (a measure that seems to have been quite effective as a permanent institution in some schools with very large enrollments). All these may serve well to get one over a period of a seasonal peak demand, but in the majority of schools they are not just emergency measures; they are continuing or recurring indications of the fact that the available staff time is not adequate for meeting the students' needs. At present this situation is made much worse in many places by the financial squeeze in the schools, but the data and the situations reported here antedate our present difficulties. They reflect the nationwide lack of imagination that makes us neglect one of the best methods we have for raising the level of functioning of the college-educated group and thus significantly improving, in the near and crucial future, the quality of our human resources.

What kind of growth can a college counseling service expect if its resources are, and remain, adequate? Given a competent staff and policies that ensure student trust, the use of the service by the students will grow, and grow steadily. Places comparable in that respect to Brandeis have reported similar experiences. Many a director of quantitatively inadequate facilities must have found, with exasperation, that any increase in the ability to provide service leads to an increase of demand. Ordinarily, however, the growth is a slow one; in a small school the growth curve may reflect even minor events, such as the staff's being joined by a particularly talented counselor or an unusually inept one. At Brandeis it took a decade for the attendance to rise from the initial 10 percent to 20 percent— an average of 1 percent a year (though actually this period saw one major jump and one setback). It stabilized slightly above this level for a few years, while we were struggling to keep up the necessary staff-student ratio. There is no way of telling whether this growth would have resumed and continued had our resources remained roughly adequate, but my guess is that the growth curve would gradually have flattened out and students' yearly participation stabilized at the level of 25–30 percent of the enrollment. The type of growth we have observed does not justify the panicky expectations of some of the pressured campus mental health workers that, given any encouragement, the students' demands for counseling will grow in leaps and bounds until all the students in school will be spending their college years in free analyses, "terminable or interminable." In a mental health service situated in a large outside community, the fear of insatiable demand might be based on reality, but provision of services to a limited population in the closed community of a school is a realistically manageable task, not a never ending Sisyphean toil.

Certain limitations must of course be accepted even by well-provided-for programs. At Brandeis I have met many highly gifted graduate students, who, being much more settled into their neuroses than the undergraduates, could not be helped decisively in the course of one school year; for their sake, I would have liked to extend our counseling facilities even further. Still, we were happy to be able to provide well for the undergraduates; for many of them the difference between fifteen and thirty sessions spelled the difference between merely beginning maturational work and completing it. I was satisfied to define adequate service to the student community as helping all those applicants who could be helped within these limits and working with the others as long as was necessary to prepare them to accept an appropriate outside referral and profit from it. The students as a whole accepted the limits dictated by these definitions, as insuring a fair chance to all; the counselors were attuned to the anticipation of termination by counselees and tried to put it to good use. In some cases, of course, termination was justly regretted. Some of those whose time had been spent in dealing with a crisis, or in solving a delimited problem, expressed regret that for them the service had been no more than a "repair shop": "There was not enough time to go beyond a bit of the surface, to come to grips with the sources of these problems." "I was just beginning to get into things." At the time I am describing now, however, such comments were infrequent. The hearsay stressed the positive, not the negative, aspects of limited work: "I have heard that counseling has helped many to solve immediate problems, such as schoolwork; it put others on the right track directing them to private therapy; it showed others that they did not need therapy after all." During that period the absence of waiting lists and of undue hurry was taken for granted; it was mentioned only occasionally in the context of praising the service's availability and informality, the absence of red tape and professional airs: "I am made to feel that I have a right to ask for help, which is then freely given." "Counseling was arranged right away, just when I needed it." "The counselor always seemed to have time for me, and never did I feel like just another case."

In replying to the questionnaire sent by us in the spring of 1966 to the members of the graduating class, the majority felt that ideally help should be given according to need, without any extrinsic limitation of time. If a time limit had to be imposed, however, most students indicated that the equivalent of one school year of weekly sessions, which we guaranteed at the time, was adequate for most purposes.

As the decrease of the staff-student ratio described in Chapter 1 started undermining our ability to provide an adequate allotment of time to all comers, seeing them without delay and without haste, the character of the questionnaire comments changed: complaints became more and more numerous, more and more bitter.

I shall quote several of them in order to cover a variety of the consequences of crowding and the wide range of feelings expressed.

When I appeared and asked for help, I was told to make an appointment for several days later. In moments of distress it is not comforting to be told to come back later when we can fit you in. I realize that the limited number and time of the counselors and the size of the overload can make it impossible to help someone who appears suddenly, without notice. Nevertheless, it is precisely that initial, unforeseen moment of need when help is of the utmost importance.

I fear the counseling center is so busy with near-suicide cases that it will be unable to help the rest of us, whose problems are not so manifestly severe.

I feel there should always be at least *one free* counselor who can be seen on the spur of the moment. You would never know how much that might have helped me and possibly many others.

I definitely do not think that the psychological counseling service should be curtailed. If anything, more money should be allotted to it. I, for example, had to wait over a week for an appointment. I really went to pieces. I did not consider myself an emergency, but psychological help should be available at the time it is desperately needed. Fortunately, I survived but I fear for some students who, not realizing the seriousness of their crises, depression, etc., might, during that time of waiting for help, take some drastic measures.

I was seen twice, by two different counselors. The second time was more profitable and encouraging. However, when I needed to see this counselor again, I was turned away.

The counseling was good, but my experience was so minimal that any comments would be poorly based: I can say this—it was upsetting to be shut out because of overcrowded facilities at a time when I needed help.

I had four sessions and was refused further contacts. To have free counseling is outstanding and I commend the school for this. But this privilege could be carried further, perhaps for a small fee. There are no inexpensive therapists around, and I have the choice of spending everything I own and working to get something I am unsure of.

There might have been progress the second time around, with X, but my time was used up; only "irregular" appointments were possible now, and I figured I might as well leave X's time to those he had time for. . . . I feel that if successful therapy had been possible at the time when I most needed it, I would have changed as a person in a way that is no longer possible. . . . I am extremely bitter about this.

These examples do not include the extremes of bitterness and discouragement which the situations of crowding produce. Such reactions are reported by friends more often than by the students themselves; many of those who have been hurt most do not return and do not answer questionnaires. The intensity of the hurt is not astonishing if one considers that approaching the center is often a momentous step, perhaps the first important decision the person has made on his own; he may have come after a hard inner struggle, despite strong misgivings and fear. The nature of the reception he receives will either increase his hopes or confirm his fears. This unknown setting comes to represent the total world to a disturbed student; the effects of the first contact, good or bad, will be out of proportion to realities as we see them. If the student has mobilized himself, against great odds, to reach out for help, he may not be merely disappointed and annoyed if he is put on a waiting list or sent away; he is likely to feel: "They do not care, no one does." He may then withdraw his tentatively proffered trust, even if situational realities are explained to him: "I was in need of help, yet I received no encouragement to return; I left dismayed and feeling turned down. I didn't come back till a year later; fortunately, I had enough confidence to return; some might be turned away for good." "Going to the center will do more harm than good if students are refused attention because of the tight schedules, especially underclass students who have been encouraged to go to the center for the first time." Such outcome of the search for therapy is clearly antitherapeutic; it is indeed irresponsible to advertise a service that cannot meet any increase in demand.

For the staff, particularly when they have known better

times, the situations resulting from crowding are both frustrating
and demoralizing. When time allowance is ample, an experienced
and competent counselor meets every new client with the confident
feeling that some amount of effective help can be given to him. The
client senses this confidence and is therefore able to respond more
easily to the counselor's attempts to involve him in a productive
interchange. To work out any plans *with* the student, not *for* the
student, requires not only time but a relaxed attitude toward time.
Shortcuts attempted by the counselor may result in failure or in fake
performance. He may try, when the center is crowded, to refer the
student outside in short order, with the result that the student agrees
but does not go; in asking the student to postpone his visit to the
next term, the counselor may underestimate the seriousness of his
problem and/or appear unfair: "My roommate came to you last
month with a similar problem and you didn't tell him to wait till
fall!" He may terminate the contact abruptly or arbitrarily, or attempt a premature, poorly prepared transfer. I know the situation
well, having been shocked by student comments into discovering
some of my own blunders of this kind. The pressure to find some
seemingly rational reasons for sorting students out endangers the
integrity both of the individual counselor and of the service as a
whole. Our failure to test our hunches and to evaluate the results
of our work is a very real flaw in the way therapy is taught and
practiced today, and college counseling is no exception, though one
might expect it to be. This absence of controls enables us, under
pressure, to adopt some assumptions about who can and who cannot
be helped in a limited time in a college setting—assumptions which
may sound plausible, and may be congruent perhaps with some
theories, but which are in fact unverified. But because they have
been in use for some time and have helped us to survive, they become unquestioned axioms.

One occasionally hears the advice not to counteract the development of waiting lists, since they can serve as good argument for
an increase of staff. Nothing is to be neglected that can fulfill this
purpose; but one cannot rely on waiting lists to appear without fail
when one needs them to bolster one's arguments. At Brandeis, as the
staff-student ratio kept rolling down, so did the proportion of applicants, slowly but surely. The shortcomings caused by the lack of

time, experienced and talked about by applicants, inhibit attendance just as other defects of the service do (defects such as involvement with the administration or incompetence of staff) : "I did almost feel that unless there was something seriously wrong or something terribly disturbing me, there was no time for the doctor to see me. I would like to talk to a doctor on a regular basis but I do have this feeling that I shouldn't come unless I am really down." Thus, when supply stops responding to demand, demand starts roughly adjusting to supply. As a result, if the downward movement continues, the center does not suffer from overcrowding, except for brief periods after the staff-student ratio has taken an unusually sharp plunge. The trend is revealed in statistics, but to many people statistics do not feel like realities. The work goes on as usual, since students come in sufficient numbers to provide work for all counselors, and the staff may not become alarmed until the self-regulatory reduction of attendance is no longer sufficient to keep the situation balanced. When this happens and waiting lists become unmanageable, a sharp curtailment of the length of the counseling period has to be officially sanctioned and threatens to make the service a merely diagnostic one, largely useless to students. Eventually, even such service may prove to be "adequate" to meet their needs—at least as judged by the absence of waiting lists; it will not be overcrowded.

3

Influencing the College Environment

Counseling of various kinds, conducted with or without the help of testing, is not the only activity that college services engage in. Some counseling and mental health centers attempt to supplement their direct service to the students by activities aimed at influencing the environment of the school. In following the description of the college psychiatrist's activities given by Kahne and Schwartz (1975), I shall distinguish three "environmental" functions that a mental health worker may be trying to carry out on campus: to be an agent of change, working to influence policies and arrangements so that they might be more conducive to the students' mental health and emotional growth; to act as consultant to the administration; and to intervene in the educational system, usually on a student's behalf. These are overlapping activities, but I believe it is worthwhile to try to keep their different foci, pointed out by Kahne and Schwartz, as separate as possible. Their implications and consequences are quite different and it is precisely their merging so easily into each other that should give pause to those mental health workers whose attraction to such activities is based on their growing awareness of the inadequate and destructive features of our school systems, colleges not excluded.

Agent of Change

The goal of furthering institutional *change,* while most ambitious, is, in a sense, least controversial. Even the best schools have room for improvement: in administrative policies toward students, in methods of teaching and testing, in living arrangements, in modes of interaction between students and faculty, in the total atmosphere of the place. What can the director of mental health work and his staff do, *as such,* to further such reforms, even when their opinion about what should be done is supported not just by speculations but by demonstrable facts? I believe the realistic answer is "nothing"— unless the person in question is a truly outstanding politician-persuader and his proposals do not conflict with vital institutional interests. At Brandeis, for example, the efforts of many concerned people to further informal student-faculty contact were to no avail. Everyone agreed that such contact was highly desirable, but most faculty members felt that they could not afford to give students extra time; they needed it for research and writing, on which survival depended. This is not an atypical situation. Those asking for the change of policy necessary to give teachers more time with students were told that the school's investment was in scholarship and research. It may be difficult to get a school to finance a good counseling service, but nowhere near as difficult as getting it to change its fundamental policies.

The clinician-teacher can best influence educational practices by developing better teaching methods in his own classes— mainly by applying the psychological principles he has formulated and found useful in his clinical work. He is most likely to be heard by his colleagues in schools that are committed to educational experimentation, where teachers can afford to take time to learn about the methods that seemed to have worked for others, or even to learn to work in such new areas as personal counseling of students. Such a path was taken by Richard Jones, who, some time after leaving Brandeis, worked out an interdisciplinary course of studies focused on human development, which he and his colleagues then implemented at one of the new schools experimenting with novel programs. As part of this program some of the methods developed originally in the clinical field are used for the assimilation of instructional material. For example, reflecting on the language of one's own dreams is utilized in studying the work of those medieval writers who expressed themselves via dream imagery; Jones's "dream reflection" seminars seem to have had a vivifying effect on literary perception and were received enthusiastically by students and faculty (Jones, 1978). The mobilization of individual personal imagery, even when it is done for the sake of assimilating the subject studied, is bound also to increase the person's self-awareness. I imagine that many of Jones's students at Evergreen would act as his students did at Brandeis and follow the seminars with a period of personal counseling, which at Evergreen several teachers are prepared to give. In this and in similar cases of the spread of psychological enlightenment in a school, the spread occurs via faculty members as teachers, not as administrators, a mode of influence that is very effective but cannot be expected to occur in a large conventional school. Still, as a hope for the future, the collaboration of psychologists with educators, not just in colleges but from nursery school or kindergarten on, together with psychological consultation for normal parents of small children, offered even earlier, by pediatricians or by workers in healthy baby clinics, is probably our best chance to do effective preventive mental health work on a large scale. Gordon (1970, 1974) has developed a very successful training program in which psychologists work with parents and teachers. The focus in this approach is on developing attitudes that can provide adults with effective tools for resolving problem situations involving their pupils or children.

But to return to what one can do to bring about changes in a traditional college. Not having seriously tried to do so, I cannot speak with authority. Yet the few instances of such attempts I have observed left me with the conviction that this is not a profitable enterprise for a counseling service. Here is one example. At one point, the dean of students decided to change the students' living arrangements. This dean was in a state of war with the students, so that they opposed all his plans indiscriminately. A student delegation came to me, presumably for consultation on student life issues but actually in search of ammunition with which to fight the dean's plan: Wasn't it based on false psychological assumptions? What were my views on the issue? I told them, truthfully, that I had no views, since I had never given a thought to the matter and had certainly never studied it. But if I did have any views, I told them, I would not discuss them at this time, when I felt they were interested merely in fighting the dean. To discuss my individual views would serve no good purpose and might compromise the proper work of the center, which was counseling, not fighting. The students left, disappointed perhaps but not astonished; they had known very well what they were about. One of the center's counselors, unaware of the situation with the dean, proved less cautious; he had had experience with various dormitory organizations in a different school and saw no reason not to tell the students the conclusions he had drawn from it. His views, which happened to be the opposite of the dean's, were built up in the student newspaper, causing the center a great deal of trouble. I subsequently reaffirmed my position to the students and to the dean: The center would stay out of fights and would not act as an expert witness, usually a fake role anyway. Should the fight subside to a point where people were willing to discuss the various plans calmly, members of the center's staff would be glad to take part, contributing whatever they could, along with everybody else. I had no reason ever to deviate from this policy, which was accepted and appreciated by the administration and students alike.

Even those of us who believe that they are the privileged possessors of some valid mental health principles, defining what is best for everyone, must admit that these principles cannot be easily translated into concrete policies and arrangements without a great deal of thought and study. If they believe that some of the school's committees are seriously tackling issues of importance to students and wish to participate, they should be prepared to put at least as much work and study into their contribution as others do, and not yield to the temptation to act as "universal" experts. It is all very well for a clinician to give his faculty colleagues a lecture on adolescence or on psychological roots of racism; they might listen with some interest in a time of quiet. But when the school is faced with the problem of how to handle a takeover of a building or negotiate the demands of a minority group, these general theories are much less useful than certain skills, which today's traditionally trained clinician is no more likely to possess than anyone else. Some of those concerned with the fate of college counselors advocate a radical switch to a new professional role—that of a specialist in social and institutional dynamics, who, by helping solve a range of problems arising in a school, contributes to the institution as a whole (Warnath and Associates, 1973). The psychologists' hopes to qualify for such a role in a variety of settings were raised decades ago by the pioneering work of Kurt Lewin—by his advocacy of "action research," meant to solve social problems while studying them; these hopes are well worth reviving. But even if our theory and methodology were adequate to the task of acquiring and applying relevant knowledge, a whole new program of training would have to be developed to provide those aspiring to this role with a firm basis for claiming the status of experts. Starting with psychoanalysis, the technique of "action research" has been developed in relation to dyads much more extensively than in relation to institutions.

To return to the present reality, the college clinician may occasionally be able to use his research skills to conduct a study of some school situation, the results of which, if applied, could influence policies affecting student life. As I myself have found out, under favorable conditions such a project can be gratifying and profitable (Hanfmann, 1970). Here too, however, the issue of time is a crucial one. A clinician who has a chance to work with students directly, who knows how much can be achieved in this way, will weigh very carefully the pros and cons of a project whose results may or may not be conclusive; may or may not be listened to; may or may not be acted upon; and, if acted upon, may or may not have beneficial effects on student life. If the staff of a counseling center have some time for research, the obvious way to use it is to evaluate systematically the effectiveness of their own work.

Consultant to the Administration

What services is the counselor sometimes asked to perform for the administration? Let us start with the one that I find most objectionable—that, essentially, of an informer. In this view, clinicians are regarded as depositories of secret knowledge about the potential trouble spots in the school, and an attempt is made to persuade them to divulge such knowledge, with reassurances that it will not be misused. To take a situation from the not too distant past: Before the homosexuals made their bid for social acceptance, the administration of many a school, afraid of the effect of a scandal, would have been grateful to the clinician for helping to screen out homosexuals. Any clinician who cooperated by breaking his promises and reporting confidential information would, needless to say, violate the principles both of professional ethics and of interpersonal behavior, which he might be expected to demonstrate to his clients. Even if a mental health worker were sincerely concerned about the spread of homosexuality in the school, considering it a dangerous deviation, he would not have to inform the authorities, since alternate ways of taking action would be open to him. Suppose that a faculty member was reported, by a student in counseling, for homosexual activities with students. The counselor could face this person with the information without revealing its source, and simply ask him to do what he could to stop such rumors from circulating on campus. This warning was bound to be heard.

It is easy for a counselor to fall into the trap of "informing" in a situation that causes anxiety to the administration as well as to himself. When a student's safety seems to be at stake, one often fails to weigh as carefully as one might the consequences of various courses of action. Some counselors, however, have been able to safeguard their working relationship with their clients by resisting the pressure to disclose information about them at the time of an apparent emergency. One such crisis arose when a student disappeared from school. The counselor had some hunches about the situation and therefore was not overanxious; he also knew that the information in question could and would be obtained from those not bound by a confidentiality agreement. However, if an administrator's anxiety triggers anxiety in the counselor, discriminating judgment may fall victim to it. I myself caused the major catastrophe of the period when the Brandeis center was well established and confidentiality taken for granted; at that time, however, the critical situations that might justify breaking one's confidentiality agreement had not been clearly defined. An anxious dean, who had somehow found out, or inferred, that some very disturbed students were being seen at the center, wanted to know who they were, so that he could independently instruct the dormitory counselors to keep an eye on them. I gave in because the dean, at the time my direct boss, was getting excited, feeling that the situation was dangerous and my resistance unjustifiable. Before the day was over, his assistant and confidante, after a few drinks, divulged the secret of the dean's victory at a party where some students were present. These undergraduates, in possession of a secret which, if confirmed and made public, would be the end of a valued service, went for advice to some trusted graduate students; the latter, ignorant of the facts, merely vouched for the integrity of the staff members they knew and advised restraint. Their advice was taken; given the reformist zeal of the students, the magnitude of the requisite restraint was considerable. No one came to ask us questions that spring, and nothing appeared in the campus newspaper. But rumors continued into the next school year, and it was the only year in the first decade of the center's existence to show a marked loss instead of a gain in student attendance; it dropped from 16 percent to 10.5 percent of the year's enrollment.

Such episodes helped to convince the administration that confidentiality and integrity are not just principles to pay homage to but are absolutely essential qualities for the use of a mental health service by students. Faced with the results of his exercising pressure on me, the dean was more than willing to have me define emergency situations; that is, situations where a "clear and present danger" (an imminent major breakdown or a serious threat of suicide or violence) might make it necessary for us to discuss a student's condition with the school, the family, or both. More important than any definition was the agreement that its interpretation was the

job of the center's staff. It was up to the counselor who knew the
student to decide whether his situation and state of mind warranted
a departure from the rule. The issue of "informing" vanished once
it was granted that although anyone, the administration included,
could ask the center's staff to consider the situation an emergency,
the decision whether or not to do so was legitimately the clinician's.

Much more frequently the administrators look not for an
informer but for an *adviser*. They may hope that the mental health
worker, by sanctioning or modifying some proposed action of theirs,
will take responsibility for its outcome. This is justifiable in cases of
severe or acute disturbance, but in other situations advice seeking
too easily becomes a device for shifting one's own job onto someone
else. I can quote an amusing example from my early years at
Brandeis. I was working with a girl who was a "protester," of a
harmless kind, long before social protest became a student movement. The daughter of an influential man, she was adept at calling
him to the rescue whenever she was threatened with disciplinary
action for her frequent infringements of minor rules. At one such
point, the father called the student personnel office and said that his
daughter was seeing me for emotional problems and that her mental
balance might be greatly endangered if she were "dormed" at this
time. The student personnel worker, justifiably annoyed, asked me
whether the student, if confined to her dorm for a few days, would
in fact have a mental breakdown or commit suicide. I felt on the
spot—though sympathetic with the personnel worker's plight. I
wrote to her that it would make no sense for me to approve, in
effect, the proposed punishment, since I did not consider it useful in
anyone's case; but she could draw conclusions, if she wished, from
my not having approached her with any suggestions concerning the
treatment of this student. (I was referring to an earlier agreement
that the center would get the agenda of the administrative committee, so that we could intervene in disciplinary cases where we felt
that the student's mental balance might be endangered.) She did,
and the student was dormed. I subsequently discussed this event
with the girl; she did not resort to this method again, tempted as
she often was. It was, however, too much to expect from this revolutionary not to quote some authority when attacked. In defending
herself to the student judiciary committee, on the subject of proper

dress in the dining room, she blurted out that Dr. H. said it was all right to walk barefoot in the cafeteria. A telephone call from the personnel office followed, sternly reminding me that my obligations were not just to the students but also to the school. I could not recall having made the objectionable pronouncement, but the girl had probably concluded from my expression—and rightly—that I was not impressed by the magnitude of this particular crime.

This episode is not quite typical of the consultative interactions with the administration that cause trouble, since the girl herself was the initiator and knew what was going on. Because she was in counseling with me, all these interactions became useful material for elucidating her customary ways of dealing with authorities. Much more typically, the student who gets into trouble is not personally known to the counselor; and the administrator, often a novice, is faced with a difficult decision and wants an "expert" to take the responsibility for it. A student is asking for financial assistance, claiming that her father has broken his promise to finance her studies. Does she deserve help, or is she perhaps a pathological liar? The psychiatrist should be able to tell. A student is caught for the second time cheating in an exam. Is he a dishonest character, to be expelled from school; or is his cheating a symptom of a psychological disturbance and, as such, deserving clemency or calling for treatment? A student threatens violence. Is the danger real? A student who is quite intelligent is failing his courses. Is he "plain lazy" and to be dropped, or does he have an unresolved conflict and therefore to be kept in school, provided he accepts a referral to the center or to an outside therapist? A student who has had a serious mental breakdown is applying, or reapplying, for admission. Should he be admitted or rejected or told to wait? A student is one of the many who request single rooms, which are scarce. Is it true, as he claims, that his mental equilibrium will be seriously endangered by sharing a room with two others? A student takes a long time to recover from an illness. Should one grant his request for a reduced course load, or does he use his past illness as an excuse? Should one waive the physical education requirement in the case of a student who claims that to him the gymnasium represents a severe emotional threat? And so it goes.

Since I had decided very early, on good evidence, that any

attempt on my part to meet such requests—in fact, any indication of dealings with administration, very visible on a small campus—would undermine the slowly developing student trust, I took a stand that successfully discouraged such requests. I encountered many of them, however, during the period when the first college psychiatrist, not bound by the center's policies, was strenuously trying to implement his belief that in a fine progressive school such as Brandeis the goals of faculty, students, and administration were one and that he could benefit the students most by advising the administration. Accordingly, he agreed to a general policy that the dean of students could refer students to him for evaluation at all critical points of their careers, to be followed by a report and an informal recommendation to the dean. Promising as this plan seemed to its authors, it resulted in havoc. Humorous renditions by students of psychiatric interviews meant to discover the unconscious motives and the hidden pathologies of some delinquents—who often "cooperated" to the hilt—found their way to the center. So did the delegations that came to protest the psychiatrist's power to decide the fate of students in a variety of crucial situations—a state of affairs nowhere stated as the school's official policy.

The center did not take part in the psychiatrist's consulting activities and was not included among "the axmen for the administration" attacked in the student paper. Students were aware, however, of our close working relationship and consequently withheld from us any information they did not want to reach the psychiatrist. Free communication was restored only after the psychiatrist reformulated his policies so as to avoid administrative entanglements. The new policy offered, rather than required, a psychiatric consultation at crucial points in a student's career. If the student accepted, the consultation took place only *after* an administrative decision had been reached and communicated to the student: after he had been permitted to stay in school, or disciplined, or asked to leave; after the student who had had a major breakdown or had left school for a period of therapy was admitted or readmitted. It was up to the student and the clinician to use the meeting to the student's best advantage. For those students who made use of this opportunity, the new policy was beneficial. The administrators, however, had to give up their original hope to get "expert" help in making decisions in administrative matters. The new policies, made known to the students, restored their willingness to use clinical services freely.

The confidentiality agreement of a counselor with a student causes difficulties primarily because it is alien to the fabric of institutional expectations and values. The counselor's refusal to share his knowledge with the colleagues who have a legitimate interest in his client may make him appear unduly officious, odd, or unfriendly. The cost of keeping one's own counsel with administrators is greater still. A clinician who yields to pressure for the sake of keeping his job may find that he has forfeited it by his "tactical retreat"; for few students will request his services if such basics as minimal safeguards of confidentiality are not guaranteed from the start. Yet to guarantee them may not be simple. At Brandeis, in spite of the strong backing I had, I initially had to be satisfied with little. What students told me was to be confidential; but I had to agree, much against my will, to give the dean the names of students who were seen for more than four or five sessions. This "safety measure"—it was meant to enable the dean to consult with the center, if necessary —was consistently protested by students. It could have greatly delayed acceptance of counseling were it not for the saving grace of the "brief consultation" clause; the initial, nonreportable sessions gave the students a chance to become involved in counseling to the point when, for the sake of continuing, they would accept the medical checkup and the report of their names. Eventually, under pressure from many sides, the dean agreed to scratch these rules; better means were found to insure attention to the medical aspect and the possibility of unobjectionable consultation.

To speed up such developments, one can arrange contacts between the administrators and outside representatives of professional opinion; but there is no substitute for bringing disagreements into the open, experimenting, comparing notes, and learning from shared experience. This is a slow process, and it may be further slowed down by the turnover of the staff; one may have to renegotiate agreements or to defend them forcefully. Willingness to take a strong stand, readiness to resign if conditions needed for effective work are not granted, may prove an asset.

At Brandeis, the final outcome of all this work and struggle was rewarding. After the policies tightening the safeguards of confidentiality were clearly spelled out and observed for a period of time without a break, the center's reliability was not seriously questioned, even though frequent changes of deans often gave students cause for concern. Students came to us to check on the rumors. The dean said that maladjustment was widespread on campus. Did he get this information from the center? Is it true that the center will be closed soon? Are counselors legally obligated to report drug users? Student delegations usually accepted our answers and left reassured. Only a few questionnaires returned during that period mentioned the issue of confidentiality. A few stressed it because they had special reasons to be concerned: "I had the utmost confidence that the sessions were confidential; even when serious incidents occurred, my counselor always asked my permission to discuss them with authorities." Others reported rumors reflecting past events or concerns for the future: "I heard rumors that the psychiatrist was first appointed because the psych center really would not give any information on students to the administration." "I have heard a rumor that counseling will no longer be confidential next year, perhaps in an effort to obtain information on drugs. Nothing is as unnerving as evidence to support such suspicions. It would cripple counseling. The strongest action possible should be taken to continue the present policy." In these comments, current confidentiality was taken for granted, as indeed it should have been by that time.

All in all, I have come to believe—on good, quasi-experimental evidence—that the role of consultant or adviser to the administration is incompatible with clinical work. The ambiguity of the counselor's double orientation makes confidentiality safeguards very unsafe—in reality as well as in the students' perception. The counselor himself may be able to keep distinct his treatment of those students who come to him on their own, and to whom he owes full confidentiality, from his treatment of those who are referred by the administration for assessment; with the latter, he may try to minimize the secrecy aspect by dictating his report in the student's hearing. He cannot, however, expect the students to react to this double image without confusion, and confusion about the counselor's role is the surest deterrent to the student's use of that role. A clear public explanation of differential policy might counteract confusion, and the distributions of the two roles between different persons or different units of the mental health service might help. The effectiveness of such measures, however, is limited. This is not astonishing, since a student who regards the administration as an enemy sees the two roles in question as not just different but emotionally incompatible: "If he is for them he is against us."

These views of mine are shared by many counselors and many directors of counseling or mental health centers, but obviously not by all; the staffs of many college services seem to have no misgivings about acting as consultants to administrators, big and small. The size of the school may be a factor here, but I doubt that it is a major one. Interactions with administrators are less obvious in large schools, and news may travel more slowly; but when vital to students it gets around just the same. I know of both large and small schools in which student attendance at mental health facilities dropped drastically after the college clinicians supported some of the administration's views. It seems that the clinician's role as a "double agent"—a role denounced by Szasz (1967) and, after some experimentation, discarded at Brandeis—is still being sanctioned at many schools.

If advising the administration is clearly detrimental to clinical work on the campus, why is it permitted to continue? The lack of clear-cut evidence of its consequences may be one of the reasons. Single protesting voices carry little weight, and to get massive feedback from students one must actively encourage and invite it. Unless the staff of a mental health service is well known and easy to approach, students will find it simpler just to stay away from a suspect and unsatisfactory service than to try to get it to improve. But this behavioral evidence, the decline in student attendance, does not always cause a counseling service to examine itself for factors that possibly could be causing the drop. Reduced demand is not upsetting for a service that is suffering from a shortage of staff time. In attempting to explain the students' moderate or decreasing use of mental health services, one can invoke a variety of reasons: increased, or decreased, pressures on students, such as academic demands and vocational concerns; political activism and social protest, resulting in rejection of "adjustment"; the lure of drugs and of novel methods of fostering personal growth. All these doubtless have some effects, but the reality of these "distal" causes should not make us overlook the possible "proximal" causes within the service itself. The experience of many schools demonstrates that, if certain conditions are observed, students' yearly attendance will grow steadily—certainly to 25 percent of the student body, possibly beyond. It is plausible to assume that some of the college services registering decline or no growth of attendance have counteracted growth by their involvement in the administrative activities which make confidentiality uncertain.

Providing the administrators with authoritative advice may also have other undesirable consequences, particularly if the advice is not well founded or the information not well documented. Readiness to provide such advice endangers the clinician's proper functioning by making him appear a magician to some, a humbug to others. Even when advising within his proper area of competence, the school clinician may meet with great difficulties. He may be able to attach a proper diagnosis to a rare student who is diagnosable; but when it comes to understanding his client in greater depth or detail, his success in eliciting pertinent information depends on the subject's frankness. A clinician who is cast in the role of a gatekeeper, who must pass upon problematic admissions or possible severances, cannot expect frankness from his client. For the mental health worker himself, the worst effect of getting caught in the administration's requests is that he either develops the illusion of omnipotence or, on finding himself unable to do what somebody confidently expects him to do, starts feeling grossly inadequate.

Feasible Consulting and Interceding

Must we conclude, then, that the clinician on campus can do nothing for students other than through counseling and nothing to prove his value to the administration? To my mind, not at all. The guideline to follow in deciding what can and what cannot be done is clear if one believes, as I do, that our most valuable work is done with the students themselves. One must attempt nothing that is likely to interfere with this work and with its continued growth. If one fully accepts this priority, much of the ambiguity disappears; it is not too difficult to figure out what one can profitably do in a given situation within the limitations this consideration imposes.

A counselor can often intervene with the authorities in favor of an individual student if two conditions are fulfilled: he must know the student well as a present or former counselee, and the responsibility for initiating and shaping intervention must be "legally" the counselor's. Further, if the administration requests a consultation about a student, the counselor must have the right to accept or reject it. With these conditions fulfilled, it is up to the counselor to decide what to do in a given case. The need to involve the administration, or the parents, can be determined by the student and the counselor together and carried out as a common project. If the student consents, exchanging information with administrative officers may help him a great deal in crucial situations. Especially in cases of necessary severance from school, the counselor may initiate a chain of events that turns a punitive situation into one of cooperative reflection and planning. These episodes of cooperation also show the dean something of the clinician's work and, conversely, provide the clinician with an opportunity to be useful to the dean.

Among students in counseling there will be instances, or episodes, of serious or acute disturbance which make it mandatory for the counselor to take over in one form or another, though always explaining matters to the student and trying to obtain his consent. (Examples of such situations will be given in Chapter Five.) These cases, however, are a small minority. One must take care—particularly in a paternalistic environment—not to let methods appropriate for dealing with the problems of these few spread to the majority, for whom they would be demeaning or infantilizing. One is much more useful, in the long run, to a student who has to face a difficult situation if, in counseling, one helps him prepare to be his own spokesman than if one offers, or agrees, to intercede for him with the authorities. Since the primary aim of counseling is to develop the student's own initiative and independent thinking, the counselor must have very good reason, indeed, to deviate from this guideline. I recall the case of a student whom I saw in relatively "long-term" counseling. This student was repeatedly on the verge of academic failure and acting out with me the dependent expectations she had of her mother. The mother always intervened in times of trouble, only to be soon faced with more trouble. Through periods of counseling distributed over three or four years, I never followed her example. I would tell the girl and the sympathetic dean, truthfully, that I could not possibly know whether, if given another extension, she would manage to complete her work. By her senior year the girl had made good progress in counseling, which was reflected in all aspects of her life; then, as happens often before completion of therapy, there was a relapse. She was in my office, greatly discouraged, when the dean called to ask what he should do about this student's overdue work, which prevented her graduation. I told him in the girl's hearing: "I would take a chance on her now; give her another extension." He did, and she delivered. At this point, expressing my faith in her was more important than anything else. If the counselor intervenes for students infrequently, and with good reason, his well-founded recommendations will be taken seriously by those responsible for the decisions.

To avoid confusion, the kind of consulting I have been cautioning against as a general policy might perhaps be called "advising," defined as giving authoritarian or "expert" advice routinely or on request. The kind of consulting that is potentially much more productive is not based on the assumption that the mental health worker, as an expert on human behavior, knows how to do everyone's job better. He provides information, or expresses his opinion, only on the topics and situations he is very familiar with, limiting himself in all other discussions to the role of one of the participants or—if he possesses the requisite gifts and/or skills—to that of a facilitator of discussion. One way in which the clinician can benefit students other and more numerous than his own counselees is to teach members of various groups that have dealings with students to identify symptoms of serious disturbance and to make effective referrals to mental health services in other than emergency cases. The incentive for developing this latter skill will be absent as long as the service accepts forced or semiforced referrals—where the student is simply told or advised to report to the center and is expected to do so. I used to tell those who came "because the dean sent me" that this was not reason enough; if the student had agreed because he wanted to come, what was *his* reason? If semiforced referrals are refused by the service, the people concerned quickly learn how to mention the center to the student at an appropriate time and then leave the decision to him or her.

To sensitize many groups on the campus to the existence of emotional problems and to ways of directing students to the sources of help is a manageable task and one essential for maximizing safety. It is not, however, a large-scale preventive measure able to cut down the need for clinical services proper. It will, to be sure, help prevent some individual breakdowns, but it will do so by increasing the service's load, not by reducing it. Any program that increases faculty sensitivity to mental health problems and faculty receptivity to the students will increase identification of such problems. "This leads to more referrals for direct service and increases pressure on the counseling center staff" (Oetting, Ivey, and Weigel, 1970, p. 35). Some schools reportedly omit from their catalogs any mention of the mental health facilities on campus; the omission apparently reflects someone's fear that the students will "overuse" these facilities if they are advertised. But whether the issue is viewed as overuse or simply wider use, the improvement of the environment, which is the hope of social psychiatry, should mean something more than an increase of referrals. The idea of working via the environment has one of its roots in the shortage of the mental health staff in schools and the wish of those concerned with student welfare to use the clinicians more effectively by having them initiate and supervise mental health activities carried out by others. Supported by the work of some community psychiatrists and by reports of excellent performance of some volunteer groups, the idea of "outreach" has caught on. According to Oetting and his associates, the "consultation model," which would make the staff of counseling centers function primarily as mental health consultants to the campus community, is currently being tried by a number of established centers as well as new ones. One of the criteria Glasscote and Fishman (1973) used for selecting effective mental health services for their study was a certain amount of success achieved in this type of work. To judge by these signs, the "consultation model," an application to the college setting of the ideas of social psychiatry, is probably viewed by some people as the hope of the future.

The idea of a "therapeutic environment," in which serious emotional problems do not develop or are quickly and effectively resolved, is indeed an attractive one, and there is no doubt that environments do vary in the dimensions that further and maintain sound psychological functioning. As clinicians we are not entirely justified in telling our patients, as we often do, that a change of environment can do nothing for them, that they will take their unresolved conflicts with them wherever they go. This is only half of the truth. Once a favorable atmosphere is established in a setting, it strongly affects the individual members; it increases their satisfaction with their life and can greatly change their behavior as well as their attitudes and beliefs. It would be fine indeed if, as college mental health workers, we could increase our effectiveness by mobilizing and shaping the resources of the community and facilitating their use. But I am of concrete bent of mind and have no real understanding of such talk until the actual operations for implementing these goals are spelled out in detail. Otherwise, the words "prevent problems before they arise" bring up memories of administrators anxious to know "everything that is going on" and plaguing clinicians to provide lists of names, Rorschach indices, test results; or else, instead of clutching at talismans, requesting psychiatric consultants to screen out all potentially difficult students.

"Environment" means a lot of things, but the part of the college environment most relevant to our concerns is people and their activities. Most of the other relevant aspects—physical and social structures, policies, traditions, methods of teaching, contents of courses—though they have an existence of their own and can be studied as such for their effects on the students, are implemented, maintained, and changed by people. People are also the agents who have the strongest immediate effects on each other. When we talk, for example, about making the environment more cohesive, responsive, growth furthering, and so on, we talk primarily about changing people's attitudes and modes of interaction; from these changes many others will result. To improve the college environment, to make it a growth-promoting, high-morale setting, one must first improve the quality of the persons who constitute it, particularly of those who have a say on a variety of issues. No one doubts that people in key positions who wield some official power can strongly affect the atmosphere and morale of a given social setting, but the college clinicians are not likely to be asked to help choose presidents or heads of departments. For the time being, our best chance for improving a social environment is to develop the people who compose it: helping them to strengthen their assets, to remove obstacles to good functioning, to learn methods of dealing constructively with students and colleagues. In other words, we are back in the business of counseling, treating, or teaching persons, individually or in groups; but we are now dealing with clients much less promising than the students, and we are in the much more difficult situation of having to convince them first of the potential value of the project.

Actually, the situation is not always that difficult. A clinician may have smooth sailing if he has been accepted—voluntarily, not on an order from above—into a group of people who are competent in their jobs, or are developing competence; who like discussing their work among themselves; and who expect contributions, not directions, from the consultant. Staff members at the Brandeis center have had many pleasant and unproblematic contacts devoted to the discussion of their work with student personnel workers, teachers of the college nursery school, some infirmary nurses, and of course also among themselves and with the center's trainees. Most of the members of these groups are accustomed to focusing on the "client"— the student, the patient, the child; since they share many of the mental health workers' assumptions, there is a natural give and take. A similar situation obtains when one meets, as a teacher, with responsive groups of graduate or undergraduate students to discuss their fieldwork or, as a "facilitator," with problem-centered student groups discussing issues arising out of their common life situations. How productive the discussion will be depends to a great extent on the leader. In the future the college clinician may be able to apply his skills to a novel task; in line with the recent efforts to utilize volunteers and paraprofessionals for mental health work, some schools may start programs to train students to be counselors. There are intriguing indications in the literature that by giving selected groups intensive, imaginatively planned practical training, one can develop good therapists in a much shorter time than is required for the traditional professional training. The development of such programs is a major enterprise requiring special staffing and funding, not a project for the counseling service alone, and certainly not a solution to its own problems of maintaining an adequate, relatively permanent staff.

In addition to consulting with interested, task-centered

groups, the counselor will occasionally get requests for consultation on some baffling problem by someone whose work is not in the interpersonal area and who, while not renouncing responsibility for decisions, hopes for expert advice. Sometimes it can be given in the tentative form of "have you thought" of this or that, but it is more useful in the long run to elicit from the person an active participation in the process of getting out of blind alleys and finding solutions to his dilemmas. If a researcher cannot decide, for example, whether to fire an excellent, efficient assistant or to spend his time disentangling the interpersonal tangles this man has a talent for creating, he may be both shocked and pleased to discover that he need not do either. There is something else he can do: find out the reasons, separate the man from his favorite adversary, warn him for the next year. Unexamined assumptions, false alternatives, narrow perspectives, evidence disregarded or distorted, communication refused or neglected—these obstacles to problem solving can make even highly intelligent people feel stuck at times. If the one asking for advice uses the counselor's questions, musings, and comments to get out of some of these boxes and start moving again, this situation is analogous to those of students—to be discussed in Chapter Six—who come to the counselor with a circumscribed problem and get a handle on it after one or two sessions. Like the groups discussed above, these colleagues want assistance and have no trouble accepting it—perhaps because they function well themselves and do not need help badly. It may be challenging to the counselor to find ways to stimulate their thinking and satisfying to feel that he has contributed to their growing competence. He cannot, however, claim to have made a great change in the college environment by helping people who are insightful and competent to start with and are moving ahead on their own. Working with those who would really have to change a great deal to become constructive agents on the campus is quite another matter. It would be analogous—perhaps identical—to working with confirmed neurotics who take a long time just to start seeing that change might be desirable and feasible. Even if they were willing to put time into seminars, group work, training sessions, and the like, their ability to make use of them would be nowhere near that of the students; for many it would be time wasted. Actually, in most of today's traditionally run colleges the faculty and the high-level administrators, whether or not personally rigid, would not think of taking time from their proper tasks to engage in such pursuits; it is unreasonable to expect a mental health worker, no matter how capable and personable, to motivate them to do so.

To sum up, I don't think much of the promise of social or community psychiatry on campus, even if the clinician eliminates its destructive, self-defeating aspects by decisively renouncing the authoritarian mandatory advising of anyone, the administration in particular. He can pull a string here and there for the benefit of his counselee; this may be an important function in those schools where individual students get little attention. He can also judiciously disseminate to various groups information that will help troubled students reach the clinical service or other sources of help. He can try to promote change on the level of policies by sitting on the committees of the school, but he is not likely to exercise a great deal of influence there and may soon conclude that his time is much more profitably spent in the counseling room. He can use some of his professional skills to conduct exploratory or evaluation studies, the results of which might be pertinent to decisions on programs and policies; here too he will do well not to embark on any time-consuming projects unless he has good evidence that they may be productive. He can assist some self-selected staff groups or individuals in developing greater competence in their dealings with students or in their jobs' interpersonal aspects. This is a chance for him to improve and expand some of his teaching and counseling skills, although he will not be using them on people who wield a great deal of power in school, or those whom he would most like to change. The impact of these activities on the school as a whole cannot be expected to be very strong.

To check these conclusions against the experiences of other settings, I have read carefully the descriptions of the environmental work in the schools studied by Glasscote and Fishman (1973), both those in which it was thought to have made some difference and those where admittedly it had had little impact. Nothing in these descriptions contradicts my observations and conclusions. Take, for example, the most obviously successful program which intended to function as the mental health conscience of the school; the activities implementing this intention were of the kind I have described as feasible, potentially useful consulting. They were carried out in an egalitarian spirit, involving no secrecy and no coercion. From the sum total of my reading and from my own experience, three points stand out for me concerning the legitimate "environmental" mental health work on campuses: (1) Since the bulk of this work consists of measures that help the student to find counseling services, it subserves the primary work but cannot substitute for it; the value of this aspect of enlightening the environment depends ultimately on the presence and effectiveness of the sources of direct help. (2) These facilitating measures, which aim at providing pertinent information to the students through many channels (as well as providing information to the counseling agencies themselves about each other), are needed in large schools much more than in small ones, where the existing facilities are not numerous and the news about them and their performance travels fast. At Brandeis, during our best years, a detailed description of the counseling center in the *Student Handbook* and talks about it by the staff to freshmen in dormitories were sufficient to support and complement the student grapevine and to fill with appointments the counselors' then ample time. When almost all students learned about the center, in a favorable way, as freshmen and found it easy to approach the service and to take a friend there, it became less important for us to sensitize the faculty to our work. Students who themselves have been helped remain the best sources of "environmental" help, and the number of such helpers on campus is a function of the work of direct services. (3) The success of the mental health worker in "moving into the college community," which means informing and "sensitizing" other people or consulting with them in other legitimate elective ways, depends not so much on his mastery of clinical methods and theories as on his personal assets—those attitudes, gifts, and skills that make people stimulating, convincing, and readily trusted by others. Whenever there are indications of some impact of the mental health worker's humanistic orientation on the social environment of the school, it seems to have been effected by an outstanding person placed in a key position. This observation is in line with Oetting's insistent warning that consulting is a delicate and time-consuming task, that only the most skilled, gradual, and well-planned consulting program can have any hope of succeeding.

4

Initiation
of Counseling

The following example demonstrates the problems involved in
initiating the counseling process. A sophomore at Brandeis who
terminated contact with his counselor after ten sessions recalled the
experience in this way:

>I am at a loss as to what the purpose of psych counsel-
ing is. My major problem was academic difficulties and uncertainty about my career. It was *counseling* I desired, but all
I came out with was a sore throat from talking so much. I spent
much of my time talking to the "classic psychiatrist" who just
sat and nodded. He gave me little advice and little insight into
my problem, for these possible reasons: (1) He didn't know me
well enough. (2) He wasn't qualified to psychoanalyze me. (3)
I was too stubborn to believe what he told me. (4) The kind of
counseling I needed was not psychological.

73

I believe the main problem was that he did not know and understand me well enough; perhaps more than one session a week could have helped that. As I said before, my major problems were academically based, so when things were not going well in my classes I would be depressed, but the counselor kept insisting the depression was for a different reason. I think now that perhaps I was seeking the wrong kind of help. The psychiatrist did not recognize this and hence did not refer me to the right people. I was frankly disappointed in counseling—its lack of structure, cohesiveness, and methodology.

The young man's communication can be interpreted in a variety of ways, but let us take it at face value, as an expression of his puzzlement and an attempt to make sense of his strange experience. He may or may not have needed psychological counseling, "holistic" or specialized; he may or may not have been able to benefit from it at the time. But these issues were never even joined. Something failed to happen in the first few sessions that would have enabled the student and the counselor either to settle down to their business with a shared understanding of its nature or to part ways with a shared understanding of their reasons. The tasks of what might be called *the precounseling period* were not carried out.

The pattern of this episode deserves a close look, since it may typify the situation of the "dropouts" who leave counseling after a few sessions without discussing the matter with the counselor and are not heard from again. For this reason, in going over the questionnaires returned to the center's staff in four consecutive years, I have picked out those comments that include a time index, those pertaining specifically to the counselor's conduct of the first session or the first few sessions. These comments—not too numerous and mostly critical—are not in a class by themselves. Complaints about the initial contact are, to a great extent, specifications of complaints about counselor attitudes and ways of acting that are rejected generally, whenever they occur. Because of the crucial importance of the first contacts, however, these comments deserve special attention; they will be used here to start and focus a discussion, by no means exhaustive, of both the pitfalls and the opportunities presented by the initial session.

The first contact poses the issue of structuring the situation.

What should the counselor do to indicate to the novice the nature and the goals of the counseling process? I shall start by reviewing the students' typical comments, which define some of the difficulties, and then discuss some approaches to the tasks of the initial period, including my own, as well as some factors contributing to our all-too-frequent mismanagement of the initial contact.

Below is a sample of student comments on the initial contact, starting with the ones whose authors felt they had not been helped by counseling and progressing to the statements of those who were satisfied with the outcome.

(1) In the one session I had, my counselor merely had me talk about my problems and did not offer any explanations or advice of his own. Even though the first session cannot be expected to provide anything monumental, still I was in rather desperate straits at the time, and I hoped that I might receive some sort of help other than the satisfaction of a catharsis and of finally giving voice to my personal problems.

(2) From the first there was a lack of clarity as to what was being attempted. I observed great vagueness on the part of my counselor: strange and unarticulated assumed obligations over which we disagreed but of which I had not been informed until I decided to leave the center.

(3) The methods of counseling I found a bit perplexing, probably because I didn't understand the goal of the counselor and the method. I am still confused about what exactly counseling was.

The criticism in these comments refers to what the counselors *failed* to do. This is true of the majority of comments concerning the initiation of counseling (and also of the majority of negative comments in general). The counselors are criticized for failing to accomplish the task specific to the first session; that is, to clarify for the client the nature of this novel situation. In some instances this complaint is clearly spelled out and is justified by the student.

(4) At the start someone should explain how counseling is supposed to work. No one did this for me, and I felt nothing

was happening; if I had known what to expect I would have been more optimistic.

(5) The center ought to make clear the reasonable expectations and goals and limitations of the counseling experience, before the student commits himself.

(6) It should not be a situation in which the person just talks at random and the psychologist listens. The aims of counseling should be made very clear to the student at the very beginning; if this is not done, he will get the impression that he can just talk at random to someone willing to listen—and the knowledge of himself will not be born or furthered.

(7) Ground rules of therapy should be explicitly outlined, particularly to those like myself who tried to assimilate therapy to patterned experience. Perhaps some books on psychotherapy and/or the various disciplines engaging in it should be recommended for reading by each patient.

These students, more experienced with counseling than the ones quoted first, point out two interrelated foci of the clarification desired: *what* can be achieved and *how*. The second of these two puzzles, just how counseling works, is the one mentioned more frequently. Some students, however, mention both and keep them clearly apart.

(8) One unfortunate but necessary problem is understanding for what purpose I came to counseling, what I could expect to get out of it. Also there was the problem of what I had to do in the sessions, which kept cropping up between the counselor and myself and seemed to strain the relationship.

Some of those who have had a successful period of counseling are able to spell out their wishes more clearly. Looking back from the vantage point of experience, they wish they had been helped earlier to realize the role of self-knowledge in counseling and the importance of the client's own activity.

(9) One negative aspect of the experience, which was more my fault than that of the counselor, was that I expected

to come in, tell my counselor my problems, and then have him solve them for me. I didn't realize or admit during much of the first term that I had to do a great deal of the work myself. In some ways I am sorry that I was not made to realize this in the beginning, though it was probably better that I learned it for myself rather than have my counselor tell this to me.

The last sentence indicates that the student struggles with an unhappy dilemma. Similarly, a student who "went in order to find answers, but instead found new ways to ask questions," and who at first resented "having to wade in the morass of my personal peculiarities" instead of being given definitions, points out the advantages and disadvantages of the counselor's not clarifying his method to him:

(10) This covert direction was good in that I was sometimes led to understand things I missed before, and bad in that I had the feeling that X was withholding information from me.

This statement describes an important aspect of the counselor's dilemma.

Explicit remarks about the need to define the counseling situation at the outset are not very numerous in the questionnaire material; but I believe that the complaint is much more widespread than this frequency suggests, since many early dropouts did not respond to the questionnaire, and many of those respondents who stayed for a longer period may simply have failed to talk about the events of what by then appeared a remote past. One can safely assume that some, perhaps most, of those who left counseling after a few sessions did so because their confusion and anxiety had not been counteracted by some structuring of the ambiguous situation, and they received no glimpse of how counseling could possibly help them: "I didn't feel that the counselor could help me; he didn't tell me anything new."

Few comments in the questionnaires praise the counselor for having tackled actively and effectively the specific tasks of the initial session. Appreciative remarks are much more likely to be made then and there, in response to the counselor's comments. I can recall students telling me that I have asked the right kind of questions,

have clarified matters for them, or have leveled with them from the
start; but among the questionnaire comments the following one is
all but unique: "The most important factor in the success of the
counseling to my mind was the fact that we defined, before we
started, the purpose of the counseling and each stated his view of
what should be attempted, and how. It is painfully rare in this culture to find a situation so defined that the views and intentions of
each party concerned are clear to all other parties."

With this paucity of positive comments, we must make the
most of the negative ones like those quoted above; yet their message
is not unambiguous. Had the counselor attempted to clarify the
situation in some way, how might the students have responded? We
can conjecture that for those whose comments are listed under (1),
(2), (4), (5), (6), (8), and (9) an early clarification would have
had beneficial effects: dispelling confusion, relieving distress, giving
hope or helping to keep up hope, mobilizing the student's own active thinking, building up trust in the counselor. Yet those quoted
under (3), (7), and (10) might have reacted to the counselor's
attempt at explanation by trying to meet his wishes or by engaging
in an abstract discussion of concepts or "rules." Clarifying the situation for the client is useful insofar as it dispels confusion and denotes
the counselor's competence, frankness, and hopefulness; but some
ways of doing it carry the risk of didacticism, of setting up rules
which—whether obeyed or combated—may encourage students to
face away from their own goals and experiences. Our experience at
the center, however, suggests that the advantages of clarification
greatly outweigh the risks. The real issue is how the clarification can
be achieved in a way that takes into account the initial situation of
the two participants.

Demonstration and Its Limits

The counselor who meets a prospective client often feels
under an obligation to assess him and to do so quickly, particularly
if he feels unilaterally responsible for "the disposition of the case."
His preoccupation with the things *he* wants to get out of this session
may blind him to the vital meaning the situation has for the other
and may make him insensitive to the client's feelings and thoughts.

This might have happened to the therapist who after talking to a prospective client told her that she was not psychotic. She had never thought she might be; she had come for some help in managing her children, but she did not stay.

Students vary a great deal in what and how much they know about therapy, but for all of them the basic situation is this: In the first meeting the client tries, with the means at his disposal, to form some idea of the kind of person the counselor is and of what he has to dispense. A sophisticated, active student, if given a chance, may ask questions about the counselor's theoretical orientation or his preferred approach. Today a girl may wish to know how the counselor stands on the feminist issue; a student of sociology may want to check on his views of social pressures as causes of psychological disturbance. The content of the answer may be of some importance to the student, or at least he may think so; actually, however, unless his perceptions have been thoroughly blunted, he is more likely to be affected by the "how" than by the "what" of the answer. He may be reassured by the counselor's willingness to discuss these topics frankly; or he may be troubled by the counselor's dogmatism or by his evasiveness or, worst of all, by his attempt to interpret the question. In general, the student's impressions of what counseling may be like are determined less by what the counselor says about it than by what he *does* in this session. Demonstration is what counts; verbal definitions are often misleading or ineffective. Demonstration, however, has its own pitfalls. The particular approach demonstrated may be just one of the therapist's many "wares"; yet the client may equate it with counseling as such. Attentive listening is what occupies a major portion of many therapists' time from start to finish. The patient who has become convinced that the therapist hears all he says and will respond in time is enabled to accept periods of silence. Yet if the counselor contributes little to the conversation in the first session, the student may conclude—and spread the word—that the purpose of counseling is merely "to give students a chance to talk out things that are on their minds, thus releasing a lot of pressure and avoiding the intensification of one's problems." Or, instead of catharsis, he may visualize another limited function: "The center was no help to me, for I had no problem talking out my difficulties and crystallizing them. Other students may need help of such nature

as I believe the psych center offers, especially those who find it difficult to analyze their problems, to express themselves, and to open up
to others." Such misinterpretations of the goals of counseling are not
too serious in themselves; they can be corrected when voiced, but
they are rarely voiced spontaneously. If the client in the early sessions asks no questions, expresses no misgivings, makes no requests,
and produces a sufficient amount of "pertinent material," the counselor may relax into inactivity, assuming that the student is all set to
go. This is not always the case. While the counselor is patiently listening, the student may be forming a lopsided view of the "procedure" or a skeptical view of the whole enterprise. He may be
deciding not to return or, worse still, stoically preparing to keep
coming without getting any clearer view of his reasons for being
there or of the realities of the situation; if so, he is preparing to
waste time and to be confirmed in his hopelessness.

In some instances these uncommunicated feelings explode in
the counselor's face, leaving him greatly puzzled. In one such case
the counselor reported:

> This young man looked glum at first, but he needed no
> prompting. Once he started talking about the problems he had
> with his girl friend, he really poured out his heart. He talked
> with animation and involvement and did not give me a chance
> to make more than a couple of comments. I felt that we had
> made a start; when the hour was over, I told him I could see
> him next week at the same time. The student immediately
> puffed himself up and said: "I don't know that you will see me
> next week; you haven't told me anything my girl couldn't have
> told me." He didn't come back. In retrospect, I should have
> paid more attention to the fact that he had come reluctantly,
> pressured by friends.

Unusual as it is, this case points out that ensuring communication is
the counselor's responsibility. In particular, as the following story
illustrates, in the first session the counselor must be on the lookout
for any points that he or she has not made clear to the student.

One student who came to the center late in the year plunged
immediately into a vivid description of his uncertain relationships:

he did not know how to read people's actions and expressions, how to know if a response meant yes or no, if a friendly gesture was sincere. We discussed some possible reasons and some effects. In responding to my question about the ambiguous situations he may have encountered earlier, the student described, with great emotion, his parents' lack of expressiveness; as a child he had once asked them if they liked each other. When the hour was over, he asked me, in haste, several urgent questions: What was the matter with him? Should he come back? What could he and I do and how? Pressed for time (the next client was waiting), I said that I would like to see him next week, to talk further, and I made a mental note to work toward clarification next time. I felt that enough had happened in the first session to bring the student back, but I figured without his uncertainties. He canceled, asking for transfer to some other counselor. I wrote him a note accepting his decision and asking him, as a personal favor, to come to see me just once. In thinking about our interaction, I had got some hunches about his reasons and would like to check them out. The next week the student came and told me that he had "decided to be fickle"; he would like to work with me. He confirmed my guesses. I had not made enough clarifying input in the session, he said, even though my comments and my letter did lead to insights later on. He realized subsequently how often he chose to respond to the negative aspects of an event— like not wanting to give me another chance after the first session! What made him change his mind? "I had doubted whether you cared about me personally. Your note showed me that you did; it was more than just doing your duty." The student proceeded to work at full speed and achieved a great deal in the short period of time at our disposal.

In the first session one's repertory of useful responses is necessarily limited. Many an interpretive statement, many a confrontation appropriate at a later stage, turns out to be unacceptable or misleading when it cannot yet be supported by shared observations and insights and by the trust based on acquaintance. The counselor's attempt to use a crucial interpretation, both as an example of what therapy is like and as a means of demonstrating his own competence, may be doomed to failure and may, in fact, boomerang: "Extremely upsetting and disappointing was the interview with X. Without a real knowledge of me or my feelings X took it upon himself at the only session we had to tell me exactly what was wrong with me and that some assumptions I was proceeding on were not valid. This approach only alienated me and discouraged me from wanting to continue therapy with someone like him." "Counselor made a brilliant analytic diagnosis in the first interview, but from then on was totally incapable of understanding the context of the situation, or what I was talking about in general; he seemed very self-centered to me." Without proper preparation a valid interpretation will often sound like an accusation to the student, or at least suggest a superior "I know it all" attitude on the counselor's part. The student will hardly feel like opening up to a person who seems to cast himself in the role of detective-judge. Most of the interpretations based on psychoanalytic theory are of little use in the first session, before evidence for them has accumulated, particularly if they betray their theoretical roots; a sophisticated student immediately picks them out as textbookish: "You are thinking of the Oedipus complex." Explanations in terms of the past may be rejected as irrelevant or as showing lack of concern for the student's actual problems: "The doctor I had wouldn't let me talk about what was bothering me: insisted on talking about my past." "My counselor used the Freudian approach—what nonsense! I am not interested in what happened at age two; I want to know why I am so tense *now*!" Any assumption voiced by the counselor that the client's parents may be involved in his problems is taboo for some students, sufficient to make them leave in a hurry; even questions about family relations may be resented, particularly if the questioning is pointed and insistent. Deliberate use of methods calculated to evoke strong feelings may also frighten away a novice who is far from realizing the extent to which he suppresses emotions and what it does to his life. A "Rogerian" response of the type that merely acknowledges and enhances the feeling component of the client's statements is a much safer bet for the first session, since it has acceptance and nonviolation built into it. In fact, this approach, if the counselor is adept at it, works very well for those who come prepared to start working on vital issues and who express genuine feelings in a relatively undisguised way. But there are many others who do not provide the counselor with anything he could "reflect" simply and usefully; with them this approach does not work.

Some counselors make an active attempt in the initial sessions to arrive at a shared view of the client's problem and to reach agreement on the specific goals of the counseling period, sometimes also on its duration, or on the distribution of the available time. Such focusing has many advantages, even though the popular concept of a "contract" between client and therapist fails to emphasize the flexible nature of their arrangement. Emphasis on the purposeful, directed character of the project counteracts some students' assumption that, counseling being a "good thing," they might benefit even if they don't know what is amiss or what they would like to achieve. Setting limited goals, taking account of the available time, discussing the possibility of referral now or later—all serve to check magic expectations; the student is discouraged from harboring obviously unrealistic goals. Moreover, the process of trying to arrive at these shared conceptions and agreements can be an effective demonstration of the collaborative nature of the whole enterprise and of the style of the counselor's contribution: "In the second session it was quite obvious that X had reviewed what I told her; she came up with valid insights and with options in viewing my problems which were interesting and thought-provoking." On the negative side, one cannot—or should not—make binding agreements about the specific goals to be pursued throughout, particularly if the available time is not limited to just a few sessions. The student's goals may undergo changes in the course of a successful period of work, and the kind and amount of progress are not exactly predictable. I myself, though anticipating the general direction of change, can rarely visualize in advance just what the student will achieve. In most cases I feel that something of value can be attained even through a short period of counseling; but if pressed for a more exact forecast, I must admit that I have so often been wrong in my expectations that I have given up predicting. Since the best time to stop cannot be guessed in advance, the time limit should be stated as a general rule, not as a promise to see the student the maximum possible number of times. Agreement on goals should be no more than a tentative identification of the direction in which, at this time, the client and the counselor wish to move. Furthermore, this focusing on the "what" of the counseling neglects the no less important issue of "how" and thus may fail to fulfill one of the important tasks of the initial session or of the total "precounseling" period.

Exploration and Its Pitfalls

One method that seems to bypass the issue of structuring or demonstrating is to devote the first session to history taking or to an active exploration by the counselor. This solution to the problems of the first session, however, is more apparent than real. If it is made clear to the client that this first interview is preliminary to counseling, that he is seen "for evaluation only" and probably not by his future therapist, then the issue is merely postponed to the next session, when the "real thing" is supposed to start. Moreover, if the student has come to the first interview all stirred up and mobilized for a significant personal step and finds himself being questioned routinely, postponement of counseling proper may have the same bad effects as time spent on a waiting list. In addition, the counselor who follows an "evaluator" may be placed under a handicap; since the student expects something very different from this second counselor, a continued exploration may lead to a fiasco: "The two sessions I have had with two counselors were about what I had expected. They were informational interviews about what was bothering me and what I was like. I knew basically what was bothering me, and even how to correct it, but I just could not take the proper steps. I got nothing from these sessions, and, perhaps irrationally, I figured I would not get anything from further sessions either."

If the same counselor conducts both the formal evaluation and the subsequent interviews, the situation may be even less clear to the student, and he may have a hard time distinguishing where information getting ends and therapy begins. This is not, in itself, a drawback. A patient who at the end of the first meeting with a psychiatrist asked "When shall we start?" and got the reply "We have started" had a smooth induction into therapy. But if confusion continues, it interferes with rapport and with work: "I had difficulty being at ease during my few counseling sessions. I didn't know if the sessions were to help with my problems or to give small bits of information to the therapist, or both. I was somewhat confused by this. My impression was that the sessions were for him to find out what to do about me rather than to help me solve my problems." The last comment, with its antithesis of "for him" and "for me," eloquently expresses the main pitfall of the information-getting approach: the counselor moves in and takes over. One need not, with Rogers, proscribe all factual questions; but one must realize that the counselor's excessive preoccupation with information getting may cause the whole enterprise to start on a wrong path. The student, in coming to counseling, usually expects that some questions will be asked to clarify the complaints he presents and the situations he describes; if he tells of a depression that started a month ago, he can expect to be questioned about the events of that time. He can have only vague notions, however, about what else will take place, and the events of the initial session will help shape his conception of therapy. If the counselor takes over by embarking on an extended exploration, if he asks questions which have no obvious connection with the problem presented, an anxious or suspicious student may feel mystified and frightened: "He asked me if I got along with other children when I first went to school. What does that have to do with my problem? What does he suspect?"

Even if the student is not upset by excessive questioning, it may cause him to lose his own momentum and to develop expectations that are both false and unprofitable. He may assume that the counselor will continue to act as a medical expert, will diagnose and prescribe; the counselor's failure to do so will be puzzling and frustrating, the more so if he views the student's expectations as dependent demands. Paradoxically, the therapist himself may have initially encouraged the client to take the passive attitude which he later decries. Furthermore, if the counselor contributes more than his fair share to the client's decision about entering counseling (or about anything else) and later proves wrong, he is worse off than if he had spelled out the factors that made for uncertainty and let the decision be a shared and a more tentative one. Disturbed students occasionally reappear at the center after having been earlier told by an "evaluator" that nothing much was wrong with them or that they were at a "stage" that would pass. These students are often bitter about the wasted time and are usually unwilling to see the same counselor. (Actually, when a service is prepared to offer help with problems of all kinds and degrees, such pronouncements have no useful function.) It may be even worse for a student to be told authoritatively after a brief contact, with no sharing of points of view, that he is in bad shape and should start therapy without delay; he then starts therapy with dire expectations or is frightened away altogether.

Another serious mistake committed by counselors overeager to get the picture of "dynamics," and to get it in one fell swoop, is to ask questions the student is not ready to answer, to bring up topics he is not ready to discuss. In feeling free to ask any question he deems pertinent for "diagnosis," the counselor uses this medical prerogative to no good purpose. The student can easily be made to feel that to benefit he must tell all, but he may still resent letting a stranger in on something that he feels "ought to be private, or at the very least an earned confidence." He may "cooperate" and feel badly misused, treated not as a person but merely as an object of study. A student who came to the center with an advanced case of *anorexia nervosa* (refusal to eat), a relatively rare condition, was subjected to this type of questioning. Though usually a tactful man, the evaluator was curious about her condition and therefore explored her background and inner life much further than was necessary for practical action in this near-emergency situation. Even though this student acknowledged that the mental health center had been useful to her in a situation requiring difficult transactions with parents and a speedy outside referral, these interview experiences left an enduring bitterness. In filling out the questionnaire several months later, she checked off the statement that this contact had "made matters worse" for her by arousing both resentment and anxiety. Compare with this the comment of a senior who had a period of counseling toward the end of the year, of necessity a very brief one: "Also comforting was X's complete awareness that we only had a short time to work and that we should not dig too deeply. I don't think anything was brought up which I am not equipped to handle. I am saying in essence that I felt safe, that I trusted my life was not going to be mishandled." One novice counselor, a highly recommended bright young man, was fascinated by the glimpses of the clients' unconscious dynamics afforded him by initial interviews. He came to tell me about them starry-eyed; but his visit was often followed by that of an indignant or frightened student, who felt that the counselor's line of questioning reflected no understanding of the student's statements or concerns. The next year this counselor accepted a position in an institution where diagnostic testing flourished and where his ability to perceive and outline the unconscious dynamics was fully appreciated by the staff.

Encouragement of passivity and a hurtful intrusion into privacy are not the only pitfalls of excessive information getting, segregated from the total context of counseling. Even if specific negative effects are absent, this approach loses the counselor the unique chances that the first contact with the client provides. In fact, in the case of "evaluation only" he is practically under obligation to let some of these chances pass by. If he says something that arouses hope in the client and makes him respond, the client may then place any other therapist at a great disadvantage by regarding him as second best. Some clients will remember wistfully even a year or two after the event, the person who said the right word, asked the right question at the right moment, without having had the opportunity to carry through what he started. When he is seeing a student "for evaluation only," therefore, the experienced counselor is well advised to restrain himself from following his trained impulses; that is, he must refrain from doing anything that could induce the student into counseling—with him. He must stop after he has obtained the minimum of information necessary for his purpose, such as determining the urgency of the person's need for help. If he explains to the student from the start the reason for his restraint and his curtness, he will avoid confusing him or prejudicing him against counseling, but the potential therapeutic momentum of the first session will be lost just the same.

A formal session of evaluation, separated from counseling proper, seems to compound, rather than solve, the problems involved in the initiation of counseling. At Brandeis such a procedure became necessary when, because of the increasing crowding of the center, we could no longer see all students without much delay. Paradoxically, however, shortage of time leads to its waste. If, instead of being evaluated, those students who came "raring to go" could work intensively in the first hour, some of them would not have to return at all, and others would be through in much less time, thus helping to keep waiting lists to a minimum. To bring about this precondition of fully effective counseling is worth all the effort it may require. In the optimal situation the counselor who first meets the student can continue working with him, unless he has reasons not to, and is not under any great pressure to evaluate and to make recommendations in a hurry.

The Tasks of Precounseling

Some students, if they have the freedom to use the first contact as they wish, plunge speedily into the problematic issues. If the counselor is attuned to their concerns, a productive interchange can take place immediately. If the issue is a limited one, it may be resolved on the first try. Such one-time contacts can sometimes be highly rewarding: "My only session with X was relaxing, enjoyable, and extremely helpful. Because she treated me as a Brandeis freshman who has some intelligence and character, and not as a typical patient, we were able to reach some rewarding conclusions and to open some probing paths. It all seemed so simple after that session." Such productive brief encounters are discussed in Chapter Five. For other students, however, a larger portion, if not the whole, of the counseling period must be devoted to resolving ambivalence toward professional help.

> To me it was apparent why I felt as miserable as I did: it was simply the result of an accurate self-appraisal, based on fact. I could not see how therapy could help me, so for the first few months the central question in therapy was whether I should be there at all. The rigidity and the persistence with which I stuck to this topic and defended my view now, in looking back, really amazes me. I was afraid that if I were to agree to therapy I would fail at that, too. I was able to make a step forward when X explicitly stated that all that was required of me was to be present physically in that room one hour each week; the work itself, or at least its initiation, would not be asked of me.

This degree of fixation on the topic is unusual, but many students who apply for counseling do need a fairly extended period of exploring what this enterprise may involve if they are to start on it with some confidence. To distinguish this work from what follows, we may call it *precounseling*. Demonstration of what counseling would be like, limited exploration of problem areas, statement of policy about time limits, discussion of the direction that might be profitably taken and of the gains that can realistically be expected— all have their place among the activities of the initial period. Its central issue, however, is not what to work on in counseling but whether to work at all. That is, the client must decide whether he wishes to enter counseling at this time; and the counselor must help him explore all pertinent points in order to develop an adequate basis for the decision to be made. The weighing and the decision are the client's; but the outcome depends, among other things, on whether the counselor has provided the clarification needed to correct misconceptions, to allay misgivings, and to increase hope. If the counselor has done his part well, the resulting decision will be, in essence, a shared one, regardless of what it is and of who formulates it. The decision against counseling, even if problems are clearly present, is not to be counted a failure when it is made with an adequate awareness of reasons and does not preclude a later attempt. This was the case with a girl who had hoped that counseling would improve, or at least preserve, her current friendship with a disturbed boy. When she realized that this would not necessarily happen, she decided against counseling; but she returned to it after the relationship failed. For another example, a young man was advised by his dentist to seek psychological help because he was grinding his teeth in his sleep. When I explained to him what counseling entails, and when he could find no other problem that he wanted to work on, he concluded that his symptom caused him less distress than treatment would; I could only agree. These outcomes are not failures, and the door is left open. But any decision that is essentially unilateral indicates the failure of precounseling.

The following two reports by early dropouts may be construed as examples of the counselors' failure to tackle the tasks of precounseling. Both reports were written two years after the attempt at counseling had failed.

> I was under a misconception about counseling. I went with a problem, willing to answer any questions that would be put to me, but couldn't start the talk myself. I felt whatever I

would say would be misconstrued. So we sat for several sessions in almost complete silence and I decided this was not for me. . . . Before I am able to undergo any type of therapy or analysis I will have to overcome my suspicion of it.

I was the counselor of this girl—at an early time, before my initial style of working had changed. The stalemate may have been produced or aggravated by my first asking questions and then changing to a passive role without even attempting to explain to the student the reasons for the switch. Explanation alone, it is true, would hardly have overcome the girl's unwillingness to initiate discussions for fear that her choice of topic would be interpreted unfavorably. (Such fear can be allayed if one does no more than reply to questions, but this device precludes meaningful conversation.) Had I responded, however, to the student's implicit request for more active guidance of the session, I might in time have found a chance to explore with her the nature of this fear, its roots and its consequences. As it was, I knew merely that for some reason the student had found herself unable to talk; she never returned.

Since my first visit was my last, I can give only a first impression. I was apprehensive about going to the counseling center to begin with, and only went because I was advised to do so by someone whom I respect very highly. Only this friend knew that I went, but even so, I lost some self-esteem in asking for help in a situation no worse than average. In such a sensitive state, it is understandable that the counselor's disinterest seemed to border on uninterest. This made it even harder to talk. Toward the end of the hour this feeling gradually went away, and the next session might have been easier. It was purely an accident, and not an uncommon one, that I forgot to attend that and the next. Now, however, I feel that if I had continued, I would have lost more in self-esteem by telling what ought to be private, or at the very least an earned confidence, than I would have gained in understanding.

This girl felt humiliated because she had to ask for help and to submit to an invasion of her privacy. Handicapping as these attitudes can be when extreme and rigidly held, they reflect our cultural values, and we do well to acknowledge their positive aspects:

the emphasis on personal responsibility and interpersonal equality. But if the counselor had been more active and more personal in promoting an egalitarian atmosphere and making the situation less "asymmetrical," the student's misgivings might have been brought to light in the session itself; they might then have been discussed and reduced in strength, enabling her to enter counseling. The counselor might have approached the issue of misgivings in this case by focusing on the fact that the student had actually come on somebody else's advice, in spite of her own unwillingness. Emphasizing the conflict inherent in this situation and its bearing on the student's course might have helped her to come to grips with her reservations. If, as a result, she had decided to leave then and there, she would have taken with her a new understanding that the decision to enter counseling could be no one's but hers, an insight which is a precondition of a genuine start. She might have returned at some time, perhaps quite soon, ready to work. I have known students who had been pressed into counseling by their parents and found themselves unable to move; some of them discontinued and returned without the parents' knowledge at a later date in order to settle independently into responsible work.

The issue of the prospective client's readiness for therapy is often discussed under the concept of *motivation,* a concept I find to be of limited value if it is used in a global fashion and with no reference to how the person perceives his situation. Many students come to the center tentatively, without any certainty that they need or want counseling. This is not a result of intrinsically low motivation, whatever that may mean, and not necessarily a sign of neurotic confusion or ambivalence; the uncertainty may result also from simpler causes. The student may know that he has a problem but, not knowing what counseling is, is not sure he has brought it to the right place. Is it counseling that he needs or maybe academic or vocational guidance? He may have been talked into coming by someone else, without having felt much need for it himself or, at least, without having overcome his own objections. He may be trying, in coming, to set an example for a disturbed friend, or he may have come out of curiosity about therapy; if he is a psychology student, he may be trying to satisfy a professional interest. A few astute observers among our respondents, in describing their friends' dealings with the center, discuss such instances of inadequate reasons for coming and propose remedies.

By senior year many students begin to feel they should take advantage of the service just because it is offered—sort of why-let-free-couseling-go-to-waste attitude—and start searching themselves for problems to present.

Some people in going to the center have this truculent attitude that the psychologist must prove himself by being witty and not using the obvious tricks of the trade.

With some it gets so bad that attending psych counseling becomes a social status event, friends going and comparing visits; this turns problems and neuroses into status symbols. The staff should somehow develop an attitude of only caring for those who need help and realize it, without barring students from referring themselves.

All these motives are not sufficient for entering counseling "for real," but neither are they an indication that the student does not need help or would be unable to use it. Professional interest or flippancy may cover up personal concerns; these attitudes, if they persist, may prevent the student from making use of counseling, but at least they enable him to make the initial contact with the center without being stopped by anxiety.

Once the student is there, what happens depends not only on his own state of mind but also on the counselor's handling of the first sessions. The counselor is often advised to "ascertain" in the first contact whether adequate motivation is present and make his recommendation accordingly. This advice disregards the obvious fact that the prospective therapist cannot explore and "test" the person's motivation for counseling without influencing it in the process. Whatever the student's state of mind before he entered the counselor's room, from the moment they start talking, motivation as well as insight is an outcome of interaction. The student's experience in the first few sessions will influence the decision he makes when he is eventually confronted, or confronts himself, with his lack of serious intention and real involvement. In the very process of facing and discarding his insufficient or faked motives, he may discover some valid personal reason for giving counseling a try. But if his reservations concerning counseling are not brought to light in the early sessions, the student's course will lack clarity because of these persisting "motivational flaws." If he drops out, neither he nor the counselor can be certain of the real reason; if he keeps coming, his "decision" to enter counseling may prove to have been verbal only. The result may be a waste of time and mutual disappointment. Some students who have observed their friends take this course suggest how it could have been averted: "Students should be encouraged to switch counselors as soon as they find they cannot talk frankly with theirs. They should be made to feel that they must not only show up, but give themselves completely if they are to succeed." "I feel that more commitment expressly agreed upon by both student and adviser is necessary. Several friends felt that the counselor did not understand them or did not see through their ruses; they were embarrassed to ask for a transfer and just stopped coming." Such comments indicate these respondents' correct perception that "motivation" is not just the student's attribute but a product of student-counselor interaction; obstacles to starting and to moving cannot be removed in the absence of effective communication between the two.

Dealing with Misgivings

My own increasingly more active handling of the tasks of the initial sessions results from the conviction that misgivings must be brought to light and confusions dispelled speedily if one is to make good starts and avoid false ones. My approach also reflects a personal preference, which I believe I share with many students; that is, although I fully appreciate the reorganizing power of some primarily emotional experiences, I find that thinking, too, can be used to excellent advantage in outlining and solving emotional problems; a complete "experience" contains both components, the cognitive and the emotional. When clinicians say that college students tend to intellectualize, they usually refer to the defensive aspects of intellectual processes: substituting thinking for feeling, using theories and arguments to distort or camouflage personal realities or hold them at a distance. College students do engage in such activities almost "professionally," but in most cases these have

not yet congealed into rigid patterns, as they often have for graduate students and for many older intellectuals, including doctrinaire
therapists; their personal investment in a given intellectual device or
a given conceptual scheme is not yet very large. The older adolescent
occasionally uses his thinking as protection against emotion; but,
even when defensive implications are clearly present in his discussions, it is advisable not to hurry to point them out: "It seems best
to enter freely and lightly for a time into intellectual discussions of
the various therapies, of individualism, conformity, Zen, of the fate
of creativity in psychoanalysis, sandwiching between these discussions . . . tentative demonstration of how his particular therapy
would proceed" (Hanfmann and others, 1963, p. 54).

Much more often than some therapists assume, the older
adolescent lets his thinking fulfill its natural function of assimilating,
organizing, and facilitating experience. Several workers with college
students describe them as dealing in a vigorous and flexible way
with the newly discovered area of subjective experiences and personal valuations. Some view their great responsiveness to therapy as
a function of the central event of midadolescence: the advent of
self-cognition. My own experience with those students who chose to
engage in seemingly abstract philosophical discussions led me to discard my initial prejudice against this kind of "intellectualization."
I was pleased to discover how often these generalizations had an
expressive rather than a defensive function and how directly they
pointed the way to the student's vital personal concerns. As in some
students' literary productions, the emotional meanings were right
there; there was no need for interpretation, for any explicit translation into a different idiom. Not all students, of course, communicate in this way, via imaginative thinking; but most students' thinking can be profitably engaged in exploring inner and outer reality,
provided some connection between the topic and their genuine experience has been established first.

Keeping this condition in mind, let us take the task of conveying to the student what the counseling process will be like. Obviously, it makes little sense to try to define therapy formally or to
explain how it works; those who insist on a detailed description are
best referred to books. But popular misconceptions about counseling
can be corrected nonetheless, and there is no need to shun all ex-

planations. It is not very difficult to set straight a student who expects advice from the counselor simply because he assumes this new professional helper is like those he is already familiar with—medical or vocational counselors, who test, diagnose, and prescribe. If, on being asked how he views counseling, the client produces this conception, the counselor acknowledges the logic of these expectations and then raises questions. Can the student view his current personal problem as an illness—that is, a condition identical in all its carriers, well known to the expert, and curable by remedies known only to him? Is it not rather a problem in living? If so, might not his own experience be most pertinent in solving it? If the difficulty seems to be largely situational, what can the student, knowing the situation as he does, expect from trying course A or course B? If the difficulty is of long standing, not caused by any current situation, its whys and wherefores can probably be found in the student's experience, which is known only to him; he, not the counselor, is an expert on himself, though the other can contribute his wider experience of human problems in general. Maybe the student's trouble is an outcome of some erroneous belief, part and parcel of his personal philosophy. Would he care to spell some of it out? If he wants to limit his role to providing material for the expert to put together, the counselor might get a good case study out of it, but what will *he* get? Showing the student in this personally relevant manner why the counselor cannot always lead the way takes more time and effort than simply telling him that advice and guidance will not be given, or trying to convey this information by silence, which only too often conveys something else. This investment pays, however, if it results in more than a mere acceptance of the rule by the client or a pale intellectual realization. A student who really gets the message may, for instance, express great relief that he is not going to be dehumanized by being placed in some diagnostic category, a distasteful treatment he was bracing himself to undergo. Now things shift; and counseling, viewed as a joint exploration of his individuality, becomes an exciting, challenging prospect.

One can proceed in a similar fashion to explore other less stereotyped expectations the applicant has in regard to counseling—his personal hopes, doubts, and fears. Once they are brought up, specific misunderstandings about counseling can be corrected, and the door is opened to clarification of some of the student's more general personal beliefs and assumptions, which are imbued with feeling. The process of making these emotional beliefs explicit may produce some insights and some shifts of attitude; some obstacles to counseling may be removed as the person actually gets a glimpse of how it can work. The topic of ideas and feelings about counseling is a natural one for the initial contact, and it has the great advantage of directing the discussion to what is on the subject's mind here and now; this sets a good precedent. In dealing with this topic, the counselor has a chance both to learn vital things about the client and to demonstrate some of his own attitudes and skills. At the same time, an unforced, stimulating dialogue will be introduced in a matter-of-fact fashion as the natural mode of the counseling "procedure."

As a starting point for such discussions, one can use the questions and the requests which the prospective counselee brings up himself, but one need not be limited to those. After providing information on the externals of counseling (such as time limits and help with referral if necessary), one can, for example, ask the student what other questions he would like to have answered, what he knows about therapy, what he wishes his therapy to be like. One can try to find out what he has heard about the service, what experiences his friends had with it, or why he did not come to the center when he first thought of coming. One can also ask him directly what misgivings he has about counseling—since everyone has some. Early in the history of the center we prepared a list of questions most often asked by students and of misgivings most often expressed, together with some general answers. The list was meant to be used by various student advisers, but some students found that going over the list in the initial discussion of counseling proved helpful for them. In coming to the center, is the student afraid of the stigma, or of being thought crazy by friends, of being weak, of becoming dependent, of upsetting parents should they find out, of being disloyal to parents in talking frankly about them? Does he fear to be judged "bad," found wanting, found "wrong" in his cherished beliefs, found to be very ill, perhaps beyond help? Or is he apprehensive because he feels that his problem does *not* amount to much, that he will forget what he wanted to say and may run out of things to tell, that he will be wasting the counselor's time and may be told to leave and make room for others? If he insists on structure, on being given answers and rules, is this insistence tinged with a general fear of confusion and uncertainty; or is he afraid that, having to guess at what the counselor values and wants, he may not be able to please or impress him? Does he trust the counselor to know what to do with his confidences? Does he, in fact, fully trust the promise of confidentiality? Has he heard rumors to the contrary?

Once these apprehensions are out in the open, the counselor must respond. If he views the disclosed fears as unrealistic and highly exaggerated, he may be tempted to say as much to the student, or try to reassure him, or induce him to search for the roots of his fears in some earlier experience. These approaches rarely work, and for good reason. Though the students' misgivings about counseling may be fed by anxieties stemming from other sources, they also have a basis in reality. In the first place, the counselor is a stranger, and it is not safe to trust a stranger with the kind of power a therapist may gain over a patient. Moreover, counselors do vary in attitudes and ability, and even experienced ones fail. Finally, success is never guaranteed, some pain is likely to be involved, and some harm may be done. If, remembering this, the counselor accepts the misgivings he has invited as something more than pure fantasies, the way is paved for a potentially useful discussion. If the student is assured that he may be right on some points, he will be more ready to see where he may be wrong or shooting beyond the mark. The nature of the discussion that ensues, while reflecting the counselor's preferred approach, must be geared to the attitudes of the individual student. A minimal discussion or a sensitive "reflection of feelings" will make some feel understood and will suffice to diminish their fears—making the feared events seem improbable, if not impossible. At the other extreme, students whose attitudes toward counseling are fraught with neurotic conflict must be confronted with the obvious or hidden contradictions with which their statements abound. A student who professes a great need and a great wish for help may also be telling the counselor less directly but clearly enough that he is well off as he is, or that he does not believe he can be helped, or both; he may vacillate between many more incompatible assumptions. Glossing over them would lead to a false start. The student must face these contradictory feelings without too much delay if a sound basis is to be found for the work to begin.

The following episode is part of a brief counseling course to be described in detail in the next chapter: A young man complaining of indecision about a major personal issue did not tackle this problem in his first regular session; instead, he used me as an academic adviser in weighing the pros and cons of some decisions he had to make about his studies. As soon as he had built up a strong case for one course of action, he immediately balanced it by equally strong reasons against it. I pointed this out and wondered if his wish to work with me on his problem was not balanced by an equally strong fear he had hinted at that therapy might make matters worse. I said it might, but needn't. Even in the short time we had, if he risked some steps toward greater clarity, he might at least gain new perspectives; therapy, after all, can work. The student brightened. As I was talking, he said, he had felt the balance shift; his hope for a wider perspective now outweighed his fear. He settled into a very productive period of work, even though, naturally, this was not the last of his doubts.

Even a tentative decision to give counseling a try requires the client to give precedence to one of his conflicting assumptions; if he does not put himself on one side of the conflict, he will be sitting on the fence, not moving anywhere. Sometimes the counselor can promote such a shift by asking the student to explicate what is implied in his or her questions or statements. For instance, one girl, a science major, who was depressed and felt lonely and miserable, said that her decision to begin counseling would depend on the counselor's answer to a question she asked. She wanted to know whether she was more unhappy than most people. If so, she should do something about it; if not, she did not need to. To let her see her extreme dependence on external yardsticks, I tried the following line of questioning. Suppose we did have all the information needed for an answer and could plot the various degrees of unhappiness of the entire world population, or at least of the American college students. Where on this distribution curve would she have to be placed to feel that her misery justified concern and merited help? Suppose her place on the curve changed because other people's unhappiness increased or decreased, without her own state being affected. Would her conclusion change? In trying to think this through, the girl realized that she could not avoid consulting her own feelings in this decision; she decided to start counseling. Similarly, a student who wanted his girl friend to take intelligence tests to show if she was worthy of him gave up the idea after having struggled in vain to decide how large a deviation from his own IQ he could tolerate in her.

Sometimes the counselor must provide more than a reflection of feeling, a confrontation with contradictions, or an explication of a confused assumption. Take those who have a great fear of becoming dependent on the counselor, knowing also that they crave such dependence. Merely acknowledging the existence of this conflict does not always break the deadlock; instead, the counselor may have to take a stand. Some of these students are able to relax and move on only after realizing that, in the counselor's view at least, such dependence would be neither disastrous nor lasting; together they could make sure that it would not get out of bounds. To a student who is afraid of being overpowered by the counselor's ideas, the counselor can make it clear that he himself considers most of his comments tentative; that he would like to share even his hunches, for what they may be worth, but can do so only if the student, whose opinion will carry great weight, feels as free to reject as to confirm them. Such an understanding is a good protection both against the counselor's errors and against tensions being built around the issue of "who is right." "X had been suggesting that I direct my attention along a line of interpretation that did not in the end prove to be central to the problem, but no damage was done through his suggestion. Not being very familiar yet with my situation, he was unable to pinpoint the source of the trouble; however, his open ear and objective mind were invaluable for my finding the answer."

Failure and Success of the Initial Contact

What makes the problems of the first session difficult for counselors? I have no statistics to quote, but my impression is that as a group we are slow to learn all we could learn from the large quota of "first sessions" which each counselor has each month. Perhaps some factors inherent in the nature of the service retard this learning or counteract its application. Students who drop out after a few trial sessions are not a serious problem for the staff; only the newcomers occasionally worry about them as their failures. There are valid reasons for this equanimity; we know that some students approach the center in a very tentative, exploratory fashion, and we have known dropouts to return when their needs become pressing. Unfortunately, some other reasons for our equanimity—related to the shortage of staff time, which has become an increasingly greater handicap—are less valid. When counseling time is at a premium and must be given to students whose needs are most urgent, the temptation is strong to conclude that the early dropouts were poor prospects anyway; their defection is seen as proof that they lacked the necessary motivation, and the matter is left to rest there. When shortage of time is most acute, one tends to act with the applicants—deliberately or not—so as to turn them away.

I believe that this factor operates even more strongly in greatly overcrowded outpatient clinics. From the students referred by me to such clinics, I have occasionally received reports about what amounts to a severe mistreatment of prospective patients. Some of them were not given appointments within the time specified or were not informed whether they had been accepted for treatment; interviewers failed to appear or were late for appointments—all of this with occasional apologies but without advance notification of possible delay; that is, with complete disregard for the feelings of the person waiting for a chance to take an all-important personal step. As one student, who had waited two hours for her interviewer, put it: "I do not mind waiting for a doctor who may be busy with emergencies, but if he fails to call up to say he will be late, I feel I am not a person to him; so how can one trust him?" Such episodes turn many a patient against a particular source of help, if not against the whole idea of therapy. When I once mentioned my puzzlement about the failure of the people in charge to appreciate the effect of such treatment on applicants, a knowledgeable psychiatrist assured me that they appreciated it fully but felt that such "obstacles" would automatically weed out the less motivated "poorer risks" and thus prevent their waiting list from reaching a monstrous size! The use in evaluation of admittedly stressful procedures, such as an interview by a group, is another effective screening device. I have known students to withdraw from the potential sources of help after such ordeals, some of them in a greatly disturbed state.

Our acceptance of such poor practices is demoralizing for patients and therapists alike. As professionals we find ourselves "selling" therapy, persuading people to try it, only to traumatize some of those who follow our advice. We also accept without proof some assumptions that are half-truths at best, because they permit us to bear calmly what would not be easy to change. Granted that among the applicants who endure mistreatment for the sake of getting therapy there will be some "highly motivated" and determined people; but there will also be some who feel so insignificant, entitled to so little, that they do not dare to become indignant. Although they may start treatment as "good," docile pupils, they may make less progress than some of those who left hurt or who revolted and turned elsewhere. We do know about some of the latter that the self-assertion involved in leaving resulted also in a spurt of self-help. The student described earlier, who left after a few near-silent sessions, two years later reported as follows: "I realized then that I must cope with my problems myself, through real self-examination and honesty. I feel I have been successful to a certain extent; I feel some satisfaction and self-respect when I am able to think a little more clearly for myself."

Such a report is not unique in our material; finding counseling not helpful, the student mobilizes his own resources. I have also known cases of long-term treatment in which the patient's taking a stand and leaving a disappointing therapist and a destructive "therapy" situation was one link in a chain of experiences and actions which eventually led to his recovery or a clear-cut improvement. Such a course testifies to the strength of the human drive for health and to the presence of health-promoting factors in the environment, but it is not a credit to the professional helpers, and its cost to the person may be much too high in more ways than one. In some instances the road from the first decisive stand—against the therapist—to more confident selfhood led through despair and attempted suicide. In milder courses typical of short-term contacts, the stakes are smaller and so are the gains. When the student quoted above gave up her attempt to get counseling, she gained somewhat in self-confidence, but the experience could not help her to overcome her mistrust of others, as a period of counseling might have done. She might have discovered, in a telling personal way, that coping with problems alone and having them solved by another do not exhaust the possibilities—that neither, in fact, works too well. Had the counselor found some way to get a conversation going, she might have had a glimpse of the third alternative right in the first session.

Some of our "dropouts" do return when the wish for help becomes stronger or the fear weaker, provided they have not become school dropouts as well. Sometimes the second attempt brings good results. In fact, I have come to believe that "distributed counseling" is the most efficient way of doing therapy, at least during adolescence. By distributing brief periods of therapy over two, three, or four college years, we can best utilize the spurts of emotional growth which occur at that age, and so achieve great economy in terms of time spent in sessions. Some students whom I worked with in this way, and had contact with years later, were able to discard a severe neurosis without any further therapy—to my astonishment, since I thought that they would need a much longer period of work. We can expect students to return for further installments of counseling, however, only if the first contact was handled well and paved the way for the next one—that is, if the student left by agreement with the counselor, or at least with a shared understanding of reasons, not because of a failure of communications. Some of those who leave puzzled, discouraged, or indignant do return later and ask for a different counselor. If it works out well this time, they express their satisfaction at having had the courage to return— with a distinct feeling that it was touch and go. This, however, is not the typical case. Many disappointed or hurt clients never return; they may not have learned what counseling was, but they have found out that it was not for them.

Whoever accepts early obscure dropouts too complacently as instances of low motivation or high resistance, besides losing a rich source of practical learning, perpetuates some false theoretical notions. If the notion of "poor motivation" is used to minimize the claims and the chances of those in whom the wish for change must be built up in the course of therapy itself, this can indeed take care of the waiting lists. The demand for strong, ready-made motivation would eliminate some of those who are fairly well off and not under any great pressure, many of those who are only initially reluctant to face their problems, and all confirmed self-defeating neurotics. We must join all those who have spoken incisively against the assumption that neurotic patients are treatable only if from the start they are motivated to change. When the confirmed neurotic enters therapy, says Angyal (1965, p. 222), "You can safely assume that he is completely dominated by the neurotic pattern, which is an all-inclusive organization with its own motivational forces, desires, hopes, and fears forming a closely knit whole. He cannot break out of this enclosing circle, nor does he want to. . . . A great deal of work has to be done before the patient can be mobilized for the process of change."

It is equally absurd to expect the patient to live up to the demands of this or that theory of treatment subscribed to by the therapist. It seems more reasonable to adapt the method to the needs of the patients. Boris (1971), in working with groups of Vermont housewives, an unsophisticated population, has demonstrated beyond doubt that one can make people willing to try an unfamiliar method of helping themselves if one succeeds in "reducing the emotional costs" of the enterprise—in his case, a problem-centered group consultation. By "reducing emotional costs" Boris means alleviating effectively, by consistently manifesting certain attitudes, the people's predominant fears—for instance, the fear that their social standing or autonomy or self-respect will be jeopardized in the process. We need not discuss here the specific actions or statements that proved reassuring to Boris's clients, but his reliance on *implicit communication* and the importance he attaches to the first contact are congruent with the ideas developed in this chapter, though Boris's theoretical orientation is different and his implementation is inimitable. The concept of "reducing the emotional costs" of entering therapy seems to me much preferable to that of "assessing the patient's motivation." Unlike the concept of motivation, this one has reference to both participants' situation; it points to what the therapist can in fact effectively do to promote interaction from the start. If he succeeds in establishing unambiguous communication with the prospective client, these exchanges will add to the counselor's comprehension of the problems of the initial stage and help him develop skills valuable in all stages of therapy. As his understanding increases along with the realization that the first session matters a great deal, so does his ability to listen for what is most urgent in the client's feelings and most usable in his own, to think on his feet, seize his opportunities, weigh the alternatives, and choose well.

Within this general framework of a developing two-way communication, a variety of approaches are possible. Here are some simple devices that have worked well for me, providing me with a chance to listen and to speak, to observe and to be observed: a light exploration of the presenting problem, going no further back and no deeper than the student can naturally and comfortably follow; some clarification of the nature and the conditions of counseling; an invitation to the student to ask questions and to voice his hopes, wishes, and misgivings; dealing with them in a way that might cut them down to size; exploring together what might serve as a good focus for work. Other counselors use different means, depending on their style of communicating and working. The difference does not matter as long as the different paths lead to the same goal: an informed decision by the client—to which the counselor has contributed no more than his fair share—whether or not to enter counseling. It is an advantage of the tentative approach, which the college setting permits, that the process of reaching a decision can be made to exemplify some important features of the total counseling process: the student's thoughts and feelings have been taken seriously and discussed frankly; the decision—though not reached in isolation—has been his; the other's participation has neither undermined his self-respect nor limited his autonomy. Such an experience is a good start; it may even mean half the battle won or—more precisely—some later destructive struggles averted.

But what if we were equipped to utilize in our work, besides the old standby of conversational interchange, the many specialized techniques, from Gestalt therapy to behavior modification, available to therapists today? Since these would be known to the therapist and not usually to the client, would not their use require a shift from the collaborative decisions I am advocating in the direction of professional expertise dictating choices to the client? Given our enthusiasm for new toys, such a development is not unlikely; if I believed it to be unavoidable, I would gladly dispense with the type of research I would otherwise value highly: a study of what fits whom; what methods work best with different patients, for different therapists, in different situations. Fortunately, a mechanical use of the probabilistic findings of such research would be neither mandatory nor justifiable. Suppose a given patient belongs to a number of classes the majority of whose members has been shown to benefit more from Method A than from Method B: say, people under 30, women, those having lost a parent in childhood, those who had no previous therapy, those whose predominant defense mechanism is denial. Yet our patient might still prove to belong to the minority that responds better to B. The counselor will never be justified in suggesting a method in a way that would exclude a choice on the patient's part or minimize the importance of personal response and of experimentation. If, when he describes or demonstrates different methods, the client responds strongly and positively to one of them, they may well decide to give it a try regardless of the research findings. Whatever techniques one uses, they must be embedded in the kind of interaction that implies and invites the client's full participation.

In my approach to counseling and therapy, I do not attach much importance to an early comprehensive formulation of the client's personality patterns. To me, our compulsion to keep several jumps ahead of the patient seems not only to counteract the therapeutic effect of shared discoveries but also to reflect several untenable assumptions: (1) that we are able, or should be able, to size up a client reliably on the basis of the interactions of the first session or the first few sessions; (2) that we can conduct this thorough evaluation without alienating and/or misleading the client; (3) that the knowledge thus acquired will unequivocally tell us what to do with the client—particularly if it justifies the use of some diagnostic label. On observing how eagerly most of our interns snatch up any bit of information that might be construed to indicate this or that diagnosis, this or that dynamic constellation, I must conclude that we are passing these assumptions to them as self-evident; we also reward them for presenting impressive psychodynamic formulations of the cases of students they counsel, though the nature and scope of the evidence on which these are based may be far from impressive. Small wonder that some whom I supervised heaved a sigh of relief when they realized that I truly did not expect them to penetrate in one fell swoop the depths of a new client's personality and to map out the nature and the origin of his disturbance; that, in fact, I myself could not do it and did not feel handicapped by my lack of gift for quick "clinical inference."

5

Productive
Brief Encounters:
Crisis and Consultation

This chapter describes brief student-counselor contacts, most of them lasting from one to four sessions, which resulted in something useful to the student and close to what he himself had viewed as the goal of the contact. Some of these contacts require no counseling proper, no psychotherapeutically oriented interventions; the counselor can meet the student's need by providing either straight *information* or some limited *intercession* with the authorities or by taking over, when he must, the *management* of a crisis, sometimes a serious one. The student's own activity may be limited to presenting and explaining his request and providing whatever additional information the counselor may ask for. Following are a few examples of such situations: A student who has made up his mind to seek treatment in an outpatient clinic comes to inquire about the facilities in the area. A student seeks information about agencies providing other types of assistance—medical, vocational, educational—either for himself or for family members. A jittery student preparing for an examination comes to get some easily dispensed tranquilizer or to renew the prescription for some other drug given to him earlier by the center's psychiatrist. A student reaches the center in a state of acute anxiety or serious depression, which makes it mandatory for the counselor to direct him or perhaps take him to the infirmary. A student may ask his former counselor, who knows him well, to support his request for a single room, or for a change of roommate, or for an exemption from some school requirement. In some rare situation the counselor himself may decide—with the student's permission if possible—to communicate something about his situation or his state to the school authorities or to the family. In all these instances what is needed is clearly defined either by the student himself or by his situation and his state of mind. If the staff member can meet this need, and sees no reason not to, he can do so without involving the student in any attempt to rethink his situation or redefine his request.

Even though the staff member in such cases does not function as psychological counselor proper, he may have to use his specialized knowledge, his skills, and his personal assets—ingenuity, eloquence, rapport—to provide what is needed, particularly when he has to deal with emergencies. To persuade an acutely anxious, or severely depressed, or obviously psychotic student to go to the infirmary without delay and/or to call his parents is easy in some cases, very difficult in others. It is, however, always worth the counselor's effort; much may be gained for the student's future if, without jeopardizing safety, one can avoid using coercion.

Sometimes elaborate planning is necessary, the participation of the student's friends often being the key to success. One example is the freshman whose suicidal attempts were reported to me, in confidence, by a friend. I called the college physician, who then called the student in, under the pretext of having to repeat some tests; he used the opportunity to elicit from the boy an expression of unhappiness and to make a counseling appointment for him. During the latter, a review of the student's responses to the sentence-completion test made him confess suicidal thoughts, if not the attempts he had made; he agreed to go to an outside therapist, and a successful referral was made. This case shows, among other things, that concealment is unavoidable at times.

When I have already established some rapport with a student, however, and do not want to risk losing it, I will go to great lengths to avoid deception or concealment—refusing, for example, to listen to potentially useful information offered by families or friends on condition of secrecy. I have never had cause to regret this policy. Some worried friends, it is true, have managed to pass information to me by writing or calling, without waiting for my permission, and in some cases I was glad they had done so. But, when one has had little or no personal contact with a student, one has no choice but to take one's cues from those who know him. In the case of one graduate student, to prevent the repetition of a near-fatal suicidal attempt, we had to go through the following steps. His girl friend, a former counselee of mine, persuaded the young man to see me in order to discuss the attempt, which, without his knowledge, she had reported to me. He did come, but minimized the importance of his action, pretended a complete change of mood, and agreed to return for a further discussion of his problems. The girl, however, confirmed my impression that he was planning to repeat the attempt; therefore, we had to present the young man promptly with a well-worked-out plan that would insure his safety and speed his recovery. While the girl, provided with our telephone numbers, kept a close watch over her friend's moves, the college psychiatrist located a good program for acute cases in a teaching hospital, which might dispel the student's horror of hospitalization. I called the student in and told him that on reflection I had come to view his breakdown as serious, requiring more help than I could provide, and requiring it urgently; when the house is burning, it is not the time for repairs. Next the psychiatrist described the hospital program, in which the student could be received at once. The young man put up a fight, but we were determined that he should go and found ways to meet his objections. The psychiatrist reassured him about his right to leave the hospital program if and when he wanted, and I secured his department's agreement to postpone the examination he soon had to take. Within hours, the student, accompanied by the girl, was driven to the hospital for a stay of a few weeks, which proved very beneficial. He returned to his studies, and I found out from the girl a few years later that things had gone well for him after that. It seemed essential in this instance to conceal the girl's collaboration with the feared "shrinks" and also not to make the student himself lose face. But avoiding these pitfalls would hardly have helped us to obtain the student's consent if the only resource for speedy hospitalization had been the nearest state hospital, feared and shunned by many.

In cases of serious risk to life, should one always pursue safety first? It is easy to subscribe to this maxim, but it is not always easy to know how to implement it if one's concern for the student's safety extends to a longer period of time than the next twenty-four hours. The steps one decides on must differ from case to case. In the case of another graduate student, whose suicidal impulses became stronger during a period of personal crisis, my colleagues urged hospitalization, which the student was set against. I made preparations for it, but since the young man was keeping his appointments with me, I decided to wait. I knew that our tenuous rapport would not survive an attempt at coercion and that I would lose my chance of being of use to him, as many would-be counselors had already done. We weathered the crisis. The resources of the school, including student and faculty friends who occasionally consulted me, proved sufficient to help this very resourceful student get back on his feet. In other instances I made agreements with students I was working with that if they felt in danger of harming themselves they would go straightaway to the infirmary and call me from there.

Sometimes an impending suicide, although averted by prompt hospitalization, is successfully carried out after the student is released, a few weeks or months later, perhaps at home. This causes less disturbance in school than does a suicide on campus; but the person who decided on using forced hospitalization as a shortcut to safety may well wonder whether his excessive caution prevented him from doing something more beneficial for the student, even though the disaster can now be blamed on someone else. Yet if well prepared and handled, forced hospitalization does not always cause the student to reject the staff member involved or prevent him from benefiting by his stay in the hospital. The chance of making the right decision is maximized if the counselor is familiar with the resources and practices of the hospitals to which he can send students and can compare them with the resources available on campus. Campus resources are not to be underestimated, particularly if the student has good friends among fellow students and faculty, who can be mobilized for help in emergencies. In one case of attempted suicide, before the student passed out, he called a faculty friend and asked her to notify the counselor; in another, the student stopped herself from repeating her suicidal attempt by confessing her intention to her student friends, who then called in a counselor. Friends have also called me, sometimes anonymously, to alert me to something that was happening with my counselee. In several instances of urgent calls from my counselees themselves, I was able to get their psychology teacher to substitute for me, or to stand by until I arrived on campus.

Some schools have facilities for hospitalizing disturbed students for periods longer than a few days. An advantage of this alternative to off-campus hospitalization is that one can work on the issues involved in the crisis while they are alive and workable. The therapeutic leverage provided, for example, by the student's emotional state after a suicidal attempt may be lost when, many weeks and many "diagnostic evaluations" later, he starts seeing the therapist provided or recommended by the hospital. If the relationship with the school counselor has been good, it is of great advantage for the disturbed student to be cared for by the person he already knows and trusts and to maintain his ties with the environment he may soon reenter. The counselor can use the student's stay in the infirmary to carry on intensified therapy, seeing him several times a week, or to provide help in working out arrangements for the future, or both. In one instance, before constructive plans could be worked out for a severely disturbed anxious student, she had to live for weeks in the infirmary, from which she went to her classes, accompanied by fellow students. During this period her counselor worked with the student herself, consulted with her family, and instructed and reassured the infirmary nurses, who were upset by the student's abnormal behavior and whose cooperation was essential for the success of the project. The required investment of time and effort does not appear excessive to me in the light of the very favorable follow-up on this very difficult case. It is obvious from this case and many others that crisis management can at times be combined with genuine counseling; their integration, if well handled, can be very effective.

Other kinds of "brief encounters" involve no management. They consist of episodes of genuine but minimal counseling which can be described as *consultation*. According to my conception of genuine consultation, the value the client derives from it is obtained with his participation. The contact is productive if this participation enables him to accept as his own the solution of the problem he has brought in and to act on the insight he has achieved; this is also what happens in counseling conducted on a larger scale. Following are a few examples of such small-scale counseling, some of them given in more detail than the rest.

A girl came to the center in distress about a falling-out with her boy friend. She had hurt him unintentionally by something she had done, and he had stopped calling; she wanted to know what she could do to regain his friendship. When I asked for the details of the crucial episode, it soon became obvious to both of us that she was not at all sure of the cause of the trouble but was merely guessing at it. If so, why wouldn't she try to find out what was wrong from the young man himself? The idea shocked the student at first; in the 1950s girls were not supposed to be forward. Then it began to intrigue her; she left saying she would think it over and did not reappear. In describing this contact in the questionnaire several months later, she wrote: "Dr. H. imbued me with the courage to approach the issue directly and the problem solved itself." Her experience is somewhat similar to that of a boy, who after consulting me broke the taboo on talking to his parents about a brother who had died a year earlier and thus got over his preoccupation with this death. In both cases reestablishing communication served to resolve the situation.

Another episode from the distant past involved a girl engaged to a man who, like herself, was in favor of postponing intercourse until they were married. Now that the wedding was only a couple of weeks off, they suddenly found it very difficult to resist their impulses, and the girl started doubting the wisdom of trying. Could the counselor tell her whether premarital intercourse is good or bad? I disclaimed having any generally valid answer and invited her to talk about whatever seemed pertinent to the development of her attitudes toward sex and of her feelings toward her fiancé. In what she told me two things stood out: (1) she still resented her mother's prudish attitudes, which she felt had slowed down the development of her own interest in men; (2) she felt tempted to have intercourse only in her home, particularly if her mother was in the next room. I made no comment except to remark casually, when she talked about the date set for the wedding, that she did not have much time left to engage in premarital sex, if this was her wish. The next week she came in only to report that the temptation had disappeared; she did not seem too astonished by what she termed a "miracle."

To continue with the same general problem area, in more recent times several girls urgently requested a consultation when an imminent visit from parents forced them to decide whether to continue to conceal from their families the fact of their living with their boy friends—now that it could not be done by mere silence. On reviewing with me the viable courses of action and their probable consequences, these girls made their decisions then and there. These decisions varied from case to case, depending on the circumstances and the people involved. One girl postponed communication until she was more certain that the relationship would last; another informed the parents of the situation by letter so as to enable them to change their plans if they wished; the third took care to keep this information from the one family member whose heart condition made upsets dangerous. In the course of reaching a decision, some conflicts about the situation were reviewed and, if not resolved, at least brought closer to a resolution.

Parents, by insisting on some of their wishes or by strongly opposing some of the student's own tentative plans (the plan to marry or to marry a particular person, to drop out of school, to change one's major, to spend a year in Europe or in Israel, to change one's living arrangements), may create situations that urgently demand decisions. One student made straight for the center after receiving an appalling announcement from his parents: if he carried out his plan to move from the dormitory into an apartment, they would stop paying his college tuition. He vented his fury, then came to grips with his fear of abandonment and his viewing of financial support as the only valid proof of his parents' affection; for this proof he had been willing to pay a high price. He decided to carry out his plan and to postpone, if need be, the completion of his education. The parents gave in—as parents often do when they realize that the young person has made up his mind and is no longer divided within himself. In other instances, the parents do not actually oppose their offspring's plans, but the student himself feels compelled to carry out their real or presumed wishes. In such cases a joint frank exploration of the issue may resolve the conflict experienced by the student.

The crisis, or the discomfort, that brings the student to the center can be precipitated by some aspect of the school situation. Friction with a roommate may lead to an acute conflict: should one always give in, or leave, or start standing up for oneself? A sophomore girl increasingly disliked some features of dormitory life: enforced sociability, no quiet for studies. A competent young woman, though at first enjoying the relative freedom from the chores of daily living offered by the dorm, she gradually came to dislike the familial, infantilizing features of campus living. Her one visit to the center was spent in a realistic discussion of her plans to move out to an apartment and of the obstacles she had to overcome to do so. Before leaving, she asked me, very directly, whether she seemed to me to be maladjusted, and I said she did not. Three years later she gave the following description of this contact: "I went to the center just once, when I was quite upset and depressed. I hated dormitory living, and my friends could not understand it; they thought something must be wrong with me. All I needed was to be told I am not batty and to make some plans for the year; I was and I did; and I have not been depressed since, which is what I wanted."

Freshmen often have difficulties in coming to terms with new situations; in some cases a brief counseling contact can speed up this process. Thus, one boy, awed by the school's intellectual atmosphere, was worried not only about his studies but also about making friends with girls. Having attended a boys' boarding school, he felt doubly handicapped. He had been constantly if mildly depressed but came to the center only after a second girl broke up with him, telling him he was too possessive. We discussed a belief that the student shared with his father: that to get anywhere one had to try very hard, never relaxing one's efforts. His description of how he went about it in school provided plentiful evidence that this unremitting self-driving effort reduced his receptivity to the subjects he studied and deprived him of ease in his social contacts; this formulation made sense to him. We agreed that the student would let me know after the Christmas vacation (which was coming up shortly) whether he wanted any further counseling. About a month later he reported that he had been able to relax and to catch up with his accumulated school work and was now taking pleasure in his studies. At home he had had some good talks with his parents and had accepted the fact that some of his views were different from theirs. He no longer felt or looked depressed, and he felt no need for further help. In replying to the questionnaire a few months later, he said that the two sessions had helped him to fit together the contradictory advice he had been getting from family and from friends: "I was helped to see my problems in a different light and things have been fairly smooth since then."

Examinations and other crisis points of academic life bring several students to the center each year—some hoping for an intervention on their behalf, the majority in search of counseling. For some of those who seek counseling, the occasion serves to initiate a more prolonged period of work, the goal of which may be formulated by the student as the resolution of a repetitive pattern: "Why do I always freeze up in exams?" In other cases, the resolution of the current crisis is of crucial importance for the student and can be achieved with a minimal amount of help. I recall, for example, several graduate students who sought help because they found themselves unable to study for an important exam, or to work on their theses, or to decide whether to change their field of study, and to what program to apply. At that time graduate students were seen at the center for no more than three or four sessions; since we had found that the ones who were chronically troubled could not be helped within the relatively short time that was often sufficient for helping undergraduates, we had decided to limit our service to consultation. Yet several graduate students were able to get out of their blind alleys in the course of this short contact and to start moving toward their goals, old or new. In each case the resolution

of the acute conflict that immobilized the student was preceded by
a review of the salient motives involved: a recurrent fear of entering
each new stage of his career; doubts about his ability, or originality,
or maturity; mixed feelings about his teachers; disparity between
his own wishes and those of parents and spouses; resentment of the
obligations and sacrifices demanded by graduate studies and by an
academic career.

The crisis created by an acute conflict may express itself not
only in an unproductive preoccupation with the issue but also
through pronounced symptoms of emotional tension, either mental
or physical. One first-year graduate student, whose self-doubts in
relation to her new enterprise were greatly increased by her family's
disparaging views and dire predictions, became unable to work and
was tempted to drop out, even though she had actually been progressing well in her studies. She came to the center in an anxious,
agitated state and eventually agreed to take a tranquilizer and a
rest in the infirmary before making her decision. The next day she
appeared in a normal state, having decided to stay in school; we discussed how she could protect herself from similar upsets in the
future. In the questionnaire she filled out a few months later, she
gave a good progress report. Another student complained of acute
gastrointestinal symptoms and of strained relationships with his
dormitory companions. The upset was precipitated by the impending breakup with his girl friend, which he both wished for and
feared; he feared it because, in his "alienated" state, he could not
afford to lose her or, rather, to lose the acceptant group of which
she was a member. After two sessions, in which he vented some of
his feelings about dependency, the student talked his situation over
with some friends and became active in his own behalf. In the third
and last session, he reported that he had broken up with the girl,
had obtained permission to move off campus, and had arranged to
live with congenial friends. He said in his questionnaire that his
talking out the conflict he was caught in and the counselor's "questions and brief analyses" had enabled him to look at things "in a
calmer and clearer light." His symptoms disappeared, and his customary cheerfulness returned.

Though many of the examples given above could be described as crisis counseling, others hardly deserve this designation.

Opportunities for consultation can arise as a result of crisis, sometimes in the context of crisis management, but they can also develop from rather routine requests. A student, for example, who approaches the center in search of some service other than counseling may take away with him not just the address of a testing service or a note to the dean; in addition, or instead, he may get a clarification of some of the motives behind this request or of some of its likely consequences, which may influence his next step. In some cases such clarification is a must, although the counselor must take care to make the need for it obvious to the client and not try to push it down his throat. In cases, for example, of requests for referral to outside therapists, I usually let the requester know that in my experience such referrals are rarely successful if the student's wishes and expectations are not sorted out and clarified in a consultative contact.

Although occasions for "minicounseling" are not limited to crises, in most of these instances the client brings in a relatively circumscribed and concrete problem, usually of recent origin, which he is currently facing; it may or may not be very disturbing to him, but he feels some urgency about it. When consultation is productive, it results in a solution of this problem—not necessarily similar to the one the client had anticipated, if any, but accepted by him as appropriate and his own; it has not been forced on him by some outside agent, nor grasped at desperately just to put an end to indecision. The student commits himself to a course of action with some insight into his reasons and some foresight of its likely consequences —thus, with a degree of confidence.

Is the client's focusing on a concrete problem sufficient to insure such a favorable outcome, to make the consultation productive? Obviously not; otherwise, psychological consultation would be effective much more frequently than it actually is. Many students who present circumscribed problems of recent origin, or can trace their disturbance to a recent event, either leave dissatisfied or settle into longer periods of counseling. Relatively few leave the first or the second session with a solution they are ready to act upon. In looking for factors that enable students, or others, to benefit from consultation, we naturally think first of the client's characteristics; that is, we say that he will benefit from consultation if he is well

balanced and relatively mature. His problem then can be thought of
as situational or minor, not indicative of any enduring disturbance.
This factor cannot be contested, but it is not the only, perhaps not
even the main, determinant of a consultation's success. In my experience the client's "good adjustment" or high level of maturity is
not a necessary condition for making consultation productive. Some
of the students who readily enter consultative discussions and benefit
from them do impress one as very well put together, but others very
clearly do not. The brevity of the encounter excludes lengthy exploration and limits the basis of judgment; so we cannot estimate in
most instances the solidity of the clients' adjustment or the degree of
their disturbance. Wide variation, however, is suggested by the fact
that their reported predicaments have varied greatly: some were
stopped in their tracks by an obviously difficult problem or a sudden
blow; others felt paralyzed in a routine situation or one easily foreseen. With some of the graduate students mentioned above, for
example, the particular crises of indecision and work inhibition—
which, with help, they were able to overcome—were part of a recurrent neurotic difficulty. In many of these cases successful consultation turned out to be the first step toward acceptance of
therapy, then or later. The students figured that since minimal
counseling had enabled them to overcome their difficulty in one
instance, prolonged counseling might provide help on a larger scale.

Since the student's general level of maturity is not all-important in making consultation productive, it must be the momentary psychological constellation that makes the difference. This
constellation may be clarified if we consider one of its varieties: the
major crisis, such as the breakup of a marriage, a drastic change of
family fortunes, a death in the family. By calling for external and
internal readjustments, the disruption created by such events offers
the person a chance to experience, review, and rearrange some of
his emotional attitudes and behavior patterns. A person in crisis,
whose well-practiced ways of functioning have been made partly
inoperant by the loss of their customary supports, may become more
open emotionally and better able than previously to benefit from
therapy. Short-term therapy focusing on a crisis and working around
it in widening circles, while also providing temporary support, can
be very productive at times; it may achieve much more than a

mere restoration of the emotional balance. (In many instances, of course, the word *mere* is hardly appropriate: to get out of a state of depression without much delay is in itself of great value.)

Large-scale crises that bring students to the center are not easily resolved in two or three sessions; in most cases they serve to initiate a more prolonged period of counseling. Some of the characteristics that make crises productive, however, are present also in the less weighty problematic situations of recent origin, which are clearly delineated and urgently demand resolutions. In terms of Gestalt theory, one can conceptualize an activated need as a system in a state of tension tending to discharge (Lewin) or as an incomplete Gestalt seeking closure (Angyal). Both formulations imply the likelihood that something new will emerge: a new channel for discharge, a missing piece that will make the Gestalt complete. This missing piece cannot be provided gratuitously by the environment; the person himself must restructure his "life space" so that some part of it acquires relevance to the problem. This discovery may be based on something he himself has perceived or recalled or on some comment he has heard. In some studies of thinking, the subject has to solve a mechanical problem by using various materials at his disposal but *not* the tool that is conventionally used in the operation he has to perform. Familiar things may thus acquire new meanings; a book is now seen as the needed weight, a hammer as a potential lever. Similarly, one can view the process that takes place in a productive consultation as an assisted restructuring of the client's experience so that he finds new ways of tackling the problem he is facing. This restructuring is what distinguishes a solution actively reached, or a suggestion insightfully adopted, from an unthinking acceptance of an idea provided by someone else.

Experience shows that an urgent problem can mobilize for some internal reorganization even people whose entrenched personal patterns ordinarily function as an obstacle to change, although this reorganization may not go very far. My guess is that the process is facilitated not just by the urgency of need but also by the particular cognitive delineation of the salient problem. Since it is specific and concrete and often has a strong situational component, the client can view it as something separate from himself. It is a problem he *has,* not an expression of who or what he *is.* To seek help with a specific problem, or with a difficult task, does not threaten one's self-respect as much as would the need to change one's "personality," to reconsider one's basic beliefs; to use Boris's term, the emotional cost of a consultation is not too high. To take an example from group work, it is much easier for the clients to enter a problem-centered group than one advertising itself as group therapy. The Vermont housewives described by Boris (1971) were willing to discuss the problems they had with their children before they were gradually led in these meetings to view the problems as caused, in part, by their own attitudes. The important role of cognitive structuring in reducing the threat to self-esteem and in facilitating personal discussions was made very vivid to me by those students who, after profiting from a consultation or from a brief period of crisis-centered counseling, decided to try "therapy" with the same counselor but found themselves stopped in their tracks by anxiety. (I shall return to these cases in Chapter 13, on referrals.) Another effect of focusing on a problem which, though urgent, seems to be limited and well defined is the client's expectation of being helped to solve it speedily. Relatively unthreatened and undefensive, the client is ready to work at a clip. Some students make this expectation explicit by applying for just one session with the counselor. To minimize the importance of the environmental factor to the client, or to declare his expectation invalid right from the start ("You really need long-term therapy"), does not serve any useful purpose.

Given the presence of an urgent localized problem to be solved, what is necessary to make the consultation productive? How the counselor handles the situation is of crucial importance. As in the initial sessions, it is easier to point out the obstacles that we ourselves often place in the path of "minimal counseling" than to enumerate all the ways in which it can be facilitated.

Some of the assets the client brings to the consultation are quickly destroyed by poor handling. Certain routines do this without fail. The state of mind created by a disturbing recent experience, the feeling of urgency, the readiness to get involved in an intensive discussion of an issue that is now to the fore—these things do not easily survive delays and distractions. If a student who has just broken up with a friend or has received news of illness in the family is asked to take some tests first, or to get a medical checkup,

or to provide a detailed life history, he is likely to tell you to forget
it. Even if he does not, much of the impetus is lost through the
delay. For such situations a "walk-in" facility is of vital importance,
if it is a well-functioning one that does not require long hours of
tense waiting.

Once the counselor has met the student, he must join him
in focusing on the problem at hand and avoid deflecting him from
this goal. This means abstaining from an exploration of his background or of any topics that have no plausible relevance to the
issue. In particular, one should not try to minimize the environmental factor and make the problem appear more "personal" than
the student assumes it to be. To do any of the things that would be
appropriate at some point in a longer period of counseling, with
ample time for preparation and explanation, would mean in effect
to pit one's own conception of the goal of the contact against that
of the client, a situation that is highly confusing. The counselor may
err in this way either because he actually believes that the student
needs more help than he thinks or simply because he is using the
kinds of intervention he is most practiced in, unaware that in this
case they do not answer. At the other extreme, a counselor who
realizes that a brief contact requires him to modify his approach but
does not know how may be tempted to meet the client's expectation
of being told what to do and start dispensing authoritative advice.
By doing so, he takes the matter out of the student's hands and
makes a satisfying solution less likely.

Negative recommendations, however, are not very useful.
What can a counselor actually do to make consultation productive?
What guidelines is he to follow in dealing with his client? A person
who is stuck with a seemingly unsolvable problem is not unlike a
young child glued to a fence that separates him or her from a
favorite toy; he sees it, but it is outside his reach. Were he able to
turn away from the beckoning object, while still keeping his goal in
mind, and to explore what the environment offers, he might discover
a way around the fence or a stick that could be used for reaching.
The consultant's task is to lead the client out of his blind alley by
helping him to extend his inner field of vision, to explore the implications of the situation he is facing. To do so, the counselor must
first make certain that he understands the situation as it is experi-

enced by the client. His dominant attitude must be that of "active listening," a term introduced by Thomas Gordon (1970, 1974) for the process of deciphering another's message; it is much more descriptive of the process of putting oneself into another's shoes than is "reflection of feeling," the term once used by Carl Rogers for this main tool of the client-centered approach. By feeding back to the client what the counselor has heard him say, the counselor can check on the accuracy of his perception of what the client meant to convey. Such feedback gives the client a chance to correct the counselor's errors and stimulates him to amplify and develop his own thoughts. This is a most effective way to maintain contact with the client while letting him proceed with his search without fear of any hampering intrusion. Those who have become good at active listening are often rewarded by seeing the client arrive at a solution with the help of this facilitation and nothing else. Of course, the consultant cannot always limit himself to following his client's thinking, excluding his own completely. While one learns and practices "active listening," the advice to abstain from all comments beyond the feedback (beyond the acknowledgment of the client's own feelings and thoughts) is quite reasonable, a useful discipline. But once the counselor has become adept at following the client as guide and is no longer tempted to take over and to substitute his own thinking for the client's, he can safely be active in ways other than listening. He may be able to help the client expand his perspective by asking for clarifications and implications of his statements, by tentatively suggesting—or implying—connections between different factors, or by asking him to imagine the likely consequences of one or another way of acting. He is guided in this process by his understanding of human situations in general and his knowledge of the given type of problems in particular; but the way he proceeds must always reflect his understanding of the client's feelings and views and his attention to the other's explicit and covert responses to his comments. The counselor's general knowledge of unconscious dynamics can be useful occasionally, but not if it makes him lose touch with the flow of the client's thoughts and feelings or greatly limits his own imaginative exploration of the situations presented; the richer his offerings, the better the chance that one or another will strike a chord. This type of participation is best described as an invitation to the client: "Let both of us have a good look at this situation."

If the counselor's own activity has remained in close touch with the client's thinking, if they have been conversing with each other throughout, then the articulate student will often acknowledge that the help he was given consisted in stimulating *his* thinking.

The solution I finally adopted was not one of those the counselor had thought about. Yet it was a great help to have her bounce back at me some of my questions and comments that I was unable to bounce back at myself—partly because of defensiveness, but also because of lack of experience and wider perspective.

The counselor treated me not as a standard "case" but as an intelligent, thinking human being. Together we were able to ask some probing questions and to open some new paths; one of them led me where I had wanted to go. Everything was so simple after this session.

Since most of the problems presented in consultation involve other people besides the client, the consultant must be able to put himself in their position also and to keep in mind that a viable solution must take their viewpoints into account. This statement, obvious as it is, touches on an issue that is problematic to some therapists. Focusing on the client's feelings alone has been a maxim in many approaches to therapy—with excellent reason, particularly when one is dealing with people who have become so adept at being guided by the wishes of others that they are unsure of their own. The Gestalt therapist's "prayer" exhorts each one to do *his* thing; if you and I do not happen to find common ground that cannot be helped; neither of us is there to meet the other's expectations. The truth contained in these statements makes them a good guideline for many, but it is of course a partial truth; we are not there *just* to meet the expectations of others, but we must fulfill at least some wishes or needs of those who matter to us. Few people will expressly deny this; if the client proves willing to pay some attention to the viewpoints and claims of the others, it is usually not just because of the power some of them wield. But to acknowledge the need to reconcile conflicting points of view is not the same as to implement this goal. People vary greatly in the traits that facilitate such implementation: empathy, imagination, a sense of fair play. I have observed some people, including some four- or five-year-old children, skillfully resolve interpersonal conflicts without attempting to exercise power; others in similar situations failed dismally. This difference, however, is not purely a matter of personal gifts. Some of the recent attempts to train parents, teachers, and counselors to deal more effectively with their charges provide us with good evidence that problem solving in the area of interpersonal relations, substituting for the "win-lose" method of conflict resolution, can be taught and practiced until it becomes a reliable skill (Gordon, 1970, 1974). This is a very useful skill for the consultant to have and to demonstrate to the client. Not every client, of course, will concede that at the very least he must consider another's claim to be well founded if he knows that he himself would make it in a similar situation; the majority, however, will appreciate the logical validity of this statement and will feel some trust in a counselor who is following this guideline even if they are unable at the time to follow his example.

Even for those possessing the requisite skills, consultation, or minimal counseling, is an exacting task; no wonder it so often miscarries. While there are ways to learn one important component, active listening, no equally simple guidelines can be given for making productive the activity that goes beyond it. Yet the consultant cannot afford to blunder. There is no time to make and correct false moves, to make too many guesses that are either wrong or unacceptable to the client or not relevant to the problem at hand. Some of the difficulties are those of *all* first sessions, which have been discussed in the preceding chapter, but some of the advantages of the initial sessions are absent in brief consultations. For most of those who come to the center with an awareness of some chronic problem, an important though often unvoiced issue is whether to commit themselves to a period of counseling. The counselor can structure the initial session around this issue. Once confusions and misgivings are uncovered, he can take some time to convey to the student what counseling is about, to indicate or exemplify how it is likely to proceed; these are the topics specific to the precounseling period. In consultations identical problems do not recur often enough for the counselor to be able to map out the variations and the possible implications of each kind. In this respect, the counselor who does some specialized topical counseling has the advantage over the "generalist," who is not in a position to amass such background knowledge. He must grope his way to pertinent factors in each case anew, and he does not have much time for this groping. Nor can he take time to explain his procedure; he must deal with the client's expectation to be given an answer by involving him in the process of problem solving by whatever means he has at hand.

As a final point, the shortness of the contact makes it more imperative than it is otherwise for the counselor not only to get or spot the right idea, without too many false moves, but also to communicate his meaning effectively, which sometimes means strikingly. Occasionally the problem as presented by the student turns out to be a search for a method to do something that cannot be done: to do in one week the work of three months; to be in two places at the same time; simultaneously to hurt and to pacify an ambiguously perceived parent. The situation is not obvious to the student, however; and, since he is set on his project, he is not receptive to having the difficulty pointed out to him. If the consultant says it cannot be done, this means that the consultant is no good, that he has no solution to offer. How can one make one's communication penetrate? With one capable and enthusiastic graduate student (not a counselee), it gradually became clear to me that the new projects he kept adding to his work load were seriously endangering his chance to complete his doctoral thesis in time, but my direct comments to that effect made no impression on him. Finally, his undertaking a major new project struck me as so preposterous that I made a preposterous remark: "That is all right," I said, "you can probably do quite well without a Ph.D.; lots of people do." The young man was thunderstruck. He promptly rearranged his affairs and completed his thesis. In brief encounters it is both particularly important and particularly difficult to find words that will make an impact.

6

Cases of
Striking Progress

The courses of counseling I am about to discuss are the ones that
made me into an enthusiast of college mental health work. They
are characterized by vigorous movement toward a resolution of long-
standing personal conflicts. After a few months, or even a few weeks,
the student has progressed to a position of a much greater emotional
maturity. These courses do *not*, however, produce identical results.
How close the student comes to the achievement of maturity depends
on the position he has started from and on the length of the counseling period, which in turn depends on many factors, external and
internal. In favorable cases the student gets out of this period of
counseling all he needs to continue developing without again re-
sorting to formalized help—ever or at least for a long time to come;
my informal follow-ups of many such cases, implemented by occasional letters from former counselees, cover periods up to fifteen
years. In other cases this brief period of assisted work is repeated

later on, when new developmental stages bring new tasks or new crises. It may also serve as an introduction to a more intensive and prolonged therapy undertaken in later years. Typically, however, these students do not seek therapy immediately after completing the counseling period. Having profited much, they are usually eager to carry on on their own. If this proves to be too difficult, they may be disappointed, but they are not likely to become despondent. They have the best evidence there is that effective help is available. For those who have achieved more, not less, than they realized, the period of "going it alone" brings increased confidence: "All in all, this year has gone amazingly well. I am not shy, though I still have moments of shyness. I feel confident and competent in many more areas than ever before, though I still lack confidence in some. . . . Thanks again." This girl kept in touch with her counselor for several years; he had the satisfaction, as he put it, of seeing her "change from a shy, frightened girl who was considered a problem to have in class to a productive professional with a gift for understanding other young people with problems of expressing too much or too little."

The question "What kind of client is most likely to move vigorously in counseling?" has no simple answer. These students come to the center with problems no different from those of other clients. Some come with complaints about chronic or recurrent difficulties —for example, in their relationships to people or in their studies. Others come during crises; they have a major decision to make or are feeling anxious or depressed without knowing the cause. Even if they come with a specific problem, however, these students do not seem to expect to solve it in one or two sessions as frequently or as definitely as do those who center on such problems exclusively and who essentially are asking for a consultation. The readiness to commit oneself to counseling work on a regular basis, even if not for a very long period of time, is either present from the start or easily developed in the first session. This readiness is a correlate of a certain kind of perception of the initial problem or complaint; even when it is quite as specific as those presented as topics for consultations— say, a quarrel with a friend or a depressed mood that won't pass by itself—the person almost from the start is ready to view the trouble as "psychological," in the sense of having some roots not in the external events but in his or her own feelings, attitudes, and resulting ways of dealing with problems. The student therefore does not focus for long on what to do in this particular problematic situation. The question is quickly replaced by: "Why do I have to feel or to act this way in such situations?" Sometimes the student has acquired this readiness to try the "psychological perspective" from his courses or from previous therapy or from an earlier interest in introspection; sometimes he or she has simply reached an appropriate developmental stage.

Whatever the reasons, these students almost from the start become very actively involved in the work of therapy and pursue it with dispatch and strong personal participation. They use their minds, their ability to think; but many of the insights they experience in sessions are not "mere insights"; they are "complete," full-bodied experiences involving a strong emotional component along with the cognitive one. This completeness makes them both vital and productive. "Intellectual insight, which is simply a statement of facts and their connections, has only an indirect bearing on motivation for change; because the patient now sees the situation differently his feelings about it also may change" (Angyal, 1965, p. 219). Feelings and emotions, according to Angyal, are experiences "of the state and of the situation of the person under the aspect of value. . . . Situations are constantly evaluated by the organism from the point of view of their significance for the life process. The emotional tone is the experience of such significances . . . given in a very intimate and immediate manner as joy and sorrow, depression and elation, pleasure and pain" (p. 32). When the emotional evaluation of some item or aspect of one's behavior changes—when, for example, this behavior comes to be intensely felt to be futile or to be harmful to oneself—the stage is set for behavioral change, which is not likely to result from a mere intellectual understanding of origins and effects.

The courses of counseling under discussion, then, present no strong obstacles to the emergence of insights and emotional reevaluations, nor to the immediate application of these insights. These promptly appearing results are gratifying to counselor and student alike. Their path is not always smooth. Letting go of the familiar, taking a chance on something new, may give rise to anxiety, to a period of moving back and forth. For some students, however, the process of change is spontaneous and not self-conscious, not marked by struggle or even by any deliberate effort; things just change as counseling proceeds. By the end of the counseling period, the student may have effected—and may be aware that he has effected—a self-reorganization of wide scope. The questionnaire comments reflect this awareness of change: "Counseling has done an enormous amount in helping me to straighten out my problems—and they were pretty deep rooted; I felt like a changed person when the year was over." "It is a truly enriching experience; I would not trade it for any other part of a Brandeis education." "It has been the most fruitful and beneficial experience of my life."

As a basis for discussing further these gratifying courses, I shall next give detailed summaries of three of them. Two of these students were counseled by me, so that I know what kinds of interventions were used and when. I have selected them from many other available cases for two reasons. First, both contacts were relatively short, slightly shorter than the average for courses of this type; while this makes them somewhat atypical, their limited length prevents a detailed presentation from becoming too long. Second, although these students were not confirmed neurotics, their personality problems fell into clear-cut patterns: hysterical in one case (Rosalie), obsessive-compulsive in the other (Benjamin). These characteristics enable me to demonstrate the types of interpretation that I have used in my work with increasing frequency, those stemming from Angyal's formulations of these two main dimensions of neurosis. The third student, Jim, was counseled by one of my colleagues, an experienced, effective counselor whose general therapeutic orientation did not differ much from mine. His write-up was selected for presentation here because it includes the student's own detailed questionnaire report of the course and the outcome of counseling. As in all cases I have quoted at some length, some of the characteristics that might serve to identify the students discussed have been omitted or changed.

Rosalie: The Pattern of Vicarious Living

When Rosalie entered Brandeis, everything augured well. A gifted and outgoing girl, the only child of a cultured family, she was delighted to find the school environment congenial to her intellectual and artistic interests; she was enthusiastic about her courses, read avidly, and made the Dean's List in her freshman year. Yet when she came to the center in the middle of her sophomore year, complaining of recurrent depressions, she had failed two courses, was constantly tense and nervous, and felt unable to talk to her fellow students. Rosalie sought solace in frequent calls and trips home. Her parents were alarmed and supported her decision to seek help. She herself was at a loss to find the cause of her trouble, feeling that until recently she had been prefectly adjusted and happy. The only flaw that could be discerned in Rosalie's past adjustment was the lack of close friendships: though socially active, she had never felt accepted by her peers and preferred the company of adults. In the fall of her sophomore year, for the first time in her life, she had had a few dates with a boy she liked. She had felt only slightly disappointed when he stopped seeing her; yet it was then that her relations with all her friends became strained, and depression made its appearance. The failure of this first attempt at closeness with a man made acute all the doubts she had long harbored about herself.

As Rosalie began talking about her current concerns, these doubts soon came into focus. In the third session she broke down and, crying bitterly, poured out her innermost fears. She felt that she was aggressive, selfish, and mean; that her sweetness was just a disguise of her "true nature"; and that she had adopted this disguise for fear of being rejected. But the pretense did not work: she could not help being loud, talking out of turn, and ridiculing her companions. She felt that she was not feminine, neither pliable nor affectionate, and did not know what love and mutuality meant. Consequently, she feared, she would never find the happiness she craved. But she had only herself to blame, since her parents had brought her up lovingly, giving her both plenty of guidance and sufficient freedom.

I made explicit and emphatic Rosalie's assumption of a basic flaw in herself and then suggested that there might be some alternative explanations for the flaw that she had described. Rosalie then started wondering about the origins of her fears and of her awkward, overassertive behavior. Her parents had provided her, from early on, with a wealth of cultural stimulation and with exacting rules of conduct; she recalled how impressed she had been with the great expectations they must have had for her. Both parents, especially her father, claimed that she had all the gifts and virtues of their respective sides of the family. Rosalie admired her energetic, somewhat impatient father and wanted to live up to his ideal of strength; she also felt that she had to compensate him for the lack of a son by being nothing less than a perfect daughter. She eagerly absorbed everything her parents had to offer; but, as she now realized with a shock, she had never felt that the resulting achievements were her own. "Between the two of them, between having my father's mind and temperament and my mother's tastes, there is nothing left of myself. I feel empty inside; whatever I have is theirs. I am not even a replica of my father—I am a formless shadow of him." Rosalie's concentration on her parents' interests and activities had estranged her from other children, whom she could not view as her equals. To make up for her feeling of emptiness and unimportance, she felt compelled to parade her superior knowledge, making her companions feel inferior; she was unable to live up to her parents' rule of never hurting others. She secretly concluded that the pretty picture her parents had of her was not a true likeness and that she had deceived them badly.

After Rosalie had vented in sessions her anger at her parents "for having made me, by subtle coercion, into a well-rounded nothing," she began to realize that she did indeed possess something of her own: her bitter feelings for one thing, her dancing for another. Modern dance, in which she excelled, was the one activity her parents did not share, and she had always felt whole and serene while dancing. As this feeling of personal "ownership" spread to other areas, Rosalie began realizing that it was she who had been "dispossessing" herself by quickly suppressing all feelings and wishes that did not fit her idealized self-image. She suspected that she might have exaggerated her parents' expectations of her. She no longer felt the need to cling to her image of herself as a perfect daughter, a supremely cultured and refined young woman, and began to have feelings and thoughts formerly excluded by these roles.

In a session which marked a decisive turn in counseling, Rosalie expressed her conviction that, in order to get anywhere, she had "to take a chance on movement"—movement that could result in a "flop or in an elegant landing." She demonstrated her point by performing a dance movement, a graceful leap. From then on, she "took chances" and made quick progress in developing new ways of behaving. Her earlier attempts at emancipation from authority had had the earmarks of a half-hearted revolt. She would, for example, surreptitiously break a dormitory rule and then debate with herself for hours whether or not to confess it to her parents. Now she was no longer tempted either to break rules or to spend all of her time writing home. She started making her own plans; during a vacation she asserted her separateness from her parents by joining only some of their activities and faced them with her decision to take a summer job instead of accompanying them on a trip. When her parents, while accepting her plans, expressed some hurt, she took it in stride. She no longer felt that it was selfish of her to be growing toward independence.

Next Rosalie turned to the issue of her relations with men. Putting aside her fear of being too forward, she asked the boy in whom she had earlier been interested about his reasons for dropping her. At first she was hurt by discovering that this casual relationship had been much less important to him than to her, for whom it was the first. But then she realized with relief that this difference was not a proof of any basic flaw in herself. She began wondering why she was unable to get any response from the men who attracted her, men who seemed to be as strong and capable as her father. Her self-exploration brought to light various unrealistic fears, among them the fear of being dominated and molded, of being completely "taken over." To ward off this imagined danger, she had been overasserting herself and antagonizing the boys whom she liked. On discovering this, Rosalie relaxed into more natural behavior; the response she obtained made her increasingly certain that she was an attractive girl, capable of both giving and accepting affection. She no longer felt compelled to keep testing and proving herself and looked to the future with confidence.

The present was also gratifying, and Rosalie could hardly believe that she had felt a wreck less than three months before. By the time she decided to terminate counseling (after ten sessions), her academic work was back to its earlier high level; and she was free from preoccupation and worry, felt accepted by her companions, and enjoyed her old and new friendships as never before. She felt that she had matured a great deal in a short time; in the last sessions her interchange with me was marked by a new freedom born of a feeling of equality. She knew that she could return for more counseling, but she did not reappear at the center during her remaining years at Brandeis. I have not heard from her since.

Although I have almost completely omitted my own contributions in this case, I was not entirely inactive; yet the reader will be right to assume that I did not have to work very hard to find points of view to suggest and to have the student respond. From the start this girl moved under her own steam and, while doing so, erected no walls between us. After only two meetings she trusted me with her worst misgivings about herself and with her undisguised emotions; her belief that she was flawed was expressed to me not as a cold theory, but through a hot attack of despair. The insights that followed this outbreak, and for which I provided some stimulation, were very much her own, eloquently expressed in her own personal idiom. Her demonstration of needing to "take a chance on movement," which marked the turn from exploration to action, was made through her preferred medium of disciplined and harmonious body movement. Finally, it was on her own initiative that Rosalie, in the last few sessions, confronted the crucial item of relations with men, bringing to bear on it what she had just learned about herself; she came full circle by resolving this issue, which had precipitated her breakdown.

Rosalie's course in counseling displays in clear-cut, telescopic form the structure typical of successful therapy, its characteristic stages and turning points. The outcome also demonstrates the efficacy of holistic insights, produced or furthered by holistic interpretations. If the therapist helps the client discover some generalized assumptions and expectations behind specific disturbances, the discovery may lead to the review and correction of these assumptions. The resulting changes in broad attitudes can make the details of behavior fall into place more or less automatically, without an excessive expenditure of thought and effort—even in areas that have not been worked on in therapy at all, as was true of Rosalie's academic failures. Contrary to the recently reinforced dogma of behavioral specificity, "one changes significantly in one's roots, not in one's branches" (Angyal, 1965, p. 205). My main contribution to the development of the holistic insight which led Rosalie to reinterpret and rearrange her life was simply to make explicit the assumption of a basic flaw implied in her despairing self-accusations and to encourage her to question both its truth and its origin, pointing out that a belief of this kind cannot be taken as its own proof.

When Rosalie delved into the possible origins of her globally negative self-image, her findings showed a strikingly close fit with Angyal's formulations of the method of "vicarious living," which he identified as the hysterical dimension of the modern character neuroses. An individual resorts to "vicarious living" after he or she has discarded not just some tabooed areas (like sex and aggression) but virtually all genuine feelings, thoughts, and impulses—so that the whole personality may be said to have been denied or repressed. This sweeping suicidal repression is based on the person's hidden conviction that his naked self is unacceptable, totally worthless. Experiences conveying to the child that he is of no account are many and varied; as a result, the loss of self is ubiquitous today. It can result from the child's being belittled, overpunished, overopposed, disregarded, or abandoned. It can also result from his being overprotected (implying that he is weak, incompetent, sick) or cast into a false role by parents and faced with expectations that he cannot fulfill without totally disregarding himself. Whatever the original cause, the repression of a person's real emotions, wishes, and thoughts makes him into a nobody. He vaguely feels that he is an empty shell—or, in extreme cases, practically an empty space; some students tell me that they feel astonished when others notice and greet them on campus. To escape the feeling of emptiness, of nonexistence, the person must find or construct some substitute for the banished self. He can live "vicariously," by attaching himself dependently to another, often chosen for his "strength" or prestige; this desperate dependency may masquerade as love. Or he can build up a pseudopersonality in one of several ways: by imitating some admired person; or by identifying with some popular ideal; or, like Rosalie, by accepting and cultivating a false role.

No solution, however, can do away with the feelings of vacuousness, of artificiality, of being a fake, of not knowing who one is, or with the need for continuous validation from outside. In some cases the fight against one's own suggestibility, a correlate of one's felt emptiness, leads to an extreme negativism, which is meant as protection against being influenced and "molded." When the supports that constitute the pseudopersonality break down or fail, the person may become extremely anxious, feeling as if he were disappearing or dying. Rosalie was unable to keep the expurgated, stylized version of her personality functioning smoothly at all times; she paid the price of concealment in her awkward, self-protective assertiveness and in her avoidance of closeness, which would lead to the detection of her false front. When her repressed genuine feelings found a reinforcement in her growing heterosexual interests and impulses, her artificial personality collapsed, and she rightly took this breakdown as a call for a thorough self-reappraisal.

Once her assumption of worthlessness (which is the nucleus of all neurotic developments) became clear to her, Rosalie moved vigorously from insight to insight. I merely underlined some of the connections she had made—pointing out, for example, that her feelings of emptiness resulted more directly from her pushing down emotions and thoughts than from her parents' claiming ownership of some aspects of herself. Such comments can help to prepare a shift, usually occurring during a successful therapy course, from dwelling on what has been done *to* the client to centering on what is being done *by* him. Properly understood, this shift raises his belief that he has the power to change; that is, although he cannot undo what has been done to him, he may be able to change what he has done to himself, under the pressure of circumstances, and to learn new ways of feeling and acting.

Jim: Finding Oneself

Counselor's report: Jim was a soft-spoken, intent person, who talked in a constrained, quiet way. He complained that he did not know himself, what he was or what he could become. He was about to graduate and felt uncertain about his future and goals. He was dissatisfied with his lack of intimate, genuine relationships. He believed that he was "using" girls. He felt inferior and held the idea that if people really knew him they would dislike him. He made certain teachers into idols and eagerly sought their wisdom and opinions.

At home he was considered a perfect gentleman. His mother was proud of him and counted on him to bring fame and honor to their good name. She often stated that he could do no wrong and that she "knew" he would never disappoint her. She was prone to preach to him the virtues of being good and dutiful. His father, a hard-working professional man, was proud of his son's achievements but shared little else with him. As Jim was growing up, his father would occasionally poke fun at his physical appearance, belittling his developing masculinity. He joked about his son's dating and would say, "To me you'll always be my little boy." Such statements would arouse vague feelings of unrest and anger. However, out of respect and fear Jim would say nothing, merely blush and smile.

Jim and the counselor met for twenty sessions. It became increasingly clear that the student was terrified of displeasing either parent. His early memories of his mother's hurt look and her crying at some misdemeanor and of his father's half-joking, half-angry remark, "I'll cut your head off," were reminders of the need to please them. He felt he must never disagree with them, only feel love toward them and achieve academic excellence for their happiness. In effect: be a perfect little boy.

As he realized his need for perfection and his anger toward his parents, he began to experiment with people and practiced some self-assertion. Simultaneously, he began to work out his tangle of feelings through his relationship with the counselor, first raising him to great heights, then challenging him, then distrusting, then feeling frightened, and finally adopting a more realistic appraisal of himself and the counselor. He realized that he had enjoyed the role of good boy and feared to grow up. In effect, being independent meant for him being alone and unprotected. He developed confidence that he could take care of himself, and his fear of displeasing his family and others slowly dissipated. He decided to go into graduate school and looked forward to the challenge of the future.

Jim's report: I feel a change has occurred, and is occurring now within me. One of the most predominant characteristics of this change is a sense of myself as a unique person.

I no longer feel nervous about myself—about my desires. I no longer play-act, or pretend, or act according to a preconceived formula; I am just myself. The reason I am able to be myself is that I no longer fear other people and their possible censure of me. I no longer worry about the impression I am giving others, because being myself is more important. Previously I felt an estrangement from other people. I felt inferior to them—and yet knew in my mind that often I was not inferior to them in any way. As a little boy I would always listen and never venture an opinion. I would never enter an argument because I lacked conviction of my beliefs; indeed, I was scarcely courageous enough to form my own ideas and to reason for myself. If I did actually experience a conscious feeling for something, my problem then was to express it. I had a tremendous fear of expression because I felt people might dislike me, or be disappointed, or be angry with me.

By giving up all my previous gods—that is, by finally realizing other human beings are mortal—I was now in a strange situation. For one thing it is exhilarating and exciting and challenging—but on the other hand it is also terrifying. I no longer have anyone or anything to lean on besides myself. That is why I must be true to myself as nearly as I am able. By realizing there are no gods—I become an adult. I assume consciously all responsibility for what I do and become. I am no longer satisfied with not progressing or growing, and so I must go in the world and finally face my fears.

If my outlook on life has become more mature, more realistic, and more sober—so too my joys have been multiplied many times. I feel a genuine and at times sad type of happiness—it is not the wild ecstasy of youth. I also feel more secure. I feel that I am building a citadel within me that will no longer be hurt and affected by stupidity. I feel a much greater sense of self-reliance—I feel more capable, more confident. I feel more safe and more content. There has been a remarkable decrease of anxiety in my life. I realize now to what extent I had been plagued and paralyzed by anxiety and fear. But I feel free now. I am now no longer paralyzed. I have begun to probe the reality around me. I have been able to do this because I feel safe, I feel that I will not be destroyed by being myself.

But perhaps an even more fundamental change that has

occurred within me (and one that is closely related to my feeling of oneness and integration) is the fact that I no longer fear *myself*. That is, I do not think that underneath my external nice-boy façade I am evil and bad, rotten and worthless. It is for this reason that I have always feared most the people I was most attracted to. Not only for outward rejection but because I could not let anybody get too near to me. I could not allow myself to like anybody too much—for fear that they would find out the truth about me and hate me for it.

I do not know how much credit to give to analysis, or therapy, or what you will, for this change. My first impulse is to bow down and kiss your feet as a miracle worker. But I realize that it is I who have changed. My ultimate belief is that the potentials for my betterment were there—and that my talks with you have fulfilled them or rather helped me to fulfill them and to realize them. What analysis has done is actually very little—simply changed my focus on things—that is about all. But it is this slight change which makes all the difference between life and death. It is like a drop of oil—without which the huge machine cannot work.

I have no illusion about the future. I think it will become increasingly difficult for me as I will have to assume many more responsibilities—but I feel this trip forward, the process of growing, is a one-way ticket—and I can no longer turn back.

This is a moving presentation of the trials and triumphs of an adolescent who has chosen to leave behind the childish things that had had a strong hold on him and start moving toward true adulthood. Though he touches on more aspects of this process than most students do in their reports, the changes that Jim describes and his reactions to them are quite typical of those students who feel that they have greatly matured during the period of counseling. Following are some variations provided by several other students on the themes outlined by Jim:

Initially I was upset as I felt that X would neither give me advice as to what to do nor care what I did; I was used to leaning on people. For the first time I was forced to make decisions and to recognize the real reasons why I felt as I did; it was a painful experience. But as time went on I began to feel that my problems were not unsolvable and that I had taken a big step in recognizing and facing them.

I have achieved a certain basic trust in myself, which has enabled me to enter into relationships—with boys, girls, men, and women—in a much more honest and open way than before. I no longer become defensive during rough periods in a friendship, and my own naturalness puts others at ease. I am much more casual, too, with my professors. This may be one reason why I am enjoying my courses so much more and getting such good grades this year.

I was afraid in coming to counseling that it would make me into a totally "different person," rob me of my sense of identity. Instead, I was led to distinguish between the "myths" through which I saw myself and the deeper, stronger motives behind my behavior. This strengthened my sense of myself, which now makes it much easier for me to deal with all problems involving people and decisions. As far as I am concerned, those results have been optimal.

After I had formed good relationships with friends, family, and my boy friend (whom I am now married to), I started feeling that I knew what the remaining problems were and could work them out myself. I asked X to tell me I should not come back. He replied that it was my decision and I could come back next week if I wished. It was very painful saying I would not return because I had to rely on myself then. I felt very weak at first, but then I felt strong and very good.

I learned a kind of thinking and a capacity for feeling which I enjoy now and find essential to living life as fully as possible. Because of the short time, there were many things I did not feel relaxed enough to discuss. But the general attitudes I discovered in counseling carried over even to those areas I talked very little about. I now feel in general more self-accepting. more genuine, more real; I no longer feel I am a child playing at being grown-up.

While Jim's descriptions of his course of counseling reflect the salient features of the last stretch of the road to responsible adulthood, they also make plausible the notion that in our culture full adulthood is not the fate of all people, not a natural accompaniment of chronological age. It is not difficult to imagine the kind of man Jim would have become if, together with his counselor, he had not worked "the miracle" of change and growth. Those overeager to please and propitiate are found in all age groups, and their "goodness" is usually spoiled by resentment.

Although Jim's childhood situation was not identical with Rosalie's, and his quiet temperament was different from her bubbling one, the reader will notice that his personality pattern had some features in common with hers. He too had replaced an "unacceptable" self with a pseudopersonality, the parentally approved "good little boy"; in addition, he attempted to live through idealized others. If the strategy of "vicarious living" is the essence of hysterical adjustment, are adolescents to be viewed as hysterics if they prove unable to discard childish dependence easily and gradually, without great upsets and without help? Perhaps the answer depends less on the presence or absence of turmoil during transition than on whether the child's natural dependence on the adults was reinforced by his having had to deny and distort rather than to channel his impulses. Falsification provides good soil for neurosis to grow in. Depending on how thorough a job he has done of falsifying himself, an adolescent will have a more or less difficult time if and when he starts struggling toward maturity. Jim had to struggle harder than Rosalie did. Like her, he eventually became confident that he had changed enough to continue on his own, but it took him twice the number of sessions to reach that stage. I would also guess that, in order to stimulate Jim to move, his counselor had to be more active than I was with Rosalie. Furthermore, there are indications, in his report and in his counselor's report, that Jim's methods of dealing with life's problems were not limited to those typical of "vicarious living"; he may have used a few that form a part of the obsessive-compulsive pattern.

In all these respects Jim is more typical of the majority of students whose courses in counseling we are now discussing than is either Rosalie or Benjamin (who is to be discussed next and whose pattern was predominantly obsessive and more difficult to dislodge). Viewed in terms of the two major neurotic dimensions, the hysterical and the obsessive-compulsive, the bulk of these students do not show as much predominance of one dimension over the other as Rosalie and Benjamin do. In fact, most children—not just the members of this particular group—are subject to more than one kind of traumatic experience and develop more than one strategy of coping with their consequences, so that only a few can be expected to fall into mutually exclusive separate groups. Most neurotics have "mixed neuroses." Cases that are relatively "pure" greatly further our understanding of the patterns in question, but these patterns are better viewed (with Angyal) as dimensions, rather than classes, of neuroses.

Still, when all is said, it must be acknowledged that even normally developing adolescents—by the very nature of their "marginal," transitional situation—are similar in some respects to those who are chronically engaged in shaping and maintaining substitute personalities; they are subject to identity crises.

The adolescent actually faces the situation similar to one the neurotic creates: something old is being left behind and something new is being formed. This situation of abandoning an old personality for a new one results in the adolescent's feeling that he is nowhere, that he does not know who he is. During this period of uncertainty when the adolescent tries to form a new personality, we find mechanisms at work that are similar to the hysterical ones, for instance, imitativeness. . . . The adolescent may also try to form a new personality around some absolute ideal of behavior, resolving that he will always do this, or never do that. To live up to such an ideal of perfection may require an exorbitant amount of repression. In choosing a model or a friend the adolescent often favors people of high social status. Since he is uncertain of his own feelings and valuations his choices must be guided by public opinion, and he feels safest in allying himself with people of prestige. In all these and many other features adolescents present a picture similar to the hysterical one, but in the normal course of development this stage is outgrown as new feelings and situations become clarified and assimilated [Angyal, 1965, p. 143–144].

Benjamin: The Pattern of Noncommitment

In trying to understand the plight of Benjamin—a sophomore who was having difficulties with his studies, his mother, and his girl friends—I made use, as with Rosalie, of Angyal's formulations and insights. Relevant to this case was Angyal's formulation of the obsessive-compulsive dimension of neurosis, termed by him "the pattern of noncommitment." The complex, insufficiently explored course of this pattern's development and implementation makes it difficult to present coherently, integrating theory with example. For clarity's sake I shall separate them, presenting first Angyal's views of the structure of noncommitment and then proceeding to the case itself.

The basic structure of this pattern, as viewed by Angyal, is easy to grasp. It is the outcome of an early "abiding confusion as to whether the world is basically friendly or inimical. This painful state of uncertainty leads the person to respond to significant people with both hostility and love and results in an unceasing search for ways to dispel confusion and to gain an unequivocal orientation to the world" (Angyal, 1965, p. 157). The confusion can have different origins; outstanding among them is the inconsistent behavior of significant adults, which made it impossible for the child to discover even moderately reliable ways of gaining acceptance (which a hysteric is usually able to do at the price of self-obliteration). The situation is worst when the inconsistent adult who is the source of affection also mistreats the child drastically: by severe punishment, extreme domination or exploitation, withdrawal, or neglect. A child treated in this way may grow up to view the world as a jungle, life as a fight of all against all. However, even much less drastic treatment by people or by circumstances can give rise to the trauma of confusion, if this treatment is inconsistent and capricious and the reasons for the shifts cannot be fathomed by the child.

Whatever has caused the confusion, it results in the person's harboring two sharply contrasting images of the world, which evoke in him correspondingly contrasting responses. He never knows what to expect or how to respond, and he feels powerless to influence events in his favor. The issue of strength and power becomes central in his thought, but in actual fact his conflicting orientations result in doubt, indecision, vacillation, and general inhibition of action and emotion. Those in whose neurotic patterns, actual or potential, noncommitment born of confusion plays a minimal role do not find it easy to empathize with the person whose basic experience in life is uncertainty. We can think of some trivial examples, however—perhaps one's state of mind when, waking up on the day of a carefully planned pleasure trip, one finds the skies alternating between sunny and threatening and the "probability of precipitation" being estimated at 50 percent. If we magnify a thousand times the agony of indecision we might then briefly experience, we may imagine the feelings of one for whom the choice of a course of action to be taken in an unpredictable situation, even a comparatively trivial situation, appears to be a matter of life and death. When everything is at stake, uncertainty may be so torturing and immobilizing that he will jump at any method to terminate it; actually, however, all methods fall short of their mark. Different patients use very different strategies in trying to dispel their confusion and gain certainty, but they all share in the life style of noncommitment: always eyeing two possibilities, saying yes and no at the same time. In this way, even though they hide this fact from themselves through elaborate constructions, they may turn their lives into a farce and deprive themselves of real fulfillment.

Possibly the most conspicuous disturbance of a noncommital person who is free from pronounced obsessions and compulsions is his lack of wholeheartedness in intimate relationships; the conflicting needs to approach and to withdraw lead to endless complications. It is a source of puzzlement and of tormenting guilt for the person that his love and his hate are directed toward the same object; he can never be certain that in fighting an enemy he is not striking at a friend. An unequivocal enemy may be a boon to such a person, enabling him to fight freely; some patients, however, find themselves paralyzed—not always by fear—even when facing an obvious aggressor. Moreover, a person who alternates between fearful and hopeful anticipations is likely to create enmities; in a situation of uncertainty he feels safer when he is on guard, cultivating his hostility and suppressing his loving impulses. A backlog of real guilt for mistreatment of alleged enemies, acquired during years of neurotic living and not to be dismissed as spurious, is one of the difficulties in the therapy of older noncommital patients. This accumulation may be very large if the person has been silencing his guilt by "discovering" more and more faults in the other; guilt and hostility then grow in a vicious spiral.

Glimpses of one's irrationality, one's seemingly perverse attitudes toward those close to one—added to the experiences of inhibition, usually viewed as "weakness"—prevent the emergence of a positive, confident self-image. Therefore, when choosing a method of intervention, counselors should remember that with these people self-derogation (sometimes masked by grandiosity) can reach spectacular extremes. Any intervention that confirms the client's feelings of worthlessness increases his predicament and reduces his chances for improvement. A consistent use of Angyal's concepts is an effective safeguard against this all-too-frequent course of obsessive patients in therapy. By stressing the role of verifiable situational factors over that of hypothetical constitutional ones in the genesis of this pattern, by viewing ambivalence as rooted in confusion, Angyal's conception counteracts the patient's belief—often hidden from others and from himself—that he is irrational, perverse, worthless, less than human.

The early causes of Benjamin's confusion did not become obvious during the four months of counseling, but the presence of contrasting images of the world and of his own chances in life, with a predominance of negative expectations, became obvious very soon; each happy memory immediately brought up one of grief or threat. As a child, a small but active one, Benjamin was happiest at his parents' beach house, but it was there that he was often beaten up and humiliated by a gang of other boys. A pleasure park nearby was full of attractions, but Benjamin never felt that he had enough money to enjoy them, no matter how much he had saved or been given. After the bullies left the area and Benjamin "no longer hated anybody," the beach house was washed into the sea.

In his descriptions of his parents the good and the bad were juxtaposed, and so were his feelings of guilt and fear. His memories of his deceased father were warm and pleasant, but he also recalled being chased and punished by him, sometimes unjustly. His mother's role in Benjamin's current life seemed to be largely negative, that of a nagger and an admonisher; but when, as a young child, he accidentally broke an object she cherished, he felt so guilty and cried so much that she had to comfort him.

The central role of the dual perception of people in Benjamin's guilt feelings is made strikingly clear if one compares his reported episodes of guilt with his story of the act of vengeance he eventually inflicted on his bullies. On having grown stronger than they, he provoked a fight with each of them and beat them up, hurting them as much as he dared; he only stopped short of what he felt would cause permanent damage. The settling of accounts with these unambiguous villains left no residue of guilt: "I am very glad of having done it, even now." This story suggests that Benjamin had felt himself threatened severely, possibly fantasying mortal danger from his enemies.

The issues of life and death came into focus for him at the age of ten by the coincidence of his father's death with his own rescue from a real, not an imagined, danger to life. One day, when Benjamin was visiting his father, who was dying of cancer, a hospital physician discovered that Benjamin also had cancer—cancer of the thyroid. The next day—which, although he did not know it then, was the day of his father's death—he was operated on. This was a miraculous escape from severe danger, and yearly checkups kept Benjamin reminded of it: "I had a cancer and I am still alive, and my father died unnecessarily." He decided to become a physician, one who saves people's lives, not a negligent or incompetent one who lets them die. He absorbed himself in the study of scientific subjects and, as with many other fields, displayed excellent ability.

In high school Benjamin was often depressed and had poor relations with his peers and friction with his mother. In his senior year he began a year of therapy, which somewhat lightened his depressions and reduced the fights but made no decisive impact. Benjamin had little understanding of what went on in sessions and felt that the therapist was keeping secrets from him. Later on, in comparing his counseling experience with his earlier ones, he said that with his first therapist he was doing all the talking but no thinking, one of his many pithy formulations.

In college Benjamin found himself wasting time and still engaging, at a distance, in periodic skirmishes with his mother; his grades were not high enough to assure admission to a good medical school. His main preoccupation was with girls. His initial visit to the center was prompted by the rejection of a girl friend, who had found him possessive and demanding. Although he said humorously that this was an exact replication of last year's episode, he was obviously worried by the fact that his relationships with girls ended before they could develop. In his first few sessions Benjamin appeared to be ill at ease, perhaps mildly depressed; at first he left the initiative to me, but his ability for self-observation and for precise, penetrating thinking was obvious from the start.

As Benjamin talked and thought about grades and about girls, his troubles started forming a pattern; in both cases successful initial approaches were followed by failures, causing him to withdraw and to lower his level of aspiration. This course of events belied his half-hearted claim that the desired objects were not within his reach: Brandeis courses too difficult, girls too beautiful or too mixed up. Actually, Benjamin knew that his intelligence and aptitude test scores were very high, and in his first term at Brandeis he got A's; in the second term he got B's. This year, he said, he was aiming for B's and expecting C's. He also knew that many girls started out by liking him very much. What was at the bottom of his subsequent failures, academic and social? In groping for explanations, Benjamin pursued the clues pointing to his easy discouragement, his constant expectation of fiascoes. In reading, for instance, whenever he came to a point that he did not grasp immediately, he felt that he would never understand it and stopped trying; the prospect of exams always spelled failure and made all subjects seem hopelessly difficult. His expectation of failure led to failure, which, in circular fashion, made his pessimism seem justified. With girls, the moment they did not respond as he wished, he felt rejected, as he had known all along he would be; he would then turn away, or act so as to make the girl turn away. If a rival appeared on the horizon, Benjamin without fail saw him as greatly superior to himself and made almost no effort to reassert his claim to the girl's attention. His first insights in counseling were (1) that he responded to discouragement much more strongly than to encouragement and (2) that this very response turned his gloomy expectations into self-fulfilling prophecies.

Some of Benjamin's self-observations, however, did not fit the pattern of easy discouragement, which can occur within either dimension of neurosis. He had stopped working the previous year— not after meeting with difficulties but after receiving all A's. And he often became acutely uncomfortable with a girl immediately after he had been feeling particularly relaxed and close, with everything to encourage him. This evidence of a "coactivation of opposite tendencies," resulting from a dual perception of persons and events, made me look for some less paradoxical features of the pattern of noncommitment, features that could be more easily brought to the student's attention. I was helped in this search by Benjamin's remarks connecting his grades with his mother. He repeatedly expressed regret about having related to her his difficulties with his studies, thus inviting a lecture; he should not let her in on his affairs, he said, but somehow he always did. Benjamin was also enacting a similar situation with me, which gave me a good opening. When he once again started the session by informing me—with a mischievous smile—that his grades were still poor, I acknowledged the importance of the issue—since, if he was serious about medical school, he could not afford to keep his grades down for too long. I then asked whether he might not be using his grades to annoy or worry his mother. The idea did not shock Benjamin. It turned out that he deliberately started getting poor grades last year to spite his mother after she went back on her promise to let him take his car to Boston if his grades were good. Since she had failed him after he had kept up his end of the bargain, he was withholding further payments.

We get here a glimpse of one step in the genesis or stabilization of a particularly handicapping feature of the pattern of noncommitment: spiteful disobedience. Disguised as disability, it is a natural way to fight an irrational authority. Benjamin related several other instances of broken promises, which, in his eyes, were not made good by his mother's later gifts of presents and privileges. He had come to feel that she could not be relied upon to carry out either her promises or her threats.

The real trouble begins when perceptions, feelings, and actions aroused in one situation are generalized to a host of others. Generalization plays a major role in the formation of neurotic attitudes, although at an early stage it is more aptly viewed as a lack of differentiation. For an infant the specific *is* the general; the people taking care of one *are* the world. If the person in authority seems so capricious that the child cannot predict his responses, the child comes to feel that anything he wants is forbidden and punishable; this is easily turned into "What is forbidden and bad is what I want." Wanting the forbidden, asserting oneself through opposition, is a bid for existence and integrity, but its effects may be disastrous. In the heat of battle one may lose track of one's own real desires, as when a person loves his work yet feels compelled periodically to stop working, because doing well and pleasing the boss means yielding to the "enemy."

Benjamin had felt no compunction about lowering his grades to punish his mother's unfairness; but, since he was no longer harboring this intent, he found it hard to believe that a less conscious variant of the same attitude might be responsible for his present poor grades. I wondered whether his mother's strong support of his plan to become a doctor did not tend to confuse him. Since her opposition usually indicated to him that his plans were his, not hers, and therefore right for him, couldn't her approval of them have the opposite effect? Benjamin became alarmed; he protested that he had excellent personal reasons to go into medicine. True, I said; and to succeed he would have to give up whatever attitudes were responsible for the crazy assumption that his integrity required getting poor grades.

This exchange took place in the third session, which, in retrospect, I see as concluding the initial stage, during which the main themes of the total counseling period were introduced. The next stage, central in the therapy of neuroses, is generally devoted to outlining and undermining the neurotic pattern and simultaneously discovering the healthy factors buried within the neurosis—the process of demolition and reconstruction. In Benjamin's case the interchange that started this process moving occurred in the fifth session, when he felt slightly encouraged by the attention of a girl and I used his better mood to ask him about satisfying relationships in the past. After recalling a congenial one that had ended too soon, the kind he doubted he could repeat and develop, Benjamin said that he was unable to be as aggressive as girls seemed to wish—"but I would love to be." I sensed strong emotion behind this wish and took it as just one instance of his yearning for confident wholeheartedness. "You really long," I said, "to be able to go after what you want in a direct and strong fashion that comes from a confident feeling, believing that your chances are good, expecting success, but prepared to accept an occasional failure as not much of a tragedy." To this recognition of his natural wish for confident selfhood, Benja-

min responded with emphatic agreement and with a formulation of
his predicament that matched my statement in scope: "I am scared
of failure."

The next week, our last meeting before Christmas vacation,
Benjamin reported that he had made approaches to girls without
being crushed by "rejection." Three weeks later he told me that
home had not been too bad and that he had resolved the issue of
grades by deciding to transfer next year to an easier school (a decision later revoked). Feeling that the acute problems had been
solved, Benjamin wondered if he should stop counseling—implicitly
asking me to decide. In reply to my comment—part clarification,
part invitation—he mentioned, almost in passing, that after my
"holistic" interpretation of a month ago he had experienced a
marked increase in self-confidence. He later described very vividly
how he had found himself able to make decisions, large and small,
rather than being bogged down with pros and cons. Nor did these
decisions get lost in postponements, as previously; they immediately
led over into action. Benjamin then demonstrated this new ability
by stating, without equivocation, that the advance he had made was
only the first step toward his goals and that he wanted to continue
counseling.

After making this decision, Benjamin pursued counseling
vigorously, in close collaboration with me but very much as his own
enterprise. In the first session of this period, he took up once more
the theme of easy discouragement and related it to his feeling that
he could not anyway have what he *really* wanted, what would be
worth laboring for; in particular, though he despised incompetence,
he felt that he was destined to be at best a mediocre physician. I
said he saw the world, or fate, as inimical and withholding, not
willing to give him a chance. Benjamin agreed strongly; that was
exactly how he felt, he said, and (what is more) he really believed
it to be true. Even if he saw now that he himself was doing everything to destroy his slim chances, he had no power to change his
actions. I spoke about his having been powerless to avert catas-
trophes, to prevent his father's death and its bad consequences for
the family. To become a physician who saves lives would be to
counteract his early experiences of impotence and loss. At this point,
Benjamin felt a memory working its way up—of his last visit with

his father. The father offered him a chocolate from his box; Benjamin took one but felt guilty for depriving his father. I asked if he believed, now, that his father was just being polite; and he said no, that his father had wanted him to have it.

Since his father's terminal hospitalization had indirectly saved Benjamin's life, and since Benjamin's grief for his beloved father had been inhibited and short-lived, one must conjecture that these exchanges were fraught with meanings that would evoke in Benjamin the emotions of love, fear, anger, grief, and guilt. He did not express—or probably even feel—any strong emotion, but in bringing up the memory of the treat he had received from his dying father, Benjamin may well have been accepting the gift of life, which had been twice bestowed on him by his father, overcoming for the moment his doubts and guilt.

Whatever the reasons, this session had a striking effect on Benjamin and set the tone for the remainder of the counseling period. The next week he reported that he had been direct and straightforward in his dealings with people; this behavior was new to him and brought results. In preparing for exams, he worked with absorption and pleasure and easily got good grades. With his mother, instead of behaving in ways that made him feel confused and guilty, he decided on a limited clear commitment; she was financing his studies and entitled to expect decent grades from him, but the rest of his life was his own. To have his own spending money, he took a job. He wrote to a girl who, he felt, had rejected him previously and was looking forward to her visit; he believed that he could now be more natural and more assertive with her than before. Benjamin was greatly pleased by his advance in all areas but also admitted feeling anxious, as if he might be punished for his daring and stopped in his tracks.

A reversal had taken place. The confident feelings, at long last, had the upper hand, outweighing the fearful one. This was not the end, however. The change, insufficiently prepared, did not usher in a clear-cut terminal stage, that of developing and stabilizing the healthy pattern now in ascendance. The rest of the sessions were filled with a variety of processes preceding that stage, which in longer courses of therapy typically predominate in different periods but which in this instance ran simultaneously, telescoped into a very brief span of time.

During the central period of the therapy of an established neurosis, the mode of adjustment that has sprung from fearful pessimistic assumptions gets gradually discredited and undermined, sometimes resulting in a catastrophic experience of its bankruptcy. Simultaneously, the pattern based on more confident expectations, the residue of satisfying experiences of managing and interacting with others, is gradually unearthed and acknowledged. As the neurotic pattern is weakened and the healthy one strengthened, their conflict ushers in the crucial stage of therapy, the struggle for decision, when two ways of life claim the wavering patient's allegiance, resulting over a period of time in many movements back and forth.

During the last five sessions of Benjamin's counseling period, while the work of the central stage was being continued, what was most conspicuous were these back-and-forth moves. No achievement of the previous weeks was steadily kept. Grades reverted to poor; friction with his mother broke out anew after a period of improvement. With girls, while Benjamin moved in the direction of greater closeness with one, he also maintained a relationship with another, using it for periodic retreats from the first. Although he produced a wealth of reasons to prove that his behavior with girls was both necessary and beneficial, I was usually able to point out to him on the spot every retreat from the confident position achieved, as well as the ways in which he was covering up this retreat.

My diligence in this work of unmasking was prompted by Angyal's observation that any progress in therapy can be canceled if the patient uses the gain for neurotic purposes, thus making his neurosis bigger and better. Increased self-confidence, for example, may be used to pursue neurotic interpersonal games more effectively. When Benjamin, after briefly doubting his chances with girls, would reassert his newly found confidence in a grandiose fashion, saying that he now could win any girl he chose, he may have been preparing to do just that. When, in response to my disbelief, he would take this statement back as a misformulation and replace it with a more modest one, was he in fact returning to realism, or was he merely covering up? "Difficult as it may be for the therapist to respond to these mixed expressions adequately, it is important for him to follow closely these repeated reversals. The neurotic pattern will return again and again—a wolf in sheep's clothing—and must be unmasked anew every time. The patient will not admit the defeat of his neurosis as long as a single loophole is left" (Angyal, 1965, p. 244).

Fortunately, Benjamin was highly sensitive to all inconsistencies, including his own; he soon started participating actively in the unmasking of his strategies. After a happy weekend with his girl friend, he would catch himself looking for flaws in her and in her situation—"as if I were deliberately trying to bring back the pessimistic mood and also as a reason to look for another girl." After he had stopped worrying his mother by idling in his studies, he was shocked to realize that he had merely changed the time index; he told her that he had fallen behind but was now catching up: "Oh my God, I do have to worry her first. Why can't I just tell her that everything is fine?" In short, although Benjamin's neurosis was far from vanquished, he no longer identified himself with it. He now recognized that his wishes were normal and realizable, and he was no longer a slave to the pessimistic orientation that had made him pursue these wishes in indirect, ineffective ways. He could now carry out the work of undermining his neurosis without also undermining himself.

Although this period of persistent discrediting of the pattern of noncommitment was brief, it had some lasting effects. In the follow-up letter written many years later, Benjamin reminisced as follows: "You kept pointing out that I hedged my bets in my relationships with women, protecting against both failure and success. You suggested that I would have to choose at some point. . . . I did blame you later for my unhappiness in my marriage—after all, you had told me I couldn't have two women at once—but I have also, oftener than you might think, remembered that observation when obsessing about some decision and then laughed and gone ahead and made a choice."

The work of rehabilitation went on simultaneously, as we tried to uncover the genesis of Benjamin's diffident orientation. Typically, when some cover-up was removed, some pretension punctured in the session, it was shown to hide some fearful or hostile or self-derogatory imagery, a part of the neurotic view of the world and the self: "I myself don't feel I am worthwhile, that is why I feel unloved." I would then ask for the antecedents of such images or such feelings. When had he felt worthless and helpless in the past, or else deceived, abandoned, betrayed? In this context, the focus being kept on the present, such questions made sense to Benjamin. He produced childhood memories (some of which were reported above): first the well-practiced ones; later some of the long-forgotten ones. Benjamin's childhood could not be reconstructed from these limited memories in any detail, but in hinting at some plausible sources of his confusion they tended to reduce his feelings of guilt. Clarification of original causes cannot be expected to eliminate their distant effects; yet genetic insights are valuable because they demonstrate to the client that the pathological originates from the healthy and therefore diminish the feelings of inferiority, even inhumanity, that isolate him from others: "By linking the patient's neurotic present with his past as a child with whom he can sympathize, genetic insights quickly lead over into the constructive phase of the therapeutic work" (Angyal, 1965, p. 264).

Benjamin's mood toward the end of the counseling period reflected this constructive aspect, even though he had not exhausted his hoard of unhappy memories or given up for good "daring myself to fail." He was opening new areas for exploration and dared—or almost dared—to feel and to express feelings strongly. He could be furious about some episode he reported and he could also say: "I am very happy—I think!" On catching himself in such equivocations, he would laugh and joke: "I would mind very much not to have been born!"

During the fourteenth session—a very active and fast-moving one—I sensed, and Benjamin confirmed, that he was wondering whether he could not now carry on by himself. In discussing this question, I told him that distributing counseling over more than one period could be quite profitable; his junior and senior years might bring new problems that he might want to discuss. Benjamin decided then and there to make this session the last and expressed his satisfaction with his counseling experience. He vividly described changes dating from the appearance of the self-confident image: "In walking around I used to look down to the ground; now I look around with

a silly grin. And I stopped hating people who had done nothing to
me—I see them as neutral or even as pleasant."

The next day some changes in a girl's plans had created a
problem for Benjamin, and he called me for an additional session.
After I agreed, he found the solution himself and kept the appointment just to have it confirmed; but on the way to the center he
found that even that was not necessary. "I have discovered," he
said, "that I do not have to check with you in reality; it was enough
to formulate the idea I want to test as if I were to tell it in the
session. Talking about things here has given me a standard of objectivity and honesty; when I formulate the idea only for myself I
can fool myself, but not when I do it to tell another. So I have come
pretty close to where I want to be; I think I can carry on by myself."
He left in high spirits.

I hoped that he would reappear at the center the next year
or the year after and was disappointed that he didn't—both because
I thought he would profit from another period of work and because
I had greatly enjoyed working with him. I found the way Benjamin's
mind functioned very congenial and thought that he might prove to
be one of those students who were both stimulated and helped by
reading Angyal's book. I would have invited him to drop in for an
informal follow-up were it not for the growing waiting lists, which
by that time were preventing us from offering additional time to
anyone not in crisis.

Eight years later, when I wrote to Benjamin for permission
to describe his counseling period in some detail, he had his M.D.
degree and was specializing in psychiatry. Because of the problems
he had initially encountered in medical school and in his marriage,
he resumed therapy after graduation from college. One of his two
therapists proved helpful and brought therapy to a satisfying conclusion; this profitable period of work lasted three years. A crucial
event of this period was the discovery and the discharge of Benjamin's grief for his father; after that his fear and his anger subsided.
Benjamin was very pleased with the results achieved in therapy. He
felt that he had gained more than any of the psychotherapy patients
personally known to him. About his Brandeis counseling period he
had very few specific memories, but he knew that it had been helpful
—not only at the time but also from a long-range point of view.

When, after a bad experience with an inept, distant therapist, Benjamin despaired of ever being able to change, this memory prevented him from giving up the struggle; and his next attempt worked. He was glad that he had tried once more. "It is still a source of amazement to me and to my wife and other friends how much I changed. . . . The future for us looks bright. But I don't think I would have returned to treatment were it not for the memory of your having been useful."

The three counseling courses presented in this chapter exemplify the college student's ability to engage in insight therapy and to derive great benefits from it. This ability has been widely recognized. Most outpatient clinics and many therapists in private practice like to work with college students, sometimes preferring them to all other clients. When traditional therapeutic approaches are criticized for not meeting the needs of the large population of uneducated, nonintellectual patients, college students are commonly quoted as that small select group whose abilities and needs determine our therapeutic practices to an unjustifiable extent. Yet many of those who acknowledge college students' affinity to verbal therapy might nonetheless be astonished, as I was, to discover how vigorously and with what excellent results they do in fact engage in therapy. Even some of those who actually work with students, privately or in colleges, often fail to discover the magnitude of their potential for insight and movement. Many circumstances function as obstacles to such discovery: first and foremost, lack of staff time, which makes "triage" necessary, limiting work with students to emergencies or to referrals; second, an authoritative or dogmatic or routinized approach on the part of the counselor, which puts students off; and third, adherence to theories and viewpoints emphasizing the negative aspects of this developmental period—specifically, the students' immaturity and instability, which, some therapists feel, place obstacles in the path of therapy. Admittedly, some students' unsettled state may make it advisable to postpone intensive therapy until later; but in my experience this is the exception, not the rule. For anyone who has had therapeutic contacts with a large number of college students and has been open to the experience, the conclusion that college years are the best time for psychotherapy is all but unavoidable.

One of those who have reached this conclusion is Robert E. Nixon, for many years college psychiatrist at Vassar; he estimates that by the end of ten years he had seen 1,500 students professionally. More than half of his clients, he feels, can be characterized as "growers." In a book written for the adolescents themselves, he describes these young people as at once admirable and difficult to live with:

> They are admirable because of their courage, their tenacity, their boundless curiosity concerning both themselves and their world, their unremitting use of the critical faculty, their insistence upon using their minds to correlate what they feel with what they know with what they do. They are difficult to live with because of their relentless questioning of almost everything that enters their ken, and because of their equally relentless demand that their questions be answered. . . . From the adults they demand answers; from themselves they demand growth. . . . Speaking as an adult who has spent much time with such young people, I can attest that they are more than merely stimulating—they are downright invigorating. Where they are, there is Life [Nixon, 1962, pp. xiv–xv].

The "growers' " pursuit of self-discovery would naturally bring them to Nixon's office, where they found an informal and open reception—even though in order to remain available, often on short notice, he had to limit sessions to thirty minutes. While Nixon counts 60 percent of his clients as "growers," he estimates (without indicating the basis for his figures) that in the *total* student population the incidence of the "growers" is no more than 12 percent. Most college students, he believes, are either "conformers" or "rebels" (conformers in reverse) who are not, or not yet, engaged in a search for individuality and for their own path in life and come to the psychiatrist only in the case of breakdown.

Most of Nixon's observations on "growers" are congruent with my own experience. He feels that they benefit greatly from therapy, even though therapy in their case is "semantically wrong," since these "patients" cannot be viewed as sick. Help in acquiring self-knowledge promotes their movement toward maturity, toward finding out what they like, what they want, and what they can do. It encourages them to assume responsibility for themselves.

In some areas, however, our observations differ. In describing "growers" as therapy clients, Nixon stresses their quick insights followed by speedy applications; but he also contrasts them with his other group of clients—the bona fide patients, the sick ones— noting in the "growers" the absence of symptomatic disturbances and also of defensiveness, of resistance to interpretations, and of transference phenomena in the relationship with the therapist. Such polarization of the student clientele is not part of the Brandeis counseling experience. I have seen many students who, as counselees, fit Nixon's description of "growers" perfectly, but I doubt that they are the majority among those who make great strides in counseling. Of the cases quoted, Rosalie, who was very open and moved ahead without focusing on the counselor, fits the description best; but she came because of prolonged depression. The two others did put up a fight in defense of their immature or neurotic orientation, and transference phenomena were not totally absent. In general, when not fostered by the counselor's attitude (uncommunicative or over-parental), transference in counseling work tends to be merely episodic and, in many instances, not too important. Most of those struggling with adolescent problems tend to work on their relationships to their parents directly, making maximum use of their current experiences in the family. Clarification of obviously transferred reactions represents for these students only a contributory source of insight. This clarification, together with the venting of realistic complaints, serves mainly to keep clear the path of communication between student and counselor. Generally, the students' perception of the counselors, of their attitudes, and of their intentions is quite realistic; what is asked of them is no more than what most therapists feel they should provide. The following report, atypical only in its length, spells out the generally valued aspects of student-counselor interaction.

I enjoyed talking to X. I had come to the Center once before and spoken to Y. I didn't feel that I could establish any contact with him, or he with me, mainly because he spoke very little and showed almost no expression on his face while I was talking to him (except for once when I felt his reaction to be too extreme and for a second beyond his control). It all made me very self-conscious and I felt only the negative aspects of the presence of another person. With X it was entirely different. Even while groping for words to describe something personal, I felt as though she could see the experience just the way I was seeing it. Talking to her put me back in touch with myself, with both good and bad things in me. What X pointed out about my patterns of acting with people got me into thinking actively and openly about what I was and what I have been doing. X was responsive to my thoughts; I felt she was thinking about my concerns almost as much as I was, even though I knew she had a lot of other people to think about too. She was listening completely all the time. I also felt that I could express my feelings about what was happening in that session and we could deal with them then and there. The only drawback I felt was that X was a bit too strong; some of the things she commented upon I should have had to introduce myself, but she was aware of this. The trouble was we had so little time that the whole process went a bit too fast.

This dominant pattern is not without exceptions, however. In some courses of counseling, transference does play an important role, as illustrated in the following excerpt from the report of one male student; he sought help for prolonged periods of depression and achieved excellent success in a longish period of work with a male counselor.

My first feeling about the counselor was that he was an intruder into my life, that he was paid to show concern but did not really feel concern because he was not my friend. I then came to regard him as a magician who had it in his power to offer some magic cure. I had the feeling that all my problems would end if he were to say the words "Listen, your problems really aren't that bad at all; you're actually quite a great guy." Fortunately for me, he never said anything like that. Had he done it, I would have regarded all my problems as solved and would have been happy for a short while; then I would have had to seek out some new authority and get once more "approval" and flattering reassurances. When I realized that approval wasn't forthcoming, my attitude about Mr. X shifted. I regarded him as inhuman, a machine to whom I was feeding data for professional analysis. My final attitude toward him was to regard him just as a man, rather than as an intruder, magician, or computer; this attitude proved to be most useful. My feelings about X changed because my attitude toward counseling and toward myself changed. He was an intruder at first when I felt fear and embarrassment. He needed to be a magician when I felt my problems to be unsolvable. I had to make him a computer when I felt he was never going to be a friend. Actually he only said things that were useful to say and he never said anything he did not believe. I see this now; I did not at the time.

It is plausible to assume, as Nixon does, that differences of student behavior in counseling reflect the difference between normal developmental crises and neurotic difficulties, but the observations and statistics gathered at Brandeis do not support the existence of a high correlation between "normalcy" and speedy progress. Furthermore, our sample of counselees cannot be easily divided into the two contrasting groups of Nixon's healthy "growers" and the sick ones. In the years when all students seen at the Brandeis center were rated by counselors on a three-point scale (disturbance slight, moderate, or serious), the middle group usually turned out to comprise close to 70 percent of all those applying for counseling. Ratings are not very valuable data, but I believe that in this case their bunching in the middle reflects more than the raters' assumption of normal distribution. This middle category was defined to include those in whom "the difficulties of adolescence were much more pronounced than usual" *and* those showing "chronic neurotic patterns that were neither extreme nor excessively handicapping." The dual definition (which reflects the difficulty of distinguishing the two subgroups)' makes room for large numbers. Being the largest, this group included most of those who displayed speedy maturing in counseling, but not all; some came also from the other two groups. In particular, some of the students who were placed in the "seriously disturbed" category, because they were acutely disturbed when they came to the center and not because of serious chronic handicap, proved to be strongly mobilized for work by their crises and moved very fast.

The high proportion of "growers" in Nixon's Vassar sample may be accounted for, in part, by the sex difference; that is, college women take to counseling much more readily than college men do. At Brandeis over a number of years, a larger proportion of women than of men applied for counseling, and a smaller proportion of those applying appeared to be seriously disturbed. Perhaps not as repelled as men by the passive connotations of the idea of seeking help, many women came because they wanted to, not because they had to. As to the easy divisibility of Nixon's patients into sheep and goats (unless he has sharpened the contrast for the purpose of presentation), it may be the result of the conditions determining the self-selection of his sample. Dr. Nixon, the only psychiatric counselor for an enrollment that grew from 1,000 to 1,500, must have made it easy for students to approach him; that he managed to see 10 percent of all students is quite an achievement. Given his limited time, however, he is not likely to have tried too hard to get them to settle down to a longer period of counseling; such periods must have been reserved for those who needed help badly. This is a situation very different from the one we had during our best period at Brandeis, when we were able to see 20 percent of all students yearly, quite a few of them for a long time.

Our strategies and practices, as they become known to the students, exercise a selective influence on potential applicants. Therefore, among the Vassar students who were not seriously or acutely disturbed, perhaps only the confident and optimistic ones— those with few misgivings about seeing a psychiatrist, those who were confident of being able to achieve something worthwhile in a few brief sessions, those who would come fully prepared to work— actually came in for counseling; those less confident and less optimistic might have stayed away. When at Brandeis we had to tell the applicants that the allowance of sessions had been cut down, quite a few decided against trying. At Vassar, if all comers had been encouraged to give counseling a good try and were assured of ample time, Nixon's sample might have been more similar to ours; it would include not only those who were forced to come by extreme misery and those who knew what they wanted and expected to get but also the large group in between, whose initial position was uncertain.

The literature on mental health in college contains contradictory evaluations on the status of the student population as a whole. Some studies ascribe to the students vigorous mental health; others emphasize their proneness to disturbance, breakdown, and suicide. In part this difference reflects a selective response of the observers to different segments of the college population. Some of the contradictions, however, could be resolved if we gave up viewing mental health and mental illness as opposite ends of a continuum, trying to locate each person at some point on this scale. To do so is no more feasible than to follow some researchers' request to indicate your feelings toward your parents on a scale where the two ends represent love and hate and the middle point indicates indifference. If your feelings are mixed, if you are aware that you sometimes love and sometimes hate them quite strongly, your case cannot be recorded on a unidimensional scale. In thinking about a person's mental health status, we would be less hemmed in by our categories if we viewed health and neurosis not as poles of one dimension but, with Angyal, as two different systems within a person, two different ways of organizing one's experience: one governed by confidence and hope; the other, by fear and pessimism. Since both systems are present in everyone, we can ascribe to the same person both vigorous health and vigorous ill health, though at any given time one of the two is dominant. The patient who, during the period of struggle for decision, puts a great deal of energy into defending his neurosis, may, once his allegiance has shifted, start energetically building up new, healthy ways. If one who has been "cured" suffers a relapse, this reemergence of the neurotic system does not mean destruction of the system of health which has been strengthened through previous work; it is there to return to.

The relationship of the concepts of neurosis and health to the concept of maturity is in need of clarification. In the case of adults the dominance of the pattern of health can be easily equated with achieved psychological maturity, and the dominance of neurosis with immaturity. In the earlier developmental stages this equation is not equally valid. A traumatized, fearful child is not prepared to attack new developmental tasks and is held back in his emotional growth, but a well-developing healthy child may also be viewed as immature, if judged by the standard of maturity that can be achieved only by an adult. We do injustice to such children when we call neurotics childish. Still, in the case of children, the difference between relative and absolute maturity is clear and unproblematic; we know that a healthy child, while similar to a healthy adult in some respects, is a very different creature in others. In the case of older adolescents the situation becomes confusing; young adults that they are, they are readily judged by adult standards, and their "marginality"—their unsettled, transitional state—is ignored. Suppose that a young person in the process of searching for an adult identity changes from day to day and goes through emotional crises. Is he demonstrating vigorous, healthy growth or a serious disturbance, a symptom of ill health? Sometimes it is very difficult—and sometimes impossible—to distinguish one from the other. At a particular moment under particular conditions, an adolescent may be attacking the developmental tasks facing him; at a different moment and under different conditions, the same adolescent may be retreating from them; he may even break down in the course of his struggles and then emerge older and wiser. An adolescent who has gone through such struggles (which made him difficult for adults to live with)˙ may even have a better chance to reach full maturity than many a quietly resentful or cheerful "conformer" whose maturity is more apparent than real. As Nixon has pointed out, impetuous "growers" must be distinguished from those who are merely rebelling compulsively. These considerations may help explain why we are not on safe ground when we place college students at any one point of the health-sickness dimension, ascribing to them either a high or a low level of mental health, since they are "at a stage of development that is both remarkably vulnerable and remarkably teachable" (Blaine, McArthur, and others, 1961, p. 248). We must therefore try to locate the factors responsible for each of these traits.

    There is no mystery in what makes transition to adulthood a difficult period, at least in our culture. The internal and external tasks to be soon tackled by the young adult loom large. School provides a moratorium for some of them, but the changes required are more drastic than those experienced during the years of childhood; and, like everything new, they are signaled by anxiety, which is often intense. What is not equally clear is the source of the developmental vigor that enables adolescents to grapple with these challenges, the assets they can muster that were not available to them earlier. The basic psychoanalytic theory of developmental stages offers no clear answer to the question of why the late teens and the early twenties present exceptional opportunities for modifying and correcting personality patterns formed earlier, and thus give young people a chance to catch up in their emotional development and to reach genuine maturity in a none-too-distant future. Anna Freud's (1942) description of adolescence emphasizes its negative aspects: the strengthening of defenses made necessary by the intensification of sexual drives and the revival of early conflicts characterizing the Oedipal stage. We do not learn from these descriptions what makes it possible for some adolescents to resolve conflicts at this time, though they were not able to do so earlier and are not likely to do so at a later age without a great deal of help.

The positive aspect, or the positive phase, of adolescence was acknowledged and stressed in the German psychological literature of the first decades of this century, the descriptions being based largely on the diaries and other literary productions of the adolescents themselves. Largely on the basis of such self-descriptions, William Stern and other developmentalists distinguished two phases of adolescence: (1) an early negative phase, colored by the conflicts of puberty and marked by moody introspection; and (2) a later constructive stage, when the young person is actively engaged in working out his personal view of the world and of himself. Taken conjointly, the two phases represent the search for and the achievement of personal identity, as later formulated by Erikson. But in these generalized descriptions of developmental sequences, the principles governing the different stages, or determining the turning points, are rarely spelled out. There is some evidence in contemporary American studies that psychological growth, as distinguished from a mere increase in knowledge, continues during the college years, at least in some people. There are also some indications that such growth rarely continues beyond these years. One finding of a study of Vassar alumnae twenty to twenty-five years after graduation is of particular interest to us. That is, those women who during their college years fitted the conception of "identity seekers" (possibly not too different from "growers") "have been unable to arrive at stable lives except after prolonged therapy or drastic change in the environment, or both. The families were either unstable or oppressive, or the sex-role conflict was so severe . . . that normal heterosexual relations were seriously impaired. These are the subjects who as students presumably could have profited most from currently existing therapeutic facilities on the campus" (Brown, 1962, p. 119). Without timely help in making their search for identity bear fruit, these people either relapsed into some spurious certainty which precluded progressive change or became at best "eternal maturers," people in a state of "slow and delayed psychological growth that is usually ended by death in an old age before psychological maturity has been reached" (Nixon, 1962, p. 140). It is important to distinguish these "eternal maturers" from those who might be justifiably hailed as lifelong "growers"; the present ideology of personal growth tends to disregard the distinction between growth *toward* maturity and growth *after* maturity.

Late adolescence, then, seems to present us with a good chance—possibly the last chance—to correct and overcome the inadequacies of our earlier development and escape a protracted neurosis. If that is so, why is it so? What makes this period more promising for therapy than either the preceding or the following ones? One important point is that the circumstances, internal and external, which make for stress and strain in adolescence are also challenges that under favorable circumstances can stimulate and further growth. Separation from home, coming to terms with sex, the demands of new tasks and new situations, learning more about people and ideas—all these circumstances may lead one to reconsider one's uncritically held views and change one's behavior. Moreover, at this age even the well-developed defenses are not yet so well practiced that they can indefinitely withstand the impact of acute conflicts, such as accompany adolescents' struggles with parents. These conflicts are very often open, alive, and in flux; in counseling, current relationships with parents and teachers provide both insights into the old and practice in the new.

Angyal's discussion of growth and anxiety is relevant to the issue of adolescents' vigorous advances and anxious retreats.

In breaking up the current organization of one's life, one faces isolation. What is unknown is alien, and the chances of relating oneself to this unknown through participation and mastery are less certain than in the familiar sphere that is being left behind. That is why in times of major changes, for instance in adolescence, the pattern governed by anxious expectations often comes to the fore, reviving both the earlier traumas and those past situations that now demand new solutions. These disturbances subside after the anxieties have been faced and new competencies and integrations achieved. Anxiety connected with growth becomes overwhelming only if growth requires total change, such as the breaking up of the entrenched neurotic orientation. Excessive fear of death is often a correlate of the neurotic fear of growth and change. Growth crises occurring within a firmly established healthy pattern are minor in comparison. Hope and the lure of the new outweigh the doubts, confident action reduces the risks, and if environmental conditions are also propitious anxiety need be no more than transitory and slight [Angyal, 1965, p. 127].

In many cases the "healthy" and the "pathological" are not very far apart at this age; one can be turned into another by the push of circumstances, of which counseling, good or bad, is one.

Another factor that makes adolescence a promising time for therapy is suggested by young people's great readiness to engage in abstract philosophical discussions and reflective introspective pursuits. The main feature of this period is the maturing of the cognitive capacity; this development is documented by the findings of systematic empirical research, such as Piaget's. According to Piaget (1950), the "concrete operational thinking" which the child perfects between the ages of ten and fourteen subsequently leads to the gradual discovery and mastery of "formal operations," which enable the adolescent to think not only of what "is" but of all that "might be," or to think about thinking itself. According to the Russian psychologist Vygotsky (1962), who studied the development of conceptual thinking experimentally, "true concepts" combining abstraction with synthesis do not appear before early adolescence and only gradually become predominant in the young person's thinking. Their appearance enables him not just to think but also to know what he thinks, and how; now he can question the logic of his own and others' statements, can pinpoint and correct mistakes in reasoning made by others and by himself.

All developmental acquisitions tend to be practiced eagerly and persistently; the toddler's walking is the best illustration. The adolescent is no exception. In the absence of strong obstacles to this course, young people will direct the light of their new thinking upon their own past and present, their society, their family, themselves; these explorations spell the end of the "unexamined life." Nixon's purpose in writing his book was to promote maturation by encouraging this enterprise, which may result in spotting, examining, and dismissing many untenable assumptions stemming from earlier stages. The tentative alternative assumptions that supersede them lead the adolescent or the young adult to experiment with new ways of being and acting. These experiments may help him to discover his own path to maturity.

Had Nixon's book been published a few years later, he could have supported his opinions by quoting Perry's (1968) study of the forms of intellectual and ethical development in the college years. This careful, systematic exploration based on interviews was conducted as a research study by the Bureau of Study Counsel of Harvard University. In talking at the end of each school year about their college experience, the students who had volunteered as research subjects showed a clear progression from year to year. In the course of their four years, they moved from thinking about knowledge as a collection of right answers vouchsafed by authorities, through a growing realization of the diversity of opinions and resulting uncertainty, to the acceptance of all knowledge and all values as contextual and relativistic, thus overcoming the absolutistic duality of right-wrong or good-bad. In this progress toward a nondogmatic position, the stimulation provided by a modern pluralistic university obviously played an important part. What students did with this stimulation, however, showed an identical sequence in all cases, even though this course could be interrupted by delays, sidestepping escapes, and retreats. At the end of this sequence, the students began to come to terms with a relativistic world through some form of personal commitment, as distinct from unquestioned belief in absolute certainty. This commitment, which carries with it an assumption of personal responsibilities, is based on a differentiated awareness of both the environment and one's self.

Thus, Perry's study demonstrates the role of cognitive development in the attainment of personal identity, the central achievement of late adolescence. This demonstration offers support to all those therapists who, like myself, have been impressed by the constructive role that thinking can play at this stage in the resolution of personal conflicts. Any new developmental acquisition stays for awhile in the foreground of mental functioning, or in a central position, a figure on a receding ground. During this temporary prominence of a new function, a great deal of energy is invested in developing it and making it more effective. This newly achieved cognitive power may well be the main factor that makes college students such promising clients and also such good teachers of their therapists. In counseling, they can and do use their thinking for defensive purposes, but that is not the main use they make of it. If we give them a chance by not viewing their search for clarity as intellectualization, and their refusal to accept our unproven statements as resistance, we shall find out that they can see clearly and describe articulately much of what is going on within themselves and between them and the counselor.

7

Changing Perspectives

A shift of perspective is not to be equated with the radical shift of a student's allegiance from neurosis to health; the latter is the ultimate achievement of therapy, which, for a confirmed neurotic, may take years of work. A shift of perspective is nothing so momentous as that. Yet it is important; it is weightier than a single specific insight, though it may come in the wake of a chain of insights. It is the first glimmer of the realization that there is a reason behind the seeming unreason of neurotic entanglements, that one has built one's life on invalid assumptions, that there is a way out of the blind alley or the narrow enclosure one finds oneself in. It is a suspicion, a glimpse, that reality can be better than one has dared to believe: essentially a message of hope, a promise for the future.

Not all insights lead or contribute to such shifts of perspective. If the student comes to feel that he is a hopeless neurotic, "regressed," masochistic, defensive, a failure as a patient, then his insights have provided him with a confirmation, sometimes a powerful confirmation, of his despairing, pessimistic outlook. A therapist who realizes how vulnerable many patients are and how easily a dominant neurotic system can pervert all attacks on it to its own uses will carefully consider the effect of his statements on the client, catch and clarify misinterpretations, and never permit the messages concerning the patient's distorted functioning to outweigh those that acknowledge his actual or potential health.

The shift of perspective, the glimpse of new possibilities, is integral to any successful therapy, whether easy or difficult, short or long; it is a precursor of change, which may appear early or late. The counseling courses of the vigorous "growers" described in Chapter Six manifest this phenomenon in one form or another, but the telescoping of various stages caused by their quick movement makes this experience merge with some others. It is usually more obvious in the courses of therapy that extend over longer periods of time. In this chapter we are dealing with cases where the shift of perspective is the *main* achievement of the total counseling period, though not necessarily its only achievement. The client may experience some actual improvement of mood and functioning; but these gains, when present, are neither radical, nor—usually—enduring. At the end of the counseling period, though the clients may feel less handicapped, more hopeful about themselves and their ultimate chances in life, and better able to cope with some of their problems, unlike some of the "vigorous growers," they do not believe that they now have all they need to enable them to progress on their own. They have, however, come to recognize the promise of therapy and show a greater readiness to commit themselves to this course.

Do the students who experience the shift of perspective but do not get much beyond it in counseling have something in common? A slow start is characteristic of clients with entrenched neuroses; their perspective is not easily shifted. To earn their trust, to arouse their hope, to reduce their fear of therapy may be a real challenge for the counselor—a much more difficult achievement than many a spectacular success. But there are other factors involved in a slow start, and the mistrust of therapy is not always rooted in neurosis. At Brandeis I found at least two groups of students whose strong misgivings about the prospect of therapy, and slowness in entering it "for real," were in part an outgrowth of their background and experience: foreign students in whose native countries psychotherapy was unknown or rejected, and the many students who had had bad personal experiences with therapy, in school or outside. In addition, some students made limited progress in counseling because of factors peculiar to their individual situations or simply because the crises or concerns that made them seek counseling occurred late in the academic year, when there was little time left for working. Some of the people in this subgroup did in fact move fully as fast as the "vigorous growers" and, had there been time, might have continued to work and to progress at a high rate.

Don: An Introduction to Therapy

Don, a psychology major, walked into my office in February of his senior year. He looked worried and, as he described his situation, spoke in a controlled way, but with involvement. Some time ago he had broken up with a girl whom he had lived with for almost three years. They were now back together, but Don was not ready to commit himself to the relationship; he was not entirely pleased with the girl and wished to change her. He felt guilty on both scores and confused about his course in the near future, after his and her graduation. Obviously under pressure, Don wanted a period of counseling, not a consultation, and, on the advice of some graduate students, he wanted it specifically with me. I felt that something useful could be achieved, some beginning made. As a trial balloon I said to Don, observationally, that his formulations of the problem seemed to center on the interpersonal situation, not on himself. Don replied, "Yes, I realized that as I was talking." Perhaps some difficulty of his own, he added, prevented him from finding workable interpersonal solutions. This response augured well for the prospect of counseling.

Unfortunately, because of the long waiting lists I was unable to respond to Don's feeling of urgency by starting to see him right away. The beginning was postponed for five weeks, and then there was only time left for five or six sessions. In this particular case, however, the lack of time turned out to have its advantages. When I realized that Don, though highly intelligent and successful in his academic work, was very vulnerable and quite fearful of therapy, the gamble involved in accepting him for counseling at this late date made me alert in the sessions both to possible pitfalls and to safe opportunities for movement. Knowing that there was no time to correct mistakes, I made fewer false starts than ordinarily; no session was wasted. I shall describe the five sessions one by one, interspersing the descriptions with explanatory comments about the reasoning behind my interventions.

First Session. Don was glad to get my note of invitation. He had meant to come in anyway to consult me about the various graduate programs in psychology; he had a definite interest in research and teaching and a somewhat tentative interest in clinical work. He launched on a discriminating discussion of the assets and drawbacks of the various programs, considering also the bearing of their geographical locations on his chance of continuing some research begun at Brandeis and on his relationship with his girl friend. He discussed these matters very actively for about forty minutes, then paused as if having exhausted the topic. Throughout this period I accepted the role of faculty counselor he had implicitly assigned to me, adding a bit of information here and there, mostly agreeing with his opinions. I abstained from commenting on the personal matters involved, except in two instances. When, in talking about the issue of separation, Don said that, although he and his girl were getting along all right now, he would like to break off for a few years. I asked, "You mean—and resume later?" He replied, "Perhaps—if we feel like it." My question was meant merely as a verbal raised eyebrow, marking the idea—for future reference—as not self-evident to me. A little later, in referring to his earlier statement that choosing a midwestern school would facilitate separation, Don said: "Of course, we would not have to run into each other in New York either." I replied that although New York was not Brandeis, there was some truth in his earlier assumption; if he should continue to see-saw in his feelings about his girl, then living in the same city might make it easier for him to make up after quarrels and more difficult for her to free herself from this tie, and that would keep him feeling guilty. Here I used the opportunity that Don had given me to point—in passing, as it were—to his continuous indecision and its likely consequences. I felt that I could risk making this point if I talked in terms of cause and effect, not value judgments; implied a concern for *him;* and did not forget to

say "if." Don agreed with my point, not visibly disturbed. I made
no other nonacademic comments.

Naturally, I wondered if Don's turning the session into a
vocational consultation meant a retreat from the personal counseling
first envisaged, but for me to wonder out loud might connote exercising power over him or convicting him of the "crimes" of resistance, indecision, and anxiety. I also thought that Don might have
good reasons for wishing to run the session in his own way. Having
had to wait so long for my invitation, he might well wish to assert
his autonomy by taking matters now into his own hands. In any
case, his decision was better accepted than questioned. It was more
important to acknowledge from the start his right to direct our work
than to get quick insights into his personal dynamics; the pertinent
information would keep. I felt that I had made the right choice
when, in the course of the conversation, Don was able to convey to
me simply and convincingly, without embarrassment or boasting, his
serious interest in psychology, his respectable achievement in research, the high evaluation of his work by his teachers. I came to
view him as a very bright and promising young colleague.

When Don paused in his discussion of schools, I took this as
a permission to revert to the counselor's role and to make a corre-
sponding comment. I decided on one of a high level of generality,
a "holistic" interpretation pertinent to the total course of Don's dis-
course—in fact, pertinent to the central issues of the pattern of noncommitment, which I felt was gradually emerging from the context
and style of his communications. "All your considerations are valid,"
I said, "and all factors you have mentioned are clearly seen and
pertinent to the decisions you are facing. But it seems to me that you
are unsure of your feeling about them. It has struck me that every
time you built up a strong case for one course of action, you immediately balanced your wish for this course by equally strong reasons against it." When Don agreed, I proceeded to apply the idea
of "balance" and of noncommitment to what I considered the main
issue of that session: the decision about counseling itself. Referring
to Don's earlier remark that reading clinical literature made problems worse, or made them seem worse, I said that the fear of this
happening in counseling might well act as a strong counterweight
to Don's very real wish to review and clarify his problems. If these

two motives should prove evenly balanced, progress would be impossible; he would keep straddling the fence. "And that," I said, "would be a pity. True, we cannot get very far in the short time we have, but maybe you could risk taking a few steps toward clarification. New perspectives, who knows, might prove helpful. Therapy, after all, is not hocus-pocus; it can work. Why else would I be here, trying?" In short, I acknowledged both his fears and his hopes, his shrinking and his healthy wish for expansion, and put my weight on the side of the latter. It worked. Don brightened visibly and said that, as I was talking, he felt the balance shifting, so that his wish for clarification outweighed his fear. He had valued the new wider perspectives provided by some of his teachers; now his hopes were raised that he might get similar gains through counseling.

This was the end of the session, and I felt that something important had happened. While Don had responded with a detached insight to my description of his "balanced" discussion of schools, when I related it in a personal way to the issue foremost in his mind, that of counseling itself, he experienced a vital personal involvement and an emotional shift.

In leaving, Don said he would come in two weeks. I accepted his statement without asking his reasons for skipping a week, which he did not volunteer.

Second Session. Don looked cheerful; he had been accepted by several of the graduate programs he had applied to and had made a choice that would enable him, he felt, to focus on theory first, postponing his training in practical clinical work. This statement led to a more detailed discussion of his misgivings about clinical work. In the first half of the session, Don led the discussion, and I followed with questions and brief comments. When Don reiterated his belief that clinical orientation is potentially destructive, I asked for an example, so as to understand just what he meant. He told me of a resident counselor greatly admired by students but resented by some because he would tell them, unbidden, what was psychologically wrong with them. When they objected or got angry, the counselor interpreted their response as defense and as further proof that they needed to be told the truth. Don was friends with the counselor and believed that his interpretations were mostly correct; yet he saw also that the interpretations were destructive to some students. I said that someone who analyzes people right and left is misusing his professional skills and that no one should submit to such analysis who has not specifically asked for it. Next Don criticized the clinical field for the sloppy state of its research, mostly uncontrolled and inconclusive. The only studies he had encountered that he respected were those relating certain traits of patients to negative outcomes, and it was not too helpful to know merely that some patients' chances are very poor. I agreed with this evaluation of the state of research in the early 1960s, pointing to a few exceptions. In conclusion, Don said that, given this state of affairs, he saw no way to be a good clinical practitioner, but he knew from experience that he could do good research. I asked him if his observations of the destructiveness of the clinical approach accounted for his reluctance to try to change his girl friend, to be her therapist. He said yes, that he might be tempted to use psychology on her and that such a procedure could be destructive. He thus confirmed my impression that in the issue of clinical destructiveness he identified more readily with the offender than with the victim.

Don's whole discussion, insightful as it was, had been conducted in terms of impersonal entities only: clinical psychology, methods, procedures. My task now was to shift it to the personal realm, while heeding Don's implicit warning not to let my approach be destructive, not to undermine his self-respect. "It strikes me," I said, "that you attribute a great deal of power to techniques or procedures as such, as if you did not believe that you yourself have the power to command these technical tools, change and adapt them according to need, use them for any purpose you choose." Don looked both intrigued and puzzled. I realized that to make this message vital to him I had to make it more personal and concrete; yet he had given me no personal data I could use for this purpose both plausibly and safely. So I used the device of a fictitious example, making clear to Don from the outset that it was only that. "Suppose a man lacks confidence that he is acceptable, except on the basis of his achievements. In marriage, or in a close friendship, his fear of rejection would create great tensions, which he would try to handle in some way—not very effectively—probably in the framework of achievement. If he is a clinician, he might try to influence his friend or his wife by analyzing or counseling her. This I believe is the case you have in mind when you reject clinical work; and I agree with you that, given this kind of personal involvement, such actions can be destructive. But let us assume that this man who fears rejection is a research worker, let us say a physicist. He can try to deal with his wife, or rather avoid dealing with her, by spending all his time in the laboratory; and that might be just as destructive of the relationship. But if the man has no such problem, neither clinical work nor research would have such drastic consequences for his family life."

Don said, with eager excitement, that this example happened to fit his situation exactly. "I can see now that when I wanted to know how to go about accepting the girl the way she is, I asked the question backward. I myself do not feel accepted except for my achievements, so I should ask how to change my own lack of personal confidence. Perhaps I rely more on achievements simply because they are something tangible, more clearly definable than anything else." In the interchange that followed, Don elaborated the theme of his reliance on achievement, not insisting that the reasons were "purely objective" but offering no alternative explanations. At one point I reformulated the issues of clinical training and work in more person-centered terms. Clinicians vary; some are better, some worse. Even if Don should be right in not trusting himself to do good clinical work now, does it mean that he cannot develop this ability, given good training and a resolution of his personal problems? Besides, clinical work and research need not be mutually exclusive for him. Don was cheerfully responsive. When to his reiterated question of how he could acquire more personal confidence, I remarked, "Perhaps you should ask how you lost it," he replied laughingly: "I can see now that I cannot avoid going into the past, the way I have tried . . . but I would like to leave it so." If he was to give up part of his control of the sessions, it would not be right away.

Third Session. Don stuck to his decision. He told me that the idea of his having lost confidence in the personal area had struck home but that today he wanted to talk about his girl, Alice, a disturbed child of a rather tyrannical family. She had spent years in therapy but still had her symptoms and was by turns childishly obedient to her parents and rebellious in irrational ways. Don had

tried to liberate her from her bonds by proselytizing for the Maslov-
ian theory of self-actualization, but he had been well aware of the
element of selfish interest in these attempts: the parental rules
limited his contact with Alice, and also, quite generally, he wanted
her to do as *he* wished, to be under *his* influence, rather than her
family's. This was not his greatest worry, however. The main factor
determining his feelings toward Alice was whether or not he could
see her behavior as healthy. For example, if she turned down some
plan of his because of genuinely wanting to do something else that
was of real value for her life, he could accept it, but not if her
frustrating his wish was based on fear, compulsive dutifulness, or
other neurotic trends. He had often been unable to disentangle
health from neurosis, the "good" from the "bad" in her attitudes.
In describing his mixed feelings, he said: "I love her, am very much
concerned for her, but mostly I do not like her."

In accordance with Don's implicit directions, I abstained
from probing into the details and the antecedents of this problematic
relationship. Instead—in the second half of the session—I reformulated what he had told me in a way that would permit connecting
it tentatively with some hypothetical factors in his own past. "Alice
obviously has both healthy and neurotic trends," I said. "In this
your perception is correct, but it does not seem to be stably organized. One might view Alice as a pretty OK person, though she has
her difficulties or her crazy moods, or else as a pretty mixed-up girl,
in spite of her many attractive traits; in other words, one might see
one of the aspects as the dominant one. But your confusion, the
back and forth of your feelings and plans, suggests that you view her
now as all good, now as all bad, so you cannot decide on any one
course. Granted that Alice is confused and confusing, still you have
mixed feelings about other issues as well and find it hard to make
up your mind. If this should prove to be a pretty general trend in
you, it might possibly go way back. We cannot explore its origins in
the short time we have, but we can speculate. Perhaps the good and
the bad aspects of life were early experienced by you in such a tight
mixture that you could not possibly have sorted it out at the time
and might still have this trouble at present."

In giving Don this outline of Angyal's theory of the origins
of noncommitment, I hoped both to reduce his confusion and to

counteract the self-derogation that might be aroused by the discovery in oneself of the love-hate pattern. Don expressed relief, but it was relief about not having to blame the *girl* for causing his indecision and confusion. "I am very glad to hear this," he said, "because this hypothesis throws it back on me. If there is any changing to be done, I am the stronger one, the one to do it; I doubt Alice would be able to." I saw no reason to question this assumption of responsibility by Don, which boded well for the future, even though I assumed that confident self-reliance was not its only root. This posture could also be an offshoot of the child's early desperate need to believe that he had good and loving parents; if they proved hateful, where would he be and what could he do? Suppose that Don had come to counseling tortured by doubt about his girl, uncertain if she was good or bad, unsure of his ability to make her good, or good to him. The idea that he might be in error, that his mistrust of her was unfounded, would then indeed be a relief. Over his own attitudes he had some control; he could change them; he had a chance. Similarly, in the context of therapy, the neurotic patient's conspicuous struggles to prove that he is in the right and the world—including the therapist—in the wrong tend to obscure the less obvious phenomenon: his *fear* that he might be *right,* and not laboring under transference, when he perceives the therapist, for example, as hostile, indifferent, or unreliable; he accepts the other's denial (which cannot substitute for a genuine corrective experience) because he *wants* to believe that his perception is distorted, that the world is not as bad as he sees it. I have known patients to continue for years with inadequate therapists because to see their failings would shatter the patient's hopes for the beneficent world which the therapist symbolizes and promises.

Fourth Session. Don walked into my office a few days later to make the next appointment; I had time right then and invited him to stay. He accepted after a moment of hesitation and immediately brought up what he had been holding back: the great shock and hurt of having been betrayed. Alice had been unfaithful to him twice, seemingly acts of self-assertion when she felt in danger of being controlled by Don. He knew both men. One had been his best friend, a fact that made him particularly bitter. He broke off relationships with all of them; later he made up with Alice, but now, months later, he still did not talk to the men. He felt intensely jealous and was obsessively preoccupied with these past events. He passed judgment, ideologically, on these possessive feelings of his, but was unable to discard them, so that Alice had agreed not to have any sexual involvements with others. He said it was good in a way that these things had happened; it gave them a chance to find out how he felt and to make this agreement, and now he need not be afraid that such acts would be repeated. And as unhappy as he had been about it all, he and Alice also had had very good moments together; he felt closer to this girl than to anyone, ever.

I listened without commenting. Don's bringing himself to tell his hurt to me called for simple acceptance, not for analysis. His delaying the disclosure for so long showed how difficult the decision had been. (This was confirmed by a dream Don told only later, but which he had had before this session.)

On having told his story, Don looked relieved, as if he had a feeling of completion. I asked him if he wanted to make this our last session: I myself thought it well to terminate sometime before I would be leaving, and I wanted to give Don some choice in the matter. He decided to come once more, ten days later. I was glad of this chance to learn how he had fared during the weeks of counseling and what he now felt about it.

Fifth Session. Don provided this information and rounded out his thinking on the main topics he had worked on: therapy and women (Alice). This session was more of a natural dialogue than the earlier ones had been. Don said that he now felt OK about entering therapy at some time with an experienced therapist of any "denomination"; perhaps theories were less important than personal factors. After getting information about clinics and costs and similar matters, he asked some questions about the workings of therapy, which I took to refer to conditions for success and to the best time for starting. I said that it takes something beyond mere insights to get results and that this something depends on the person's evaluation of his situation. To take his case, his wish to make changes in his life might become stronger if the situation with Alice deteriorated or, on the contrary, if it became more promising, worth doing some work for. This made sense to Don.

He then described the effects of the clarifications he had obtained in counseling. Things had been going very well in the last weeks—thus, he felt, validating his new concepts. Of great importance to him was the idea that somehow, somewhere, he had stopped believing that he could be accepted for himself, it had been axiomatic to him that he must earn acceptance by achieving and by pleasing others. He now noticed that whenever he felt rejected he had the impulse to do something "worthwhile" or something "nice." By catching these impulses, he nipped them in the bud and reduced the compulsion. He could even conceive of the possibility that some people liked him not because of but in spite of his strenuous efforts to make himself acceptable. He was no less astonished to catch himself thinking that he did not deserve the nice things that were recently happening to him. Don felt that his new insights provided him with tools for coping with difficult situations, thus making him feel less helpless. Is that what insights do? Is that *all* they can do? Did he mean, I asked, whether the managing and coping would always be so strenuous, with his attitudes basically unchanged? He said that was it. I said that when therapy is fully successful—as it not infrequently is with young people—feelings and attitudes do change, and the effortful managing of oneself is no longer necessary. Although neurotic trends may never be totally eradicated, and relapses do occur, they need not last long.

Next Don took up the issue of the hurt and humiliation he had suffered at his friends' hands. He realized, he said, that he had been avoiding contact with the two men because he could not bear thinking of what had happened. So, to test his improved self-confidence, he made himself think of it and of them: he succeeded without much pain. But then his thoughts suddenly jumped to a time twenty years hence. What, he thought, if after long years of marriage his wife were unfaithful to him? He felt shattered and could not imagine what he would do. He stopped these thoughts but was impelled to ask a friend what he would do in such a case. The friend said that he would be very much hurt but that his actions would depend on the circumstances of the case. This reply gave Don some perspective; seeing that his friend did not view the postulated event as the ultimate catastrophe, he experienced great relief.

In response to Don's disclosure of the obsessiveness and the intensity of his concerns, I tried to provide him with some useful discriminations and some tentative explanations. "It is natural," I said, "for you to feel hurt and anxious about the future; but your persistent futile preoccupation with these past events, after you have done all you could to prevent their recurrence, goes far beyond what is plausible and useful. Your thinking about this has a diffuse global character; for all your appreciation of human complexities, you seem unable to recognize that a wife's infidelity can have a variety of possible causes, some of them related less to her husband than to her own problems. You can only think of this act as an absolute annihilating betrayal of yourself. Such global emotional thinking is an earmark of very early experiences; a very young child might feel shattered when his mother leaves him for the first time, since her reasons and circumstances are not a part of his experience."

As I was talking, Don signified eager agreement. Then he told me the dream he had had two weeks before, prefacing it with the statement that he felt free both to be frank with his mother and to refuse to disclose things she need not know; but he was never rude to her. In the dream she asked him a question and he shouted at her: "I won't tell you!" And the mother turned into me (the counselor). At another time this dream might have opened many topics, but in this last session I chose to relate it to termination. I said that the conflict between privacy and self-disclosure was part and parcel of therapy, but there were additional weighty reasons against bringing things up in the last session, since one might start something one could not complete. I told Don that he could call on me for consultation or referral and that he had all it takes to benefit from therapy; his wish for clarity and his ability to think things through could be used to advantage. It was a pleasant termination. I felt that we had done well and that Don felt the same. His questionnaire follows.

>   *Don's report:* An evaluation, negative and/or positive, of my experience in therapy is inseparable from the fulfillment, frustration, or total irrelevance of my anticipations regarding therapy. At the risk of being personal (what else can I be) and maybe lengthy, I should spell out some of those anticipations and describe what came to be in light of them.

I first considered actively coming to the counseling center around November, but didn't make the move until February. There I met my first frustration, although inevitably at the time I felt relieved by my reprieve. Schedules were full, and there was no space. When Dr. H. contacted me a month later, I was less ready but came, I suppose thankfully and fearfully, anyway. Now it is about six weeks later, and the sessions have ended. That beginning was postponed, and ending so speedily reached, constitutes the negative side of the experience for me. Any feelings of regret, or of aborted hopes, are related directly to the short span of time; I accept obviously, however, that this was the reality I was aware of. The negative feelings I have are all of the sort that "this was a great thing while it lasted, but why did it have to end so soon." If there were any way of rattling around the bureaucratic time slots or salary slots so that more students could be accommodated, this would be an improvement in the counseling center. But of course you know this. I say it simply because I feel it since it hit me personally.

The positive sides are more involved, but to me also more interesting. Immediately, the first anticipation to be upended was of my conceptions of "what goes on in that little room." If it's going to be of any value, I knew, I would have to be open, so I was ready. But the first few times I wanted to say something personal, my voice choked, and it suddenly became apparent how much trust means. I guess I circumvented the problem of recalcitrance by concentrating on the debits of therapy for a while, but I remember precisely the first moment when I felt drained of my complete resistance. When Dr. H. said, "But, you know, therapy is not nonsense," I first felt really ready to open up. What I am saying is that I was surprised at how much resistance—that bookish word—I felt, how suddenly all those bookish words—trust, resistance, intellectualization, transference, insight, understanding, validation—took on completely new meanings. And as I write them now, I do not have to think of a passage in a book in which they appear in order to rattle them off in a long string. I simply have to remember back to the sessions in which I felt them.

Very comforting along these lines were Dr. H's provisional, somewhat hypothetical, yet usually precise accounts of what I was feeling at the time and about the situation I talked about. Thus, again, I remember feeling drained but immediately more trusting when she explained that I would be fearing to open up at the same time as wanting to. Also comforting was her complete awareness that we would only have a short time to work, and that therefore we shouldn't dig too deeply. At this time, I don't feel anything was brought up which I am not equipped to handle, although by analyzing problems in a hypothetical way, avenues of future investigation were brought up without the feelings of threat which would have come had we started out on them immediately. What I am saying, I guess, is that I felt safe, that I trusted that my life was not going to be mishandled, that there was hard work to be done which could not be completed now, and that I was about ready to start real therapy by the time it ended.

The astounding thing to me about all this is how real it is, how what I am saying seems so much closer to what I feel than it usually does, how all the things I underwent were as in the books, but personal, in no way detracting from the books, but adding. Of course, there were delusions of dependency, fantasies in which I felt after leaving some sessions that I should do something drastic so that I wouldn't have to wait the whole week, and so forth. But again, these were so real that I almost had to laugh at them. It goes without saying that I now feel it crucial to be in therapy before one is a therapist, which is something I've always equivocated upon.

But I'm babbling, and saying just one thing: The experience was real. Although I don't know, since this is the first time, I feel I would have reacted negatively if I didn't feel that Dr. H. was genuine, both as a person and as a therapist; from what I've said here, I suppose it was even more important that she be genuine as a therapist, since I've had ambivalent impressions of the value of therapy. But as things developed, I am grateful I had a chance to come to the center.

As a personal note, Dr. H., when you said in our last session that you'll be around and I should call if I need help, although I hope things will never be so desperate that I will call, it gave me a very, very good feeling and a note of confidence to end on. Thank you.

In the case of Don I know what happened. In the spring of the next year, after a breakup with Alice, he entered private therapy with me. I saw him twice a week for a year, until his training took him to a distant geographical area. It was a substantial chunk of work, with substantial achievements—though not marked, as the five counseling sessions had been, by a quick opening of new perspectives. Don continued to work in sessions energetically and to a great extent independently. I did not score any quick successes when I occasionally attempted to introduce new topics or develop the old ones, but he valued my ability and willingness to restore clarity whenever he felt overcome by confusion and stopped in his tracks. To that purpose I continued to use Angyal's concepts, both those explaining noncommitment and the general theory of "universal ambiguity," the rivalry of the two innerpersonal systems.

Eventually it became plausible that Don's relationship to his mother had become disturbed very early indeed, largely due to circumstances caused by the child's serious and prolonged illness, which remained undiagnosed for a long time. Don's fear and mistrust of women, as well as his longing for a woman's full acceptance, were clearly manifested in his current dealings with girls, both friends and lovers. The ups and downs of his relationships often brought to my mind Angyal's descriptions of the plight of those who, in seeking the affection of a particular person, are driven by the hidden wish for reconciliation with the early "primal mother," for acceptance by the one who once was all in all. The affection of any real person, who is necessarily limited and imperfect, leaves this need unfulfilled. Disappointed, the person struggles to make the relationship into something different, or else devalues it and renews his search. For a long time the evidence remained indirect. Don's early feelings toward his mother remained submerged until, during one of our few confrontations, he reexperienced total rejection by attributing it to me. After telling me what he was feeling, Don asked me to tell him how I actually felt about him, and I did. He saw that his fears had no basis in reality. This episode contributed to making Don's perception of me less ambiguous and more realistic. At our separation he felt sad, but positive feelings prevailed. "I have entrusted myself to you," he said, "and you let me be and grow; I came out stronger, sturdier." He never felt judged by me, was permitted to work at his own rate—in fact, "permitted not to be neurotic." He felt that in clarifying his confusions I was conveying the message to him that he did not need all this nonsense, that I was enjoying him the way he really was. This was more important to him than all the insights he achieved.

In his new location Don continued and completed his therapy in a group, with a male leader. At first his letters to me spoke of problems and invited clarifications by expressing confusions. But after a year and a half, he wrote to say that he felt he was a patient no longer; his therapy had been completed. Since then we have exchanged letters occasionally about personal news and professional topics. Don has been combining practical work with teaching and research. Several years ago he married and feels now that the marriage "is deepening in a good way." His life is clearly forward moving; it is, to quote another bit from his last letter, "incredibly full and exciting."

It is not unusual for students to decide to give counseling a try, as Don did, because they are both aware of a personal problem and interested in exploring the possibility of a career in areas related to mental health work. If the period of counseling provides them with an experience that makes constructive changes appear possible and probable, it may result in commitment both to personal therapy and to a particular vocational course. To counselors the main message of this case should be that if one succeeds in combining stimulation with caution in a way that suits the client, one can achieve a shift of perspective in a relatively short time. To me, Don's saying that he felt safe, trusting that his life was not going to be mishandled, has served as an impressive reminder of the dread some students feel in entering counseling and of the risks that are indeed involved in their decision.

To exemplify the lack of knowledge and of cultural acceptance of therapy as an initial obstacle to counseling, I shall briefly describe the case of a foreign graduate student, a scientist in his thirties, in whose country psychotherapy was unknown to most and ridiculed by those few who had heard about it.

Juan: The Effects of Culture on Therapy

Juan, a foreign scholar, came to the center for a consultation, not for counseling, seeking advice about how to handle a very disturbed woman with whom he had been living, unhappily, for several years and who threatened suicide whenever he suggested separation; because of certain factors in her background this threat was not to be taken lightly. The young man felt that *she* was his only problem, but after I confirmed his suspicion that no easy solution to this problem was available, he became willing to think in terms of himself, to try counseling with the purpose of discovering how and why he had gotten so deeply into this relationship in spite of early indications of serious disturbance in his friend. At the end of the first session he said straightforwardly that he wanted to face his share of responsibility for this miserable situation.

The first few sessions were taken up with the story of this relationship; its telling brought up many paradoxes. The young man often schemed and plotted to induce his lover to leave him; but whenever she was ready to do so, he felt compelled to get her back. This puzzled him greatly; he knew that he was often lonely and needed affection, but this was natural, not a "problem." Why was he willing to pay such a high price for her company? Why did he, a clear-thinking scientist, behave so illogically, so perversely? He had no answers to these questions of his, and no idea how to search for them. His story told, Juan was at a loss about what to do in the sessions. He had never read psychological literature or heard discussions of personal problems; the idea that irrational behavior might have roots in emotional beliefs formed in one's past was totally strange to him.

I used every avenue of approach I could think of to stimulate Juan's thinking and feeling about himself, but for a long time he responded in very limited ways. He obediently followed my invitation to talk about his past and started, on his own initiative, to read psychological literature; his reports of his reading evidenced interest and good understanding. Yet, as I tentatively connected the traumatic situations emerging in his past with his numerous present difficulties, which were also gradually coming to light, he found these ideas logical and interesting but unconvincing because incapable of proof. He became anxious as his feelings gradually came into play and threatened his detachment; yet he decided to go on. Confronted with the alternatives of focusing on one circumscribed problem or attempting to outline the general pattern of his disturbance, he deliberately chose the latter as promising greater clarity.

The familiar obsessive pattern of confusion, ambivalence, and indecision was clearly outlined and its roots tentatively traced to confusing experiences with both parents, particularly with the mother, an
anxious disciplinarian who controlled her sons by threats. These
intellectual discoveries became a vivid reality for Juan when, during
some upsets with his girl friend, he suddenly cried out to her as to
his mother in a child's voice, reexperiencing his early terrors.

There was no time, however, to develop and integrate these
discoveries, since the end of the school year was approaching. Juan
reverted to his detachment, seemingly losing touch with what he had
experienced in counseling. The situation with his lover was no closer
to resolution than ever, but there was more communication between
them, and the interaction was less tense. Two weeks before termination, Juan was plunged into confusion by the questionnaire's inquiry
about whether counseling had been helpful. Helpful in what? He
realized that he had viewed it mainly as an intellectual exercise and
was trying to be a good student, but was that really a useful personal
goal? Two weeks later things had fallen into place. The dream Juan
reported in the last session depicted his relationship with his friend
in a very insightful way, and he felt some hope that, having seen
his own contribution to the maintenance of the situation, he would
be able either to improve the relationship or drop it. In summarizing
what the twenty sessions had done for him, Juan said that our discussions had lifted the veil of complete mystery, of the darkness that
enveloped a part of himself, something unaccountable in himself
that he could not fathom and that he was slave to: "It is no longer
that mysterious or that threatening; I am very glad I came." He
now felt that he would like to continue therapy but was wary of
clinics and decided to wait until he could pay for private treatment.
The next year Juan completed his work at Brandeis and left; I do
not know whether he has carried out his plan to reenter therapy.

Lack of familiarity with the idea of therapy is not an enduring handicap; sometimes, in fact, it turns into an asset. Once a
beginning has been made, some students from cultures or subcultures where psychological concepts have not been popularized
respond to the new experiences and ideas in a fresher, more immediate, and more personal fashion than do those for whom these
ideas are not new. One young woman from the same country as

Juan, but ten years his junior, also had no conception of psychology or therapy. Though she was sad without cause, rejected all gaiety, and usually kept silent in company, she was astonished when her American friends advised her to try counseling. She came in hesitantly, and we spent the best part of many sessions in silence; in spite of all my explanations, the girl had no idea what she was supposed to do in this strange unstructured "course" and was protecting herself by silence from possible criticism and ridicule. Yet, when she grew to feel safer with me, she opened to this new experience, and it made a great impact. By the end of the counseling period, the girl had made spectacular progress; she was sold on therapy, but it did not look as if she would need it. Given enough time, some slow starters, after overcoming their initial guardedness, turn into vigorous growers.

Lisa: A Fresh Start

A bad experience with therapy in the past can be a powerful obstacle to quick progress in counseling. Lisa first came to the center at the end of her freshman year, when her parents' impending divorce threatened to disrupt her life. Her upset was not out of proportion to the circumstances. The counselor, impressed by Lisa's ability to speak freely and frankly and to obtain relief by doing so, felt that the problem was mostly situational—one that, given a minimum of help, Lisa would be able to cope with. He gave her sympathetic support and an invitation to return for a few sessions next year. Unfortunately, in conveying to the girl his optimistic outlook, the counselor made a categorical statement where a tentative one would have served. Lisa appreciated the message at the time; when things went from bad to worse the next year, however, she decided that the counselor had not taken her troubles seriously. Disenchanted, she did not return to the center.

At the start of the junior year, after some deaths in the family, her depression deepened. She entered therapy with a prominent local analyst, whom she subsequently saw three times a week for a year. It was a complete fiasco. Lisa was unable to provide what her therapist seemed to demand—childhood memories and free associations—and felt criticized by him for these failures. The long silences were painful to her; and the sessions seemed unproductive and depressing. She also resented the therapist's attempts to make her increase the number of weekly sessions; she felt that he wanted her to subordinate all her other projects to therapy, while she wanted to relate to people through shared pursuits, not just through problems. In comparing notes with a friend who was seeing another therapist, Lisa concluded that this girl's self-confidence was being built up in therapy, whereas hers was being more and more undermined. When during her therapist's vacation she started feeling much better, she decided to stop seeing him. She was at the beginning of her senior year, and she hoped that she could get along without therapy and concentrate on her studies. However, she soon became more depressed than ever, full of fears and doubts, unable to work, prey to suicidal thoughts.

She was still in this state when she came to see me, on the advice of a mutual friend. Our initial contact worked out well, and she was willing to keep coming. Lisa knew that she needed intensive help and needed it urgently. She had money for therapy, but she was terrified of making another attempt; she felt that if it, too, should go wrong, she would be left without hope. Under the circumstances, our work had to be aimed, first, at reducing her persisting depression and, second, at enlarging her perspective on therapy and on her own chances of benefiting from it. Lisa was given antidepressants by the staff psychiatrist, and I encouraged her to come in for brief visits when she felt an urgent need for contact and comfort. When she regained her balance somewhat, we discussed her recent and current troubles with family and friends and some of her attitudes and experiences that had bearing on them. I took care, however, to balance the discussion of problems with attention to the areas where Lisa was functioning well, her plans for the future, and ways in which she could stop her depressions from escalating. I wanted to provide Lisa with a conception of therapeutic work that would seem sensible and promising to her, different both from an unfounded reassurance and from an impersonal strange ritual.

I then introduced the idea of a referral to a psychiatrist who would work along the same lines. After a few weeks I proposed a candidate, a man whom I knew to be warm, active, and flexible and who could combine psychotherapy with drug therapy. On meeting him, Lisa agreed to try working with him—on the condition that she could continue to see me and would also be free to decide how often and for how long she would see the new therapist. For several weeks she saw each of us once a week; we kept in touch, exchanging our notes. When she came to trust the new relationship, she gradually stopped seeing me—after a total of fifteen sessions—and increased the number of weekly sessions with the psychiatrist. For many months, until she left the area to go to graduate school, Lisa worked with him intensively and productively, getting a great deal done. In her questionnaire reply, she expressed her feeling that the counseling service was the most valuable student service offered by Brandeis. "Through Dr. H. I was able to find an excellent therapist outside of Brandeis. I had had a previous experience in therapy which had made me doubt its value, but I feel that I have made great emotional progress this year." Several years later, in referring a relative to her former therapist, Lisa gave a good account of herself.

Phyllis: A Poor Referral

An obstacle to progress in counseling unusual in the Brandeis setting was encountered in the case of a girl who was failing her courses and was pressed into counseling by an eager new student adviser, who was not yet familiar with the center's reluctance to counsel students who have not come in entirely of their own volition. By applying for counseling, Phyllis was buying another chance, another year in school, which she could try to use to bring up her grades and avoid failure. The adviser was right in spotting emotional factors behind Phyllis's nonachievement. A bright child of a family threatened with disorganization, she doubted the love of her mother, whose hopes for success were pinned on her sons; and she felt ill at ease in the "foreign" environment of Brandeis, which separated her from the friends in her own ethnic and religious group. Although I talked to Phyllis about the mishandled referral, I was unable to fit my actions to my words: I could not refuse to see her in counseling until she herself felt that she wanted it. Phyllis talked, obediently;

but many weeks passed before she confessed her belief that, contrary to my assertions, I would be reporting to the powers that be on her progress in counseling, or lack of it.

Like some students who come to the center at their parents' suggestion but do not start working until they leave and then come back on their own, Phyllis did not start talking "for real" until she was convinced that this was her own enterprise. Then she gradually disclosed to me her loneliness, her nightmares, her despondency. The insights and the experiences accompanying this process began to dispel her suspicion that her misery was all her own fault, the result and the proof of her badness. Her discoveries were not happy ones, but clarity was better than confusion. "When my mother told me—not in anger this time—that nothing I could do could please her or distress her, I knew it was a moment of truth. I felt very calm, almost relieved, and now all decisions are easy."

Decisions had to be made, since time was running out. Phyllis had not improved her grades and expected to be dropped at the end of the year. Rather than wait, she decided to leave school at midterm on her own and take a job, thus lessening her dependence on her family. There was no question for Phyllis of continuing therapy, since she would not trust a clinic and there was no money for private treatment. Inwardly, too, Phyllis was not yet confident that she could benefit from therapy. What she had experienced was merely a "shimmer at the horizon," a glimmer of hope, and this experience had made her grope for something akin to therapy. During the last session she asked me whether there was not a substitute for talking intimately to a real person. Could she, for instance, imagine an understanding person, someone with whom there was no need to pretend, and talk or write to this imaginary person? In church she had tried to talk in this way to God, and this had helped her to clarify her thoughts. I invited Phyllis to write to me, but she did not make use of the invitation.

I next heard from Phyllis about ten years later, when she called on me for assistance in locating effective help in her fight against her progressing alcoholism, after some unsuccessful attempts of her own. She was married and had children; and she felt that her marital life was worth saving. But she had become discouraged by the failure of her own struggles and of her attempts to obtain help from a local state hospital. We met a few times to talk, and I helped Phyllis to make contact with Alcoholics Anonymous. A few months later she reported that she had stayed with them and was making good progress. That was the last I heard from or of her.

Another factor that occasionally slows down counseling is worth mentioning here: a persisting suspicion that physical factors might be involved in the student's difficulties. In such cases the counselor should insist that the student have a thorough medical checkup, and not only for the obvious reason of safety. Even when physical causes are highly unlikely, the thought of them may prevent the student from settling down to work on the psychological ones. However, I can think of a few cases where a student's physical complaint had been diagnosed and treated in so many different ways over the years that he had no choice but to write it off as psychological; yet he could not help thinking and worrying about it. In one of these cases a thorough study in a diagnostic hospital, finally undertaken at my insistence, led to a definite diagnosis of a rare physical condition that could be relieved, if not cured; reassured, the student then settled down to work on his many psychological problems. The either-or thinking often leads clinicians (with or without medical training) to be satisfied with a plausible psychodynamic explanation of a symptom, as if the patient could not be a hysteric *and* have a broken leg.

However, in most of the cases where many months' work brings a shift of perspective but does not take the student much further, obvious extraneous difficulties do not contribute to the slow start of counseling. The only obstacle is the well-established neurotic system, the self-protective way of life, which, at the beginning, has the person's complete allegiance. "The patient comes to the therapist because some of the consequences of his way of life are painful; he feels anxious, he has distressing or handicapping symptoms, he is frustrated in various ways. . . . He suffers and he wants to get rid of the pain. . . . It is not that the patient wants to be helped to change the self-defeating methods with which he pursues happiness; he expects to be taught how to succeed with these methods without suffering painful consequences. Only in the process of therapy does it gradually dawn on him that much more is involved than he had bargained for" (Angyal, 1965, p. 222).

Angyal is talking about adult patients; in their case the work to be done to get them to this point may take years, not months. College students have important advantages; their neurotic patterns are not yet stabilized or worked out in fine detail, their developmental stage dictates and facilitates change, and their newly discovered reflective thinking provides them with an effective tool of self-examination. On the debit side, they have not yet struggled with personal difficulties long enough to become discouraged or doubtful about their usual methods of coping with them. A girl, for example, who expects salvation from "love" is not likely to examine her concept of love after the failure of her first serious attempt at a relationship; it is not until failures accumulate that she may start wondering whether her ideas are realistic and whether the methods she uses in her attempts to "get love" will ever succeed. This is one of the equations that counselor and student must solve when they try to decide on the best timing of the counseling period. Does the student gain more by starting counseling early and possibly avoiding some failures or hasty decisions, or should he let experience accumulate, enabling him to make better use of this limited opportunity? Perhaps distributed periods of counseling are effective because they combine the advantages of early counseling *and* accumulated experience.

Students in whom the neurotic organization predominates, though they are more open to therapeutic approaches than are middle-aged neurotics, still face the same major obstacles to change. They cannot let go of their customary ways of doing things until they have discovered and practiced some alternative ways of feeling and acting; yet they cannot easily conceive of any alternatives that are not system-consistent as long as the neurotic system holds sway. To loosen this tight circle some work has to be done on both fronts: discrediting the neurotic assumptions and discovering some personal alternatives. This work takes time, partly because there are no standard directions about "how to do it." In each case the student and the counselor must discover by experimentation ways of implementing these goals that are acceptable to the student and give evidence of furthering movement.

Following are a few excerpts from the questionnaires and letters of students who did not show significant improvement after prolonged periods of counseling but still received something that they considered valuable: a shifting of perspective, a glimmer of hope. One of these students—who said in her questionnaire, soberly, that as a result of counseling she was not happier but felt she was on the right track—gave the following description of her initial situation: "I did not come to counseling in a 'crisis state,' but rather with long-term concerns and anxieties. I am the type of person who is well defended in a counseling situation and therefore require a great deal of patience and time." This could also be said of the other students whose comments follow:

> I began to change a lot of my previously held opinions. The value of psych counseling to me consisted not of a definite conclusion to my problem, but of a beginning of changes, of seeing some possible new directions for my life.

> I have seen the possibilities of a healthy solution and I am determined not to let shame and defenses cut me from using them.

> I will not obliterate the memories of this past year. It has been too important. The thick fog which has blurred the future for so long is slowly receding, destroying some paper castles on its way. Thanks again for everything.

> When I finally realized that my feelings of utter badness were not proof of my depravity, that they had other causes, I felt as if light had been let into a dark room; things are not hopeless any more.

> I have begun to see myself from a more enlightened point of view. In a way, though, I know less about myself than I did in January because so many points *to* view have been opened to me. Therein lies a fascinating challenge. X has given me tools and given me much more that is intangible. I am optimistic and very grateful.

Though these comments differ in the intensity of the emotional tone, they depict the same liberating realization: There is a better way. The person does not yet see clearly just what this different way is like; the realization is more like a growing faith than an articulate knowledge. One student expressed it well when he said:

"Maybe the decisive change is in sight, but I don't know yet what it entails."

What is the pragmatic value of this first indistinct realization? The answer should be clear if we accept the obvious: that *hope* is the precondition for any sustained striving. The shift of perspective which spells hope, if it is not lost and forgotten, results in a more serious commitment to guided self-exploration.

When a shift occurs early in the course of counseling, or at some point of a long-term therapy, it may lead to a period of more intensive and more active work in sessions. In retrospect, viewed from the vantage point of completed therapy, the shift of perspective may be seen as a turning point, as one of the important steps toward this successful outcome. In short-term counseling, if a student experiences this widening of perspective toward the end of the counseling period, he usually wants to continue what has been started: "I feel as if I am just beginning to learn. . . . If it were at all possible, I would have liked to begin a long-term program now." It is not always possible for the student to fulfill this wish. Those whose external situations are not favorable to this project, and whose need is not too urgent, settle for an indefinite postponement. Some among them were surprised to discover later that the experience of shifting perspectives, by increasing their trust in their own chances, enabled them to develop further insights and to move ahead under their own steam. They let me know months and years later that they had improved their lives significantly without the benefit of further therapy.

For the majority of students who experience a shift of perspective but no major improvement in counseling, further therapy is in the cards. Some carry out the plan without delay, using the counselor's help in referrals. Though I have follow-ups for only a fraction of those who postpone, it is a plausible assumption that the majority resume therapeutic work within a few years from the termination of counseling.

The therapists to whom we have referred students have reacted in two different ways. Some of them clearly understood the difficulties of inducing clients into therapy, even after they have explicitly committed themselves to it. They were impressed with their new clients' ability to settle down to productive work without fumbling and delay; in their view, these clients had been well prepared for intensive work. Other therapists have failed to appreciate both the importance and the difficulty of the initial unspectacular results achieved through patient, skillful, client-oriented therapeutic work. Believing that college counseling can offer nothing effectively therapeutic anyway, or else willing to view only *behavioral* changes as indicators of progress, these people regarded anything that preceded the client's entering "real therapy" as a waste of time, and they attributed all subsequent successes solely to their own efforts. When some psychiatrists criticized the Brandeis Counseling Center during its period of affluence for not referring the students out right away, they failed to realize that without these misguided policies of ours the students in question would not have come to their attention at all; they were, to start with, not only "unworkable" but also "unreferrable."

When one views the issue of mental health from a wider perspective, the early approach to young people who suffer from serious neurotic difficulties is perhaps the most important contribution a well-appointed college mental health center can make to the national scene. For the individual person the early start of therapy may make all the difference. Those students who hold that coming to counseling has been the most important step in their lives have a good basis for this belief. From the point of view of the counselor, the doubtful, anxious, slow-starting clients, though they do not delight us in the same way as do those who move vigorously from the start, represent a challenge which can be turned into a source of learning: learning about the workings of neurosis, of the manifold ways in which it is maintained and defended, and about the range of means that one can use to undermine it without undermining its bearer, while simultaneously starting to uncover and build up viable personal alternatives.

8

Modified Approaches

Some modified approaches, departures from typical counseling procedures, were described in Chapter Five covering brief encounters: giving information, interceding, managing emergencies, providing a consultation or minimal counseling. This chapter concerns modified approaches that occur in the course of longer student-counselor contacts but are also dictated by the exigencies of the student's situation, external or internal. I believe that most clinicians would designate these departures as "supportive contacts," but to me the term *support* seems vague and misleading. Too often it is viewed as "mere support"—necessary perhaps to prevent a collapse, but neither aiming at nor resulting in any significant improvement; in giving such support, one makes the patients feel better without making them well. In some contexts support is thought of as a "holding operation"; one stays in contact with the patient until his state, or his situation, permits one to embark on "real" or insight therapy, which aims at increasing the subject's awareness of the nature and the roots of his difficulties. In my view, however, insight is not *the* agent of change but merely one of the components of therapy; a client can make significant gains without a great increase in insight, or with insight following, rather than preceding, changes.

Other implicit assumptions concern the composition of "supportive" contacts. Some people believe that such contacts involve counselor-patient transactions that therapists are often advised to shun when conducting insight therapy: direct expressions of sympathy and appreciation by the therapist; easy availability to the patient; disclosure of the therapist's own opinions and personal traits; help in solving reality-based current problems, not excluding advice. Such a definition sharpens the contrast between "support" on the one hand and pure insight therapy, or the strictly client-centered approach, on the other. Yet, I believe, most therapists know from experience that the interventions listed above may serve as vehicles of interpersonal processes functioning as important curative agents. Their presence does not make a client-counselor contact into a "mere" something or other; and there is no call to exclude them, wholesale, from any counseling or therapy session.

To some people, however, "support" connotes not merely such straightforward, potentially useful personal interactions but also the deceptive ones, deliberately staged for the patient's benefit: bribing or charming by fake approval or flattery, taking over for the patient when there is no need, using prestige suggestion or any other form of manipulation. The motivation of those using such methods is suspect. But quite apart from how they are motivated, fraudulent interventions, even if they work for a season by enhancing the therapist's influence on the client, are destructive in the long run; they can increase the client's confusion and undermine further his trust in himself and others. It is all very well to stage "therapist variables" in experimental research in order to demonstrate conclusively the facilitating effects of shared attitudes, or mutual liking, or a hope-fostering atmosphere (Bergin and Garfield, 1971); but it would be folly to expect strenuous play acting by the therapist to have lasting beneficial effects. To avoid the confusion that permits some people to read "support" as "pleasing the client at all costs," I have rejected this term in favor of a noncommittal one, *modified approach.*

This term has its difficulties, to be sure. It is—or should be—

an axiom for us that one never uses a standard approach without "modifying" it to fit the particular person; these modifications result from the client-counselor interchanges, both initial and subsequent. The slow starters discussed in the preceding chapter have often required the counselor to change the "rules," to invent special ways to stimulate their mental functioning or to allay their fears. Some, afraid of not being able to get anywhere, were able to start only after I told them that they could remain in counseling through the year even if they kept totally silent in sessions, and I had to ask others for a blanket permission to interrupt them whenever I lost touch with what they were saying. Similarly, when one girl developed a severe headache in sessions as soon as she became afraid she might hear something derogatory, her counselor suggested that she tell him to stop whenever she disliked what he was saying—and he would stop. Are such "rule changes" modified approaches? In my view, they are not—as long as the modification subserves the general goals of shared exploration, without placing any limits on it in advance. I reserve the term *modifications* for those instances when attention to the client's wishes and needs resulted in a quasi-agreement not to explore in certain directions, at least for the time being. The area most often excluded in these explicit or implicit agreements was that of "deep" motivational analysis (that is, the personal motivation bordering on the unconscious); also excluded in some cases was an exploration of the origins and general pattern of the student's difficulties. These omissions usually resulted in a greater focusing on the current problems and on practical tasks, at the expense of wider explorations; but, as far as I was concerned, this focusing did not necessarily mean abstaining from all efforts to facilitate significant changes—if not now, then in the future. Of course, in the absence of systematic follow-ups, one seldom knows if efforts have brought end results.

Cases that require modifications have no single obvious feature in common. The conditions determining this course range from purely external ones, such as lack of time, to the client's complete inability to participate in a free-wheeling exploration or else his determined rejection of this course; usually they are a combination of both, though either the external or the inner component may be in the foreground. However, in the majority of cases, including

all those to be described below, an important part is played by some
acute crisis which prescribes the primary goal of counseling: that of
helping the student get back on his feet. One might describe this
counseling as crisis-limited, to distinguish it both from the crisis
management described in Chapter Five and from the numerous
counseling courses that have their start in a crisis situation but use
it merely as a point of departure for wide-ranging personal discussions. The cases to follow are fairly representative of the kind of
counseling courses that I have in mind.

Thomas: Solving Practical Problems

A graduate student of art, who had called urgently for an
appointment, burst into tears when invited to talk and confessed to
strong suicidal impulses as well as a desperate preoccupation with
being unacceptable to girls. He felt childishly naive, unable to impress and to compete; though he no longer believed the teachings
of the Catholic church, he still regarded sex as sinful. He had used
drugs heavily this year to obtain relief and instant bliss, though he
was afraid they would make him insane. The student's grant-sup-
ported period of study was to end in two months, and he had no
other means of support.

The young man's childhood—spent in a disunited, disad-
vantaged family, with a seriously ill mother and an overpowering
father—abounded in traumatic episodes; after each trivial childish
"sin," he had nightmares in which death threatened him. Between
the ages of fourteen and twenty-one Tom attended a community
clinic, but he did not feel that he got much help. His therapist, he
felt, lived in a different world, an ivory tower: "He could not feel
my feelings; he told me to do things I could not possibly do." Feeling judged by this man, Tom never told him—or anyone else—
about his "shameful" sexual fantasies and practices; he blamed
himself for this "cowardice" and for his failure in therapy. In pour-
ing out this confession, Tom became so upset and disorganized that
I suggested he spend the night in the infirmary. He declined, feeling
that he could manage at home if he had permission to call me.

During the next days his panic subsided, and he was able to
secure a simple part-time job. He was now less depressed and more

coherent in sessions but still preoccupied with his sexual, social, and intellectual inadequacy. His attempts to observe and imitate the actions of his peers, who he felt had the know-how, were not bringing the desired results. He felt that he could swallow any information offered him but could not "put his teeth into it" and make it his own; he felt so insubstantial that at times he doubted his own existence. Now he also revealed his intense fear of leaving school and his fear of all jobs, tracing it to his father's early opinion of him as a good-for-nothing. Although his family had been trying for some time to bolster Tom's self-confidence, he was so afraid of being scolded and humiliated by bosses that he was never able to hold a job for more than a few weeks.

In the fourth session, with only a month of the school year left, I briefly summed up what Tom had told me, pointing out that he had a good understanding of the origins and the nature of his troubles, though his loyalty to his family made him minimize the severity of the early traumas. I proposed that our priority should now be to help Tom prepare to exchange the school environment for that of the workaday world. This required dealing with his fear of jobs, but it also involved finding friends outside the school and possibly locating some opportunities for continuing counseling. Tom agreed, and in the next four sessions we adhered to these guidelines, although not too rigidly. Tom still brought up sexual issues, but no longer as major worries. He now tested his fears by confessing his sexual problems to a girl and was greatly reassured by her not being shocked and not thinking them unique. He concluded that sexual proficiency was not as important a measure of a man's worth as the conversation of his peers had led him to believe, and that the resolution of sexual issues could wait; to offer marriage or even just a good time to a girl, he would first have to earn and save. He also considered dropping the use of drugs as a means of gaining reassurance; he was induced by a friend to try a new drug and found the effects not good; perhaps his self-confidence would be raised by keeping a job more than by the false promise of drugs. I supported this testing and thinking by focusing on the probable effects of alternative courses of action. We discussed the means of reducing Tom's fear of working on a job and the best way of approaching his boss for more work. His "counterculture" misgivings that a better-ordered life might destroy his openness to impressions also came in for their share of attention and testing.

In reintroducing the issue of postcounseling referral, I described various approaches to therapy and cast my vote for one of the local groups of Recovery, Inc. I did so because participation in these groups costs practically nothing and because this self-help organization of chronically "nervous" and former mental patients—which uses as a guide the book of its founder, Abraham Low, *Mental Health Through Will Training* (1950)—teaches its members some effective methods for increasing control of their thoughts and actions. I gave Tom an article by a member, a former schizophrenic, which had been my own introduction to this remarkable, unpublicized organization. He was impressed but also frightened because the people who entered these groups had serious troubles that took time and effort to overcome. In taking down "Recovery's" telephone number, he got scared and felt that he might find himself unable to call; but he let me call for him and get the address and the time of the next meeting, which he could attend as an observer without any preliminaries. In the next session, he reported that he had gone and even participated in the discussion. He had brought up the topic of sexual problems and had found the group members neither shocked nor too interested; yet they were friendly, and he was pleased to find another Brandeis student among them, even though he once more painfully realized that both his and their problems were real and that the process of solving them would be arduous and slow. In our eighth and last session, Tom revived some of his anxieties and doubts but then acknowledged that he was feeling much better than he had two months earlier. He had done fairly well in his job and expected to be given more work there; he had cut down on drugs and was no longer obsessively preoccupied with girls; he was more cheerful and was looking forward to continuing his contact with "Recovery"; in fact, he felt all in one piece, as he had not for a long time; counseling, he thought, might have helped. I did not hear from him after he left school.

In Tom's case, the "modification" consisted in permitting him in the initial sessions to experience and express his feelings of inadequacy, loneliness, and despair, but subsequently deemphasizing both these feelings and all explanatory insights and working only on issues pertinent to the solution of his urgent practical problems, while undermining his hopes for instant magical solutions. I took more initiative than I usually do, and I advocated "Recovery" because I felt that at this juncture Tom needed help in developing self-discipline much more than he needed further insights and/or a reawakening of his emotions.

Laura: Helping to Weather a Crisis

Another graduate student, Laura, was facing the breakdown of her first serious relationship with a man. After years of therapy in early adolescence, this disturbed, brilliant girl sought her salvation, the restoration of her personal integrity, in various activities typical of the youth in the 1960s. When these attempts failed, she placed her hopes in a friendship which eventually afforded her the experience of openness and mutual acceptance, radically different from the jungle world she had lived in up to then. Eventually the neurotic patterns of the two friends came to the fore, meshing with and reinforcing one another, and Laura foresaw breakup and abandonment. She elected me, on the basis of a slight previous contact, to stand by until the situation was resolved, stating explicitly that she wanted me merely to help her keep her head above water in the next few weeks. She was still fighting her friend's growing wish for separation. If she could keep him, she would not need therapy; if she lost him, she felt that she would need much more than the center could provide. She proposed to use the sessions to tell the story of her life, "perhaps for the last time," and she meant to keep full control of the sessions: "It is about me, so I am the one to decide what is vital."

Laura told her story in concrete detail, with adequate but controlled emotion. In talking about her friend, she occasionally broke down and cried, but she quickly regained mastery of herself; she conveyed the intensity of her misery without fully expressing it. I did not remain passive, though it was rarely possible to make comments unobtrusively and I did not want to overuse Laura's reluctantly given permission to interrupt her at times. I studied my notes carefully to see which of Laura's excellent insights might be made more effective if viewed from another angle or placed in a more general framework. One of my goals was to support Laura's realistic perception that the crisis had been produced by the interaction of both friends' personal difficulties, as against her placing the whole blame alternately on herself and on the man. I supported equally strongly the rejection of another false dichotomy, a rejection expressed by Laura's anguished outcry against her friends' assertion that this relationship was all neurotic and that she had to look to herself for salvation: "Of course I myself must do it, but why shouldn't it be with help, with his help; what's wrong with that?" I agreed with her but pointed out that a good therapist was more likely to provide steady help than an overinvolved friend. I also repeatedly pointed out the two diametrically opposed world images and orientations competing for her intellectual and emotional energies. Each one when predominant was strong and clear. She could be hateful and destructive; but, according to many students' testimony, no one could be more understanding and loving than Laura in her good periods. Which one would she ultimately be? She was still unwilling to choose; and she was still absurdly trying to use intimidation, a method dictated by her conception of the world as a jungle, for the purpose of gaining love and creating the longed-for interpersonal harmony.

Much more dramatic than these fragmentary discussions, in which I was elaborating Laura's own ideas, were several confrontations—initiated by me but caused by Laura's activities outside of sessions. She no sooner started seeing me than anxious roommates, friends, administrators, and teachers began calling for information and reassurance. They urgently wanted to know whether Laura's weird actions indicated that she was actually insane and whether she was likely to do what she was threatening: kill the boy friend, commit suicide. When I told this to Laura, she said coolly: "Tell them the truth—that you do not know." Using offense as defense, she attacked me for breaking the confidentiality rule and talking about her without her permission. She started watching her friends closely to prevent them from communicating with me, or to intercept their calls to my apartment, but she earned my gratitude by refraining from suicidal threats when she called my apartment and my mother answered the telephone. After two or three weeks of this, I told Laura that if she kept terrorizing all those around her, I could not keep seeing her, protecting her thereby from the consequences of her actions; I would have to let other school offices take over. She saw that I meant it, and she drew her conclusions, though she did not desist entirely from trying to manipulate me along with everyone else—mainly, it seemed, for the purpose of impressing her boy friend with her plight. I could never be certain where Laura's real "craziness" ended and deliberate intimidation began; but, according to some of her friends, I had a good understanding both of her strengths and her weaknesses and was not fooled by her.

The strength on which I was betting in my dealings with Laura actually enabled her to pull through in a most impressive fashion. When her friend saw that they merely kept hurting each other and made up his mind to pull out, she grieved briefly but then put the whole matter behind her. In the meeting she made our last, Laura said that she now had to relearn to walk by herself. On returning to her long-neglected studies, she caught up in no time, and she elected one of her teachers to be my successor, a confidential counselor or listener. Her choice was a good one, and within the next year she completed her studies at Brandeis without further major upsets. I do not know whether the effort I had made to reawaken Laura's interest in therapy had any effects. But I believe she knew what she was doing when, threatened with a collapse of her hopes for closeness with a man and torn by contradictory wishes, she arranged for a temporary contact with people who were not likely to withdraw from her or to be drawn into her own struggles.

Bernard and Gregory: Supporting Artistic Expression

In the case that follows, the situation of crisis, though present, was less obvious than in the two cases reported above. Bernard and Gregory were two brothers, two years apart in school, both of them talented people, lonely at Brandeis and depending on each other's company and friendship. They came to the center in the middle of the older brother's senior year because their increasingly severe depressions and other disturbing inner states began to interfere seriously with their work. After they had failed to establish rapport with the counselors they were seeing, their teacher referred them to me. The counselors, impressed by the brothers' unusual fantasies and changeable moods, viewed them as very disturbed and were in turn viewed by them as unimaginative and unresponsive to their artistic concerns. The young men belonged to a very close-knit family from central Europe, whose members cultivated a wide range of artistic and literary interests and had kept aloof from their American environment. Valuable as the family's culture and closeness had been in their development, its self-sufficiency was now creating great difficulties for the growing children; it was impossible for them to visualize closeness with anyone outside the family. The professor who persuaded the brothers to try me used as an inducement my own European background. They dropped in together to meet me, obviously anticipating an enjoyable visit, and such it proved to be: I turned out to resemble their grandmother. We spoke German and talked about topics related not to their problems but to their interests: books, plays, places and travels in Europe; their plans for further training in their fields, sculpture and literature, respectively. I got a message in this meeting, and in the subsequent ones I had with each brother separately, that these topics, personally involving but nonthreatening, had to be given a prominent place in our discussions if the brothers were to consider the sessions worthwhile.

The counseling worked out differently with the two, partly because of the differences in their ages and their situations. Bernard, the brother who was to graduate in two months, had his plans for further training all made; his main concern was to get over his current disturbance and work inhibition so that he could complete his projects. Since his time was at a premium, I agreed to see Bernard irregularly, on demand; and he came only when he felt the need and had something important to say. Our meetings therefore were unproblematic. We discussed the topics of Bernard's choice, mostly his work; I commented only on the more obvious aspects of the struggles and achievements he was reporting, never attempting to go beyond the feelings he himself was willing to express. Actually, he let me see more of himself by inviting me to view the exhibition of his sculptures than he did by talking. Bernard succeeded in shedding his depression and overcoming his work inhibition; he completed his work with distinction. His exhibition was a success, and his artistic future looked bright. He showed no interest in undertaking therapy after graduation, and I had no basis for urging him to do so. He was glad, however, to be given the name of a therapist in New York, just in case. The therapist was a European, seriously interested in art and literature. (Bernard never called on her, but his parents did a year or two later, when their youngest child, a girl, broke down on entering an out-of-town college. After a consultation which included the parents, the girl's upset subsided and she was able to make plans involving a less sudden weaning from home.)

Gregory's situation was different. In his sophomore year his plans for the future were not made yet, and he doubted whether he should stay at Brandeis, where he felt isolated, had difficulties in studying, and expected to be even more lonely after his brother's graduation. These unresolved issues, which caused Gregory intense misery, led to some discussions with teachers and some confrontations with the parents, and made him willing at times to exchange literary conversations for work on personal problems. He eventually brought up and discussed, at least minimally, a wide range of fears and conflicts—many of them having to do with his being the younger brother. However, the literary and philosophical discussions continued to occupy much of our time throughout. They were, in part, performances staged for my benefit; yet some of the most revealing expositions of Gregory's personal myths and beliefs were given via a discussion of such topics as the "living theater" or Kafka's view of the role of the performing artist. Gregory's disturbance subsided somewhat; he now had enough "good days" to be able to catch up on his work. He decided to stay at Brandeis and to spend the summer traveling and working in Europe, alone.

Gregory reappeared at the beginning of the next year, looking and sounding much more mature and self-confident. He wanted to continue counseling and to make better use of the sessions than previously, but, feeling better this year, he was under less pressure; he soon started skipping sessions or filling them with literary talk. Before long, I told him that he must choose between occasional social visits and regular appointments for more continuous work on his problems. He hesitated, until, at Thanksgiving, his parents declared themselves against further counseling, feeling that Gregory's developmental problems were being adequately resolved. Through the rest of this year and the next one, his senior year, he kept in touch with me through occasional visits; no longer an isolate, he reported on his new relationships, referred friends to me, and at times used the meetings to discuss and resolve some minor current problems. The severe disturbance that brought Gregory to the center in his sophomore year did not recur; he was both happier than previously and more aware of his feelings and motives—one of his realizations being that he had tended to avoid using our sessions to full advantage.

Most of the work Gregory had done was done at the beginning, when his misery was intense. In the case to be presented next, there was, on the contrary, a clear-cut progression from a "modified" to a more typical therapeutic approach in the second year, although the lead was left to the student throughout.

Jeremy: Fostering Communication

Jeremy, who first approached the center as a freshman, had felt lonely and depressed ever since he could recall. His father had died when Jeremy was four, the son's only memory of him being that of a figure in a coffin. An only child, Jeremy grew up on his grandparents' isolated farm, while his mother went to work. There was little communication between him and these adults, who seemed not to have much understanding of children, and Jeremy made no friends in school. Intelligent academically, and eager to excel, he suffered from a severe school anxiety, had an ulcer at thirteen, and at times experienced suicidal impulses; while in high school, he saw two counselors over the period of a year, liked one of them, but did not feel helped. Jeremy came to the center because at Brandeis, for the first time in his life, he longed to make friends and realized that he did not know how. He felt basically different from all other people, inadequate in most ways but superior to them in his devotion to science and music. He was afraid of rejection and afraid that he might hurt people, particularly women; he felt that he had already hurt some—by withdrawing as soon as closeness threatened. The counselor who saw him that year subjected Jeremy to extensive exploration, postponing "real work" to the next year; he thus forfeited his chance to establish rapport with this lonely boy. In a polite, stilted letter Jeremy declined further counseling. In the middle of his sophomore year, he alarmed the two friends he had made by telling them that he was "polluting the world" and by carrying cyanide in his pocket. They eventually managed to take the cyanide from him and persuaded him to accept an appointment with a different counselor.

A slight young man, pale and emaciated, his eyes invisible behind dark glasses, Jeremy described his acute depressions, or attacks of despair, as short but extremely severe. This last one was the worst of all; the danger of suicide had been real. Asked what had precipitated it, he cited some possible causes but eventually disclosed that it had come in the wake of his realization that the two friends he had made at Brandeis, a boy and a girl, were in love with each other. He was at a loss to explain his despair at this discovery—particularly since he was not romantically interested in the girl and, in fact, was currently courting another. He was not angry at his friends, perceiving (correctly) that their feelings toward him had not changed. In following my invitation to speak freely, Jeremy voiced his doubts about the promise of therapy; he said that, being an independent person, he felt loath to accept help and would probably manage to withhold information from me, as he had done with the first counselor. I said in reply that it was Jeremy's right to decide on his course in counseling and that we could be frank with each other; it would not be "withholding" if he simply let me know what he did or did not want to discuss. This seemed to please Jeremy. He chatted about going home soon, for the period between terms, saying that his mother would take him out to dine, regardless of the expense, since she was not a good cook; no one had been, at home. Jeremy spoke lightly and I replied in kind, suggesting that he offer to cook a dinner for his mother; he had just told me that he was developing an interest in cooking as an art, not trying to make it a science, as did some of his scientist colleagues. I liked Jeremy, enjoyed his wit and his logic, and felt that this first session had gone well.

In the second session, almost a month later, Jeremy reported that instead of going to expensive restaurants he and his mother had had some real talks at home. He found out that she was not the one who had pushed him into a career in science; contrary to his assumptions, she would not have objected to his becoming a musician. But it was too late to change now; music had to remain a hobby. He then talked of saving his small allowance to buy records and best seats in concerts and operas for the girl he was attracted to and was trying to make friends with. He had not had much success, since she repeatedly refused his invitations to restaurants and musical events, telling him he was spending too much. As described by Jeremy, his dealings with the girl struck me as compulsive and coercive. Using various examples, I tried to show how his insistence and his over-spending might carry a message he did not intend; that is, although he really wanted to give the girl something valuable, share with her his enjoyment of music, the way he went about it might make her feel coerced, or else bribed—perhaps by someone who did not think much of his chances to be accepted for himself. Jeremy listened closely and admitted that he felt socially inferior to most. He had no social skills to speak of and was not good at small talk, or just talk; he could only talk—or lecture rather—on music or science. I said that the problem could be approached in two ways. We could try to find out what obstacles, external or internal, had prevented him from acquiring these skills, or he could start developing them now, practicing at first with people by whom he felt accepted, or who did not matter to him too much; to expect quick success in learning to deal with girls might lead to disappointments, triggering depressions. Jeremy chose the second path. He felt that, if his difficulties had any causes, they were too distant in time to be found; by now, he said, it was just him. He never brought up memories unless I—very rarely—asked about antecedents of some of his present ways of thinking and acting. I got some glimpses of his early frightening fantasies, but we never discussed them, or anything else, in motivational terms other than pointing to the early disruption of communication between him and his social environment. We talked only about the topics Jeremy himself would bring up, either for discussion or just to chat about. Whenever he ran out of topics, he asked whether I had any questions but more often than not this proved to be a polite way to let me know that he now wished to depart for his lab or the library. I accepted these wishes without questioning or interpreting them; some of our sessions were quite short.

Our work was centered on Jeremy's behavior in social situations. By getting feedback from others, thus substituting communication for fantasy and guesswork, Jeremy began to try to find ways of behaving that would bring him the desired results. He now talked freely to the girl in whom he was interested, and he was quite receptive to the suggestions made by her, by me, and by his two friends. If he did not know what to talk about at a party, why not draw others out by asking questions? He had never tried. In his childhood no one answered Jeremy's questions and he stopped asking; he now felt that an exchange of questions and answers would unduly obligate both parties; still he tried and it worked. The girl drew his attention to his stilted language; he often sounded like a book. At some time it might have been a means to impress people, but now it was just habit; he felt he could tackle it. The girl, sympathetic to Jeremy's problems, was a great help to his progress. She listened and gave her ideas, without pushing them too strongly, but she did not hesitate to resist his excessive demands on her time; she consistently deflated his fantasies of exclusive special friendship, and early faced him with her plan to leave Brandeis at the end of the year. This led to a flare-up of his despondency and his urgent demands. He felt that it was his duty to love and worship this girl, and he asked me to tell her not to require him to let go of her. I declined, suggesting that he talk about his feelings to his friends, whom—though I did not know them—I had come to view as effective counselors. With their assistance, Jeremy regained his earlier realization that he could do the girl a good turn by *not* becoming upset about her leaving.

There were several lesser upsets—about failed tests and unfinished course work but, despite all setbacks, Jeremy was clearly progressing in his attempts to join the world of other people; he no longer tried to coerce his friends into his own private world. In the last weeks of the term, Jeremy experienced many a "first" in his life: the first shopping trip, the first hike with friends, reading for pleasure, getting a plant for his room; he also felt in much better touch with his mother and had made good plans for the summer. Jeremy's perceptions had also changed. He had more clarity about his mother's attitudes and felt that previously he had not done her justice. He was aware of many handicapping aspects of his functioning, such as his automatic fight against relaxation, and was by now almost convinced that his atypical childhood, rather than any mysterious personal lack, was responsible for his social awkwardness. Jeremy was almost ready now to see his problems and his prospects in their true perspective, and I was sorry that further work had to be postponed until fall. I suggested that he read Angyal's description of neurosis and treatment while the recent developments were fresh in his mind.

As I expected, this book proved a hit. In the fall, in reporting an excellent summer, Jeremy spoke of Angyal's "fantastic knowledge of the workings of the neurotic mind—and I had thought that my ways were unique!" In addition to showing him that he was not alone, not a freak, the book, Jeremy said, had this important message for him: that the chronically disturbed person perceives his distorted, threatening personal world as completely real—the only reality there is. This insight, added to his steady progress on all fronts, must have helped Jeremy to distance himself from the fantasy world of his neurosis, which we never explored as such. He realized only in the summer, he said, how much he had been helped by counseling. The most important development of the summer months was Jeremy's intimate friendship with a girl whose affection he had not previously responded to. In this relationship he found himself relaxed and self-confident, no longer anticipating hurting the woman or being hurt by her.

Jeremy did not expect any major crisis this year, but he still wanted to have counseling sessions, perhaps every third week. In carrying out this plan, he worked on his feelings about his teachers, feelings which were interfering with his work: his fear of being evaluated; his competitiveness; and, most of all, the guilt he felt for devaluing some of his best and most helpful teachers and for letting them down by failing in his work. He was well aware by now that his failures were motivated ones, his own active doing. He noticed that he no longer got depressed when his wishes were frustrated by people or things; he got angry instead, mishandled apparatus, and made a nuisance of himself by criticizing people and trying to push them around. This stage soon passed; Jeremy became such good friends with several of his teachers and fellow students that they gave him a surprise birthday party, another "first" in his life. His visits at home were also very rewarding. After the Christmas vacation, in his fifth session, Jeremy decided to stop coming. He said in parting that he was amazed by the distance he had traveled since he had come to the center a year ago; "Or, more exactly, I cannot understand how I could be the person I was at that time." He said (in the spring questionnaire about the counseling service): "Speaking only for myself, it is not an exaggeration to say that this service has saved my life."

In an informal follow-up a year later (initiated by a chance meeting on campus), Jeremy was friendly, cheerful, and evidently pleased with his life. After he had stopped seeing me, he had been slightly depressed for a week or two but then regained his serenity and had had no gloomy moods since. He was now living with his girl friend; they shared an apartment and got along well. Jeremy spoke enthusiastically about his current work and his work plans; even before graduating he had several publications to his credit. He used his leisure time to read, to think, to play a musical instrument, to be with his girl and his friends; he joked about still liking at times, "not too often," to deliver lectures to captive audiences. It was indeed difficult to identify Jeremy with the severely disturbed, lonely young man of two years ago.

It was obvious to Jeremy and to me that credit for these changes had to be shared with his girl friend and his friends; we realized also that the insight-furthering function of counseling had been carried out by Angyal's book. Still, the contribution of counseling itself had been considerable, and a large part of it was made in the first period of counseling, fourteen sessions distributed over four months. During this period little effort was made to stimulate Jeremy's insight into the nature and motivation of his difficulties, to say nothing of their origins; the focus was not on the roots but on the effects of his actions. Depending on one's theoretical orientation, one can view our proceedings as practice in reality testing, or in problem solving, or as learning and practicing new behaviors. I prefer to view them as establishing straightforward, unambiguous communication with a person whose disturbance had isolated him from his environment but who now felt a great inner push toward contact and closeness. This process, an important component of any successful therapy, can be furthered, as the comments by other students indicate, by working with observable contemporary data: "X's attitude strengthened my confidence in my ability to assess my experience because his interpretations took full account of my obser-vations." "She was never dogmatic and based her comments on the present behavior which we both could observe." "His example gave me reason to trust evidence and not to fall back upon half-true theoretical clichés." Furthermore, whether or not the past is ex-plored, the sessions can be vital only if the focus is kept steadily on the client's present life situation, the source of his need to change. Jeremy's course suggests that if one must limit the field of thera-peutic exploration either to the person's past or to his current mode of functioning, the present might well yield better results.

Before closing this chapter, which concludes the discussion of the productive courses of counseling, I want to comment on the differences of the four variants of these courses in terms of what *the counselor* is called upon to do in each one. In *brief encounters,* in-sofar as they involve counseling and not merely information giving or crisis managing, he centers on the specific problem brought in by the client and tries to assist in its solution, without moving too far away from its situational aspects; he must be on his toes to find quickly a useful loose end, a workable lever. With students who are ready for counseling in depth and *move vigorously* after they start, the counselor tries to stimulate their thinking and feeling about themselves through time, not just about some circumscribed current situation. In doing so, each of us uses his or her preferred theoretical framework and the accumulated knowledge of pointers or questions that have worked with others; but some of these people require only minimal stimulation. The student takes the lead and embarks on his journey of discovery with gusto, even if not without trepidation, and the counselor can relax into active listening. These courses are the counselor's delight. With people who are slow to start, who find it difficult to respond and to *shift their perspectives,* either because they are caught in a well-developed, stabilized neurosis or because of some other obstacles to movement, the counselor has to work much harder. Here it is not enough to listen and to suggest view-points. Instead, the counselor soon finds himself attempting to un-earth the client's misgivings and conflicts, as well as his hidden assets; meeting his objections; allaying his anxieties; explaining his own interventions; wrestling with the client's defenses—and doing all of it, with variations, over and over again. He will need all of his skill and inventiveness as well as patient persistence and a measure of optimism about the outcome; his optimism will be well founded and convincing if he can look back on many successes. These courses offer good preparation for long-term therapeutic work for both the student and the counselor. Finally, the *atypical* cases or situations require the counselor not only to improvise, modifying his usual specific procedures, but even to abandon some of the general directions he usually pursues through his interventions, such as exploration of patterns and origins, reawakening of feelings, or undermining of defenses. He must, instead, identify the directions or the goals demanded by the student's situation, external or internal, and then find methods of implementing these goals that are acceptable to the student; what is at a premium here is the counselor's flexibility. I want to stress here once more that the approach appropriate for a given client cannot be decided on in advance. One must feel one's way as one goes along and be led by the student's response to one's offerings.

9

Negative
Brief Encounters:
Dropping Out

A student who is obviously in need of help does not return after the
initial contact; another leaves, dissatisfied, after a few sessions. These
negative brief encounters constitute a large category within the
unproductive courses of counseling. Most of these instances testify
to the counselor's failure to carry out the task of initiation in a way
that would motivate the student to give counseling a serious try.
The nature of this task, the difficulties and the opportunities it presents, is discussed in detail in Chapter Four. I would like simply to
repeat here that not all decisions against counseling are to be
counted as failures, even if the counselor (and sometimes also the
student) feels that help will probably be necessary in the long run,
if not now. If the counselor's comments have adequately clarified

to the applicant the nature and the conditions of counseling, and he then decides against it with some insight into his reasons, I count this contact as productive. Suppose someone who comes merely because a friend or a teacher so advised him gets a vivid demonstration of the insufficiency of this reason. He will then have to consult his own wishes in the matter. Whatever he decides, he has learned something useful (which may help him to return at a later date). Similarly, a person who has not admitted to himself his fears and reservations about counseling may have them brought out in a manner both convincing and nonaccusatory. He may then either overcome or accept his misgivings, but in either case his awareness has been enlarged. Thus, a man who had approached the center in May of his senior year wrote that his two sessions had been useful: "Having come so late in the year, I could not accomplish anything, but I saw more clearly than I did before that this delay reflected lack of real desire on my part to experience therapy; I learned something about myself." What saves these slight tentative contacts from being unproductive is the counselor's ability to lead the student to see his reservations and to accept them as his. If the counselor, pressed by lack of time and long waiting lists, quickly imparts his observations to the student and/or suggests postponing counseling, he not only deprives him of the chance to make his own decision, perhaps to overcome his misgivings then and there, but also makes his later return highly unlikely. The factor of insufficient time (and the counselor's anxiety about it) is probably responsible for a large proportion of negative brief encounters.

If this variant of unproductive courses is as large as I assume it to be, the negative brief encounters deserve to be studied in detail in any setting that provides outpatient therapy. A high percentage of early dropouts represents the clinicians' failure to connect with those people who have enough insight and initiative to look for the help they need, a failure that may forestall any further attempts on their part. Furthermore, a large proportion of useless contacts, even if brief ones, is a great waste of the staff's time, which is always at a premium. Such a situation also demoralizes the staff and causes them to resort either to wishful thinking ("They dropped out because they improved") or to blaming the dropouts for the failure ("They were not motivated"). Because of all this, it would be of great importance to document reliably the incidence of negative brief encounters in various clinical settings and to study their causes. Unfortunately, however, clinical settings usually fail to provide the conditions needed for even the minimum amount of informative evaluative research—conditions such as the education of the staff and the allowance of time for accurate recording, coding, and tabulating of a range of pertinent data. In the absence of such data, I draw my conclusion about the prevalence of early dropouts from the fact that, during my twenty-five years at Brandeis, the proportion of short contacts (one to four sessions) was quite high at all times (one-third to half of our caseload) and from the counselors' testimony that with most students they need more than a few sessions to get something useful done. Such data not being conclusive, one can optimistically assume, if one chooses, that many students leave after a few sessions because they have been adequately helped by a short contact. If, however, my assumption is valid, the college counseling situation does not radically differ from that of other community centers, where the prevalence of early dropouts is often explained by the obvious disparity between the conception of treatment held by the staff and the expectations of the unsophisticated lower-class applicants.

College students are doubtless better informed about psychotherapy than most applicants; yet this abstract knowledge does not guarantee that the student and the counselor will be on the same wavelength. Familiarity with definitions is probably less important than the client's specific expectations, wishes, and fears, on the one hand, and the counselor's ways of implementing his own conception of therapy, on the other. If these two sets of personal assumptions clash and their disparity is not reduced by clarification, counseling is off to a poor start—or to no start at all. The client and the counselor do not have to belong to different social classes or subcultures in order to find themselves at a standstill; they will do so, for example, if a student who is paralyzed by indecision meets with a counselor who believes that he is failing on the job if he as much as tries to help the client get started. That is not a fictitious example. An astonishing number of therapists—not all of them beginners—seem to adhere to this creed, but it is an exceptional student who is satisfied to talk *at*, rather than *with*, his counselor. Here

is the testimony of a student who did *not* fall victim to this disparity
of initial assumptions:

> I came with a strong need to work on a problem which
> I was not capable of solving myself. My first sessions I thought
> to be highly impersonal. There was a minimum of questioning
> and commenting; I did almost all the talking. The "silent
> listener" annoyed me very much; I had hoped to find someone
> who would take a more open interest in me. However, after a
> few sessions there was a change marked by greater communica-
> tion. I too was doing some listening now, and I believed that my
> counselor was interested, although by no means overwhelmingly
> so. . . . Had I not the determination and the belief that, in the
> end, counseling would help me, I might have left because of the
> alienation I felt in my early sessions. I overcame this, and in the
> end I believe it did not harm me. It might have harmed some-
> one who was in a greater need of a human being taking interest
> in helping him.

Since so many of the dropouts—even among the talkative
college students—drop out silently, the vocal minority may be speaking for many others when they spell out their criticism of the counselor's initial approach. Often a student remains *puzzled about what
counseling is,* how it proceeds, and what it does; he may also misinterpret it or view it in some limited way—for example, as catharsis
or as practice in formulating one's problems. He may leave because
he is at a loss or unable to proceed (for example, when the counselor remains silent) or because he does not see how what is going
on in the sessions can be of any use to him:

> When I went to the center I didn't really know what
> was troubling me; I just knew that I felt very unhappy. During
> the sessions themselves, when I would have to speak about what
> was bothering me, I found that I just couldn't, that I had
> nothing specific to say. I think that I wasn't sure enough in my
> own mind of what my problems were (or of why I was un-
> happy) to be able to formulate them clearly enough in a situa-
> tion where I had to keep the ball rolling. Due to this inability
> to express something which I myself couldn't put my finger on,
> and the resultant silent spaces during the hour, I began to

wonder whether I should go to the counseling center at all. I began to think that perhaps I was magnifying my own problems (since when the time came to talk about them they didn't seem to be there in talkable form) and that I should drop the whole thing. Which is what I did after a few sessions at the beginning of the school year. At the present time I feel, as I felt before I went to the center, that I have problems—I am overly tense, nervous, and depressed too much of the time. But I don't know if counseling could help, or if my problems will work themselves out over time.

The informational pamphlet used in the center's early years includes the following "Question" and "Answer":

> Q. Is it all right to come to the center if one has no specific problem but just feels generally dissatisfied or tense and restless?
> A. Yes. Disturbing emotions may manifest themselves in such a state, or even in specific physical symptoms, and in some cases, these are the only manifestations of which the person is aware. One does not have to present a clearly outlined problem to seek counseling help.

Thus, we invited students in the position of the girl quoted above to give counseling a try. Such an invitation implies a promise that the counselor will help students overcome this obstacle, perhaps by making it the first focus of their exploration. By not having—or by losing—her problems "in talkable form," was this girl telling the counselor that she had nothing she could call her own, not even problems? That she could contribute nothing of value to the enterprise? That she would take no chances on giving an opinion or making a claim on someone's interest and help? Whatever it was, the counselor did not fulfill the promise implicit in his acceptance of the student for counseling and did not help her toward greater clarity. Yet she, rather than questioning the counselor's performance, questioned her own fairly obvious need for help and abandoned the attempt in a spirit of doubt and resignation, without any other prospects in sight.

My guess is that failure to get counseling started is not only

the most frequently voiced complaint but also the most frequent
cause of students' dropping out early, and that this complaint points
to an important gap in our training of counselors. Psychological
counseling is different from similar situations that most people are
familiar with, such as advice given by authority or a shared discussion of personal problems by friends. It is hard to understand why a
counselor should expect a novice, even an intelligent college student,
to catch on, unaided, to the nature and the rationale of this new
situation.

Another group of complaints indicates that the counselor's
behavior, expression, and comments make him appear *incompetent*
to the student, lacking in understanding or self-confidence or both.
He may sound like a textbook; misunderstand or fail to understand
what the student is saying; seem jittery; laugh inappropriately; appear propitiative or, when the student discloses the extent of his
disturbance, overeager to refer him out. "When I told X my symptoms, he dropped me like a hot potato"; "Y seemed inexperienced,
puzzled by what I was telling her; I did not feel she knew how to
help me"; "He told me he would treat me as a mature person, but
he did not sound convincing, he just wanted to placate me"; "I
wondered if his deadpan expression was a cover for anxiety."

One particular variant of this complaint, not always easily
unearthed, deserves a detailed discussion. A counselor may give an
impression of incompetence when he fails to appreciate the extent
of the student's disturbance and tells him that he has no reason to
worry; that, considering his age and his situation, he is indeed doing
very well: "The counselor was very complimentary, blaming all my
troubles on my mother's actions; I was pleased to hear it, but deep
down I knew he missed the boat—I was far from blameless." Admittedly, certain clients—most notably, those who have developed
an extreme form of "vicarious living" adjustment—are easily misunderstood even by experienced, perceptive counselors. In trying to
fill their inner emptiness by other people's approving responses,
these clients have become extremely sensitive to the implicit wishes
of others and can convincingly deliver a reasonable facsimile of
whatever is wished for, be it conventional adjustment or unham-
pered free associations.

In one astonishing case, a competent analytically oriented

counselor, after seeing a confused girl through her freshman year, pronounced her a volatile adolescent but certainly not a neurotic. Essentially, the girl had flirted with the counselor, giving him plentiful material for analytical interpretations and acting in turn fascinated and horrified by them; she was gratified by his favorable opinion of her and felt she had learned a great deal from him. But when a year later she again looked for help—an attractive, outgoing, vivacious girl successful in her studies and with her male and female friends—and was told by a different counselor that nothing much was the matter with her, she was not reassured; she had tried many roles over the years but was still tense and miserable. She came back the next year, asking for a different counselor, and I worked with her for the rest of her senior year. Though intelligent and insightful, Debbie steadfastly held on to her identification with some set of social expectations. She was able and willing to change her reference group and eager to learn *my* set of rules, but she could no more conceive of discovering and developing her own feelings and preferences than (she said) a muffin could be baked without a form. When I started challenging this view in earnest, not merely in words but by behaving not "the way a therapist is supposed to," Debbie suffered acute anxiety, as if all her props were falling away. Following several such episodes, her perspective widened, and some slight hope for personal existence was born. She decided to continue therapy. After her graduation I referred Debbie to a gifted therapist, concerned and patient, with whom over the years she has been slowly making progress, reluctantly giving up her belief that salvation lies in living through another.

I have run into few cases as extreme as this one, but they may be more frequent than we assume. The strength of this pattern becomes obvious only through a long-term follow-up, usually missing. If some typical features of the pattern of vicarious living are combined with extreme anxiety about any dislodging of the "false front"—in fact, about any prospect of appearing less than perfect— they present a serious obstacle to movement. Greater attention to the student's inner states (as different from attainments) and a greater readiness to suspend judgment would prevent "misdiagnosis" in such cases. A sensitive counselor—one who is aware of some clients' fear that their problems, like themselves, are unimportant—will keep his initial opinion of a student's problem to himself. Most students who approach the center for help do not look or ask for an explicit diagnostic pronouncement, and hopefulness can be conveyed in other ways. I feel—and tell the student—that if the "problem" is large enough to disturb him or to detract from his satisfaction with life, it is large enough to work on. Only in the course of this work can both of us discover just how large or how small it is.

Optimistic misinterpretations by the counselor are neither the most frequent causes of early termination nor the most upsetting ones for the students. Many more bitter complaints are made about the counselors' negative comments, those felt to be *derogatory and/or pessimistic:* "He seemed pompous to me." "He kept smiling, but his comments seemed vaguely hostile." "X talked in a condescending fashion." "Y does not seem to credit Brandeis students with any intelligence." "At our first meeting, not knowing anything about me, Z presumed to tell me everything that was wrong with me." "She quickly dismissed me, telling me I could come back if I started feeling worse." Implicitly or explicitly, the counselor is accused of being, or at least acting, insensitive, arrogant, unconcerned—not the kind of person who inspires trust. Very often, the core of the student's experience is a personal hurt, sometimes openly expressed: "I left feeling hurt and indignant." "I felt humiliated by his sarcastic laughter." "I was made to feel I was a pathological case, and nothing more." "You know the way shrinks can say things. I was depressed, he called it 'regressed to childhood'—it sounds derogatory, untactful; perhaps it was true, but said in this way it hurt me."

The personal hurt is somewhat allayed if the student views the derogation as undeserved, ascribing it less to his own shortcomings than to the counselor's negative attitudes, personal or professional. Still, in the vulnerable situation of seeking help, the fear that the counselor may be right when he is seeing or expecting the worst is never far away, even if the student has some awareness of the professional jargon, on the one hand, and of his own selective perception, on the other: "In talking to my parents X called my overeating self-destructive and they thought he meant suicide; they would not let me out of their sight, and this made me very uneasy." "When Y said that what had upset me in his remarks had been reassuring to other patients, I realized he was apologizing for his mistake, but I also felt he implied that my reaction was pathological and that I was sicker than most."

A student who has an extremely negative self-image and has developed no adequate protections against assaults will refer the counselor's pessimism to himself only: "He does not expect much of *me*." Thus, the counselor's comments may confirm the client's worst fears. The student then may make use of the simplest self-protective device available to him and avoid the person who has made him feel this way. Many of those who dropped out for this reason did not communicate their experiences to the center directly; in several cases we learned from the student's friends why he would not go near the center after his first meeting with the counselor. As one would expect, there are many among those taking flight who need help badly; paradoxically, some of them are prevented from getting it by the counselor's very efforts to acknowledge this need and to meet it by effecting a quick referral. Here, as in many other situations, urgency and hurry are apt to produce effects diametrically opposed to those aimed at.

My experience with Grace, a senior who dropped out of counseling after only a few sessions, provides a first-hand illustration of our failure to retain a student who clearly needed help. Grace decided to give the center a try in her last term, mainly because of her frightening nightmares and various specific fears: of the dark, of being confined in small places. She was often homesick, did not get along as well with her peers as with adults, had no boy friends, and was indecisive about her postgraduation plans—in particular, whether to stay in her home town or to move out. About her family she said, "They are wonderful, but I always quarrel with them when I am at home." Grace enumerated her complaints cheerfully, partly humorously, as good jokes, and in conclusion stated that overall she was a well-balanced person. I asked her whether her complaints were so minor that she doubted the value of working on them. She replied that her fears were quite handicapping, and we agreed on the hour of the weekly meeting.

In retrospect, I can see that I should have taken Grace's initial reservations more seriously and have looked for discussion topics not too threatening to her self-esteem. Perhaps the problem (shared by many seniors) of her postgraduation plans would have offered both of us the chance to relax and to get acquainted. But, misled by the ease with which Grace, from the start, produced "relevant material," with insights almost there, I felt that failure to deal with these offerings would mean siding with Grace's tentative denial of her need for help. My often-confirmed belief that the most convincing dichotomies are usually false did not in this case help me steer a safe course between frightening the girl and falsely reassuring her. Putting it in positive terms, I should have looked for a way acceptable to the student of speaking, from the start, both to her health and to her neurotic assumptions. I might, for example, have acknowledged explicitly the richness of Grace's observations and their potential relevance to many important personal issues, some of them more bothersome than others, and then invited her to help me make the necessary selection of a problem that might be easiest to approach; or I might have found some other way to slow down Grace's "confessions" while offering her a measure of control of the new, somewhat threatening situation. Instead, I promptly embarked on "uncovering" and "interpreting" the pattern of her difficulties.

This at first worked astonishingly well—actually too well, considering all the circumstances. In the second session, after telling me that her parents were perfect and speaking warmly of their many admirable qualities, Grace poured out a stream of complaints against them and then convincingly described the current handicapping effects of her own attitudes as a "good," self-effacing child. As she was talking, I thought of the cases of those students who, after expressing too soon or too strongly their negative feelings about their parents, had a hard time dealing with the sequel of increased guilt feelings. I made an attempt to forestall this crisis, but it was not thought out too well. On hearing that Grace's mother was startled by the thought that her daughter might talk to me about her, I asked Grace if she was not making things more difficult for herself by reporting the sessions to her mother. I found out later that Grace, not unnaturally, took this as a statement of a rule forbidding her to discuss sessions. Thus, my intervention, instead of lightening Grace's conflict, increased it by making me and her mother competitors for her loyalty, each one seemingly demanding secrecy for the relationship.

Still, in this session Grace was undisturbed and continued to talk insightfully about herself and her family. Much of what I contributed she seemed to accept as neither strange nor shocking, perhaps as thoughts that she had not quite dared to spell out but was relieved to hear from another. I even risked implying the idea of unconscious motivation—which I am not usually in a hurry to do—by suggesting that some of Grace's seemingly irrational behavior might have served as a means of surreptitiously fighting her mother. At the same time, I tried to counteract the potentially negative effects of such interpretations by putting this fight itself into a wider perspective—suggesting that, in the early situations Grace was describing, it was natural for the child to try to make herself childishly "perfect" but that her present strong wish to come into her own, to discover her own vital feelings and values, made the struggle against her mother and her mother's expectations unavoidable. In the course of this session Grace dropped her original light, jocose tone; her expressions fitted her topics. I felt that there was genuine collaboration between us and that together we had covered a lot of ground, as if the content of a month of fast-moving sessions had been telescoped into one. I had no doubt that Grace was now "in."

A week later Grace told me that she had felt fine during the session but had become depressed later on. After having talked the way she did, she felt worse about herself, but mostly she was afraid that she had misrepresented her mother, making her seem much worse than she was. I met these typical fears—as I often do—by pointing out that Grace's present resentments did not in my eyes invalidate her affection for her family and that I never take a partial picture of the parents for the total, which emerges only gradually. Grace seemed to accept this. She proceeded to describe her frustrating relationships with her contemporaries, against whose assets and achievements she constantly measured her own and with whose opinions of her she was greatly preoccupied; she brought a wealth of illustrative episodes. Grace expressed no strong feelings, but most of her stories implied discouragement and/or self-derogation, and I repeatedly pointed out that she was overcritical of herself and possibly discouraged about counseling. I also tried to make the most of the few episodes which indicated that Grace's social behavior was much more natural and appropriate when she was less anxious, more at her ease. But in this session, unlike the preceding one, my comments made no impact and produced no relaxation; Grace failed to make use of the viewpoints I was trying to provide to help her sort out the overabundant "material" she was producing, and with which I could barely keep up. This hour left us both breathless.

It proved to be our last working session, though I saw Grace briefly the following week, when she came in to make the next appointment. There was some confusion about schedules after the period between terms, and she failed to appear for her appointment or to contact me later. After awhile I wrote her a note saying that I assumed she had decided against having counseling now but that she would be welcome if she wanted to return toward the end of the school year—for instance, to discuss her plans for the next year. Grace did not respond to this note, but she did respond to the questionnaire she received a few weeks later. In it she marked her counseling experience as "helpful," expressed some confusion about which of us had terminated the contact, then wrote as follows:

> I found myself analyzing every move I made, and it made me very uncomfortable as well as suspicious of myself. Instead of becoming happier with myself, I was becoming more and more critical. This frightened me. I was insecure enough before I decided to go to counseling, and I was upset to see that I was more insecure after a few visits. I honestly feel that I should have continued, but I lacked the courage to do so. More than anything else, I think I was afraid to find an untold number of things I dislike about myself and the people that are close to me. It was easier for me to go back to things the way they were. I felt that I was probing in a manner that was unfair to myself and my family. I was looking only at what I thought to be the bad things. Finally, I do consider myself to be a normal capable person, and I was beginning to think I was an unstable neurotic. I guess what it comes down to is that I was scared to get too involved with myself.

I believe that this is an honest and essentially correct evaluation, even though, in line with her reluctance to blame others, Grace took care to call her harrowing experience "helpful" and never hinted that her counselor had had a part in leading her to probe in an "unfair" negative way. This case is a reminder that, as one student said in his questionnaire, one may "go too fast, learn too much, and then find that one has opened the Pandora box." A student to whom this happens in the early sessions may leave more upset than he had entered, but this upset is not likely to have lasting effects, except perhaps that of prejudicing him against therapy. A student, however, who does not leave—and thereby exposes himself to a consistently traumatic situation—may be fated to become one of those who tell us later on that counseling has made matters much worse. Respondents who feel that the harmful effects have not been outweighed or mitigated by gains are not numerous, but their testimony merits attention: "Though counseling evoked much thought, it paralyzed action by bringing to the surface paradoxes and contradictions which I was unable to resolve." "The state of being in therapy has become associated with negative parts of myself, with a nonaffirmative depressed outlook on myself and my life." "The problems were adequately illuminated but the treatment was too impersonal; I was driven into deeper misery." I know of students who became seriously depressed in the course of counseling or outside therapy and did not regain their balance until they left, or changed counselors, or succeeded in conveying to the one they were seeing (directly or through a mediator) that he needed to become less interpretive, less critical or impersonal, more reality-oriented, more interactive. If the therapist proves inflexible, and the patient, as is often the case, is not too certain of his stand, the situation may drag and deteriorate. The client may be prevented from leaving not only by his confusion and self-mistrust but by some specific motives as well. One patient left a consistently upsetting and disappointing treatment only after the therapist finally agreed to give her a letter of recommendation that she needed. The moment her prolonged "therapy" came to a close, her persistent depression lifted.

Some descriptions of the therapeutic process suggest that anxiety is required for success and therefore should be fostered by the therapist. Such misleading formulations, it seems to me, may contribute to the production of iatrogenic diseases (disturbances caused by treatment). Anxiety and pain may be unavoidable if therapy is to result in radical changes, but not because anxiety as such is necessary for progress. Basically, the prospect of change—of losing the familiar props of one's functioning, or of one's self-image—is bound to arouse anxiety. To discredit neurosis, the therapist must point out certain things to the patient, *even though* they may make him anxious, not *in order* to make him so; and the therapist must at all times gauge the person's ability to assimilate disturbing discoveries. Anxiety, if it is not to become overwhelming, must be counteracted by the patient's growing self-confidence. Arousal of hope for better things, demonstration of viable alternatives is needed to energize the patient's efforts to get out of his blind alley.

Sometimes such encouragement must be provided before a student who feels discouraged and vulnerable will even risk exposure to counseling. This proved true in the case of Susan, who in some respects was similar to Grace but was looking back on a much more distressing childhood. In trying to start counseling with me in her sophomore year, she vividly described her disturbed parents, whose years of strife had recently culminated in divorce, and her own pervasive emotional problems. For several months in her freshman year, she had seen a silent psychiatrist, whom she had left when she found out that delving into the past and exploring the negative aspects of her present life made her feel worse, not better. She was so eager to leave all this misery behind that in the course of four sessions I was unable to overcome her reluctance to get involved in counseling, even though our relationship was good and I did not feel then or later that I had made any major mistakes.

Susan did use the sessions to discuss a limited but urgent problem—her wish to leave school—caused in part by a dislike of her major; she solved this problem by changing the major. After that, she acted on her decision to exchange counseling for some guided group work available on campus; this group work was designed to cultivate positive attitudes without dwelling on the negative ones. She found the exercises taught there to be of real if limited value, and she kept in touch with me through occasional visits, feeling that this contact helped keep alive her awareness of her personal problems. In her senior year Susan told me that the self-confidence she had gained through her social and academic successes now gave her courage to give counseling a try. She did so, worked well, and in the course of ten weeks benefited considerably, in spite of recurrent reluctance. She was aware at termination that much remained to be done and considered resuming therapy at some later time. In the light of this development, Susan's first brief contact with the center is not to be counted as unproductive.

Now and then, one comes across cases where a disturbed student is prevented from entering counseling by forces outside his and the counselor's control. An example is the extreme situation, well known to family therapists, of parents who, though concerned about some of the student's symptoms, are unable or unwilling to modify the interpersonal situation which nourishes and perpetuates them and to start relinquishing their firm hold on their child. In such cases it soon becomes clear, to the student as well as the counselor, that progress in counseling would in truth seriously endanger the student's relations with his parents and the whole family's functioning; a great deal of anxiety is aroused, and the attempt at emancipation via counseling is promptly abandoned.

Apart from these rare cases, the failure of counseling can be profitably viewed as failure of mutual understanding, or failure of communication between client and counselor. Insofar as the student's dropping out is also a communication of sorts, negative brief encounters are important sources of counselor learning. In fact, it was these episodes that first made me realize the value of student feedback and led to the introduction of questionnaires. When students approached me (as the center's director) with requests for a change of counselor, it was usually because the initial sessions had miscarried. I would get the counselor's side of the story and then try to persuade the two parties to discuss their differences face to face. If they were reluctant, I did not insist; but the meetings that did take place often led to a settling of difficulties and a resumption of counseling work. As a result of such experiences, some counselors (myself included) started inviting students to vent current grievances. We were astonished to discover how much was *not* communicated in sessions both by student and counselor concerning the nature of their common enterprise and of their interaction. We were often ignorant of each other's opinions of how well counseling was going, or of what was amiss.

Obviously there are many obstacles to straightforward communication between client and counselor, but most of them are surmountable. My attempts to mediate between hurt students and hurt or puzzled counselors have brought to light some typical misunderstandings that should not be too difficult to correct. Usually, when a counselor defended himself heatedly against the student's allegation that he had hurt him, declaring it to be a fantasy or a distortion, I found on listening closely that what the counselor was disclaiming was the *intention* to hurt. If I were not careful in my response, the counselor might assume that I sided with the student and that I accepted his disclaimer—if at all—only with regard to *conscious* intention, holding his hidden "true" motives suspect. Had this been my meaning, I would have been guilty of the kind of hasty, unfounded interpretation with which students sometimes charge counselors and which can be very destructive indeed. This is a widespread misuse of the concept of unconscious motivation; that is, we act as if our general knowledge that such motivation exists entitles us to dispense with weighing the evidence of its presence, its nature, and its strength in the instance being considered. Actually, more often than not, I accepted the counselor's statement at face value as much as I did the student's. Implementation is not identical with intention, and it was the counselor's behavior that the student was complaining about, not his motives. I would never suggest that unconscious motives were always responsible for faulty implementation of a reasonable intention; I know only too well that it is not always a simple matter to find effective ways of conveying one's meaning to another. As Angyal has pointed out, psychotherapy is to a large extent a special problem in communication. A counselor who keeps this in mind will not get stuck in the unprofitable consideration of blame. Instead, he will give his full attention to the student's explicit or implied complaints and, putting aside his natural impulse to defend himself against seemingly unjust accusations, examine his memory and his records for evidence of what he has said and done that could have been so interpreted by the other. He will not necessarily discover hidden motives, but, by sharing what he *does* find with the student, he can learn how to avoid misunderstandings and how to develop effective ways of communicating in sessions.

10

Uneven Courses
of Counseling

It should be clear by now how tenuous the dividing line is between productive and unproductive courses, even in brief counseling contacts. In longer contacts, some stretches or sessions will be productive; others, barren. The comments of most students show their awareness that their counselors offer them a mixed bag; some of their interventions promote movement, some are useless, some interfere with progress or set students back. Given these mixed offerings and the brevity of the contact, it is not astonishing that many students express a great deal of uncertainty in evaluating the course and the outcome of counseling: "I am still too close to the experience to give a balanced, well-considered appraisal." The changes one notices may be small and perhaps not too useful (as when the new self-assertion is practiced very clumsily); one is afraid that the old ways of behaving will return; one hopes that the work done will bear fruit in the future. Termination may come at an inopportune time: "The incomplete knowledge you have of yourself can make you more insecure than you were in the state of relative ignorance before you began." The perplexity expressed most frequently refers to the value of insight. One has gained insights but has not been able to act on them; one wonders if this is progress, or all the progress that one can expect. Having to evaluate what for many students is essentially unfinished business is a major source of uncertainty; as the allowance of counseling time becomes smaller, the doubtful evaluations increase in number, along with the negative ones. Still, the time limit is not the only factor involved; the evaluation of long periods of therapy may be fully as difficult as that of the short ones.

What balance must the course of counseling (or therapy) achieve to be viewed as on the whole productive, with the positive effects outweighing all negative aspects? Both the results achieved and the factor of time must enter into this computation. If in courses I have categorized as productive the barren stretches had been shorter, if a higher proportion of the counselors' comments had been effective, these students might have fared even better. Some of them might have shifted their neurotic perspectives sooner; those who required a modified approach might have benefited much more if it had been modified earlier or more appropriately; and even the "vigorous growers" might have moved still faster or gotten still further. Only a very disturbed, seriously handicapped person who has been helped radically and durably by therapy is likely to disregard the factor of time and expense in evaluating his treatment, since such an outcome is worth any investment. But if someone whose handicap is not severe spends, say, five years and a large sum of money on intensive therapy and achieves a slight improvement, he will hardly consider the enterprise productive—particularly if he has reason to suspect that the same effect could have been produced in half the time and with less pain by a different therapist, or a different method.

In most cases to be described below, some time-related characteristics of the counseling course made it, in my opinion, essentially unproductive, even if it contained some productive stretches or movements. In one group of cases the course was unproductive—or much less productive than it might have been—because the counselor's intentions were poorly fitted to the particular

stage the student was in—either in his course in school or in counseling itself. In the second group the counselor, after an auspicious
beginning, made a serious mistake which prevented further progress
and undermined what had already been achieved. The two categories
overlap; the fault of most faulty interventions is that they do not
fit the client's state, and this lack of fit may often be viewed as the
result of poor timing.

As an example of the first type of course, we can take the
case of a freshman girl who grew panicky in the new environment
and was seen for several weeks by one of the center's counselors,
a gifted beginner. The counselor, in his evaluation of the sessions,
was pleased with the outcome and rated the progress made as
"good." The student, on the other hand, checked the "cannot
decide" category of the questionnaire and explained her reason in
her comments. In her view, the counselor, in trying to do more than
she was bargaining for at the time, failed to do what was appropriate in the situation. Her report follows:

I came to counseling because, as a freshman, I was
terribly frightened of being totally on my own. I feared that I
was incapable of making any decisions and of acquiring new
friends. I had grown up in a relatively small and secure community and feared that I wouldn't find my "niche" here at
Brandeis. The result was a terribly panicky feeling which X
helped by being a temporary stronghold of support while I
floundered about. In that sense, counseling was beneficial. However, I wonder if in my particular case I wouldn't have been
better off to be simply told, firmly, that I *could* cope with
things—I just needed time. Instead I went through a crisis of
looking for all sorts of reasons in my past for why I was so
upset. The questions that counseling seemed to bring up got
me so confused and upset that I withdrew into myself and was
blinded to opportunities that arose to settle myself in my new
environment. I should have been encouraged to spend time
doing things rather than worrying about my past.

I think a freshman who is afraid that she will never
"belong" should not be given doubts about her past to worry
about at the same time—even if her past *is* the cause of her
fears and doubts. Maybe these things should be glossed over at
that time so that she could cope with the present. Then, later,

once the initial panic has calmed, if it is still necessary, those doubts should be reexamined more carefully.

As it was, I stopped counseling not because counseling had helped—something else did. During intervals when I had no counseling (such as vacations) I "forgot" myself and became involved with outside experiences enough to see that there really was nothing to stop me from getting used to things.

Some may feel inclined to disagree with this girl's conclusion, assuming that the explorations which increased her upset ultimately led to improvement, but it is entirely possible that her judgment was correct. The counselor—whom the student described, appreciatively, as "kind and eager to listen, offering a place to turn to"—might have quickly reduced her anxiety if he had dealt mainly with the means of coping with her "freshman panic" and had not added to it by inducing or encouraging the untimely "explorations in depth." Since this kind of exploration can be very productive in some crises, the counselor may be tempted to seize what seems to him a good opportunity for it. But to push for the "deeper work" when the student is faced with urgent adjustment tasks and/or resists this push strongly is not an economical way of working, not only from the point of view of the service but also from that of the clients. The student's energies can be better employed than in digging up problems that are not problems for him at the time. The counselor's task with most freshmen is to help them settle down to life in the new environment and to bring the "modified" contact to a speedy termination. It is not his task to prove to a student that he will be badly off unless he gets more help than he now thinks he needs. That may not be true—and, if it is true, life itself will prove it much more convincingly. Pushing for a premature recognition of this "truth" can be destructive; I have known students plunged into a prolonged depression by a counselor eager to effect a referral. However, many of those students who as freshmen were helped back on their feet by a brief contact with the center returned as sophomores, juniors, or seniors—after their self-respect has been restored and strengthened by success achieved in school—for a period of more substantial work. Counseling distributed over several periods during the college years benefits from the student's progressing maturation; it can be uncommonly productive. None of this, of course, is as cut and dried as it may sound, and the best course to take is not always obvious. The student himself may be in conflict about what he wants from counseling, and his statements cannot always be taken at face value; still, it is up to the counselor to see that some effective agreement is reached by the two of them about the course that seems most promising at the time.

The case of the freshman demonstrates one kind of discrepancy between the counselor's intention or perception and the client's needs at the time. Another less frequent and less obvious one can be best illustrated by the experience one student had in outside therapy. This gifted, highly intelligent, sophomore girl, Annie, had entered Brandeis at sixteen and had convinced both herself and those close to her that she was advanced far beyond her age, not only academically but in general maturity and sophistication as well. When in counseling she became aware of the frightened child hiding behind these pretensions, she made her parents take notice of her disturbed state by making a suicidal gesture. They were shocked into agreeing to Annie's wish to take a leave of absence from school and use it for intensive therapy. Therapy worked, and Annie returned to school a year later; during her senior year she had a few counseling sessions, both with her old counselor and with a new one. In the questionnaire she filled out at the end of the year, she viewed her counseling in the extended perspective provided by her experience of therapy. She wrote as follows:

> With the outside psychiatrist I was first and foremost a patient. When I was first referred to him I was pretty disturbed and felt a patient all right. For months we worked on my neurotic hang-ups; he was supportive and it was very helpful. But as I started getting stronger, and was looking for new ways to be and act, I found that my therapist and I were no longer on the same wavelength; he seemed unable to see the changes in me and kept interpreting all my novel actions merely as disguised instances of my old neurotic ways. It was a real setback, but luckily I was able to see more and more clearly that he was wrong; so I stopped seeing him.

Angyal has emphasized that the therapist must be alert to new developments in the client, particularly at the stage when new, nonneurotic ways of feeling and acting make their first tentative appearance. If they are not recognized at this time but, instead, are treated by the therapist as merely new variants of the old neurotic attitudes, their chance to grow and develop may be greatly limited. Failure of the therapist to keep abreast of the client's development can be a strong factor in making a counseling course unproductive, particularly because—like many a counselor error—it tends to remain hidden. The patient is rarely in a position to realize that this time he has been misread by the usually perceptive counselor. Therefore, this error probably is much more common than one would assume from its infrequent mention.

Let us now turn to the instances where a counselor's mistake—or series of mistakes—creates an impediment to movement and turns the potentially productive course into an essentially unproductive one. The first example is taken from the experience of a colleague (Bader, 1974), who quoted it in discussing the issue of responsibility for therapy.

> A major therapeutic failure was needed to make the issue of counselor responsibility come fully alive for me. A senior girl, whose problems were not out of the ordinary, seemed alive and active during the initial stages of counseling, but later lapsed into a mechanical way of talking; our interchanges lacked vitality and the sessions went downhill. My efforts to understand the situation failed completely, and counseling was terminated by the student when we both were hopelessly frustrated. In her questionnaire comments the student gave the following description of one particular intervention of mine, after which the situation was apparently past mending.
>
>> I started the year being very optimistic about both counseling and my counselor. I perceived X as someone easy to communicate with and be as honest as I could; I liked him and still do. The way we talked of my problems was in several respects new to me; the sessions were enlightening, so I hoped that I would feel something new soon. This did not happen, so in the middle of the term I found I was losing faith in both counseling and my counselor. I told X that counseling hadn't helped me to change. He said I did not want to change, otherwise I would have

with the help of counseling. That meant the fault was only with me. Once this accusation was made to me, I felt that if he would continue to deal with me with that assumption, future sessions would be pretty well near meaningless. Admittedly I sort of preferred to think I would "be changed" as a result of therapy to thinking I would have to change myself. To say it now more accurately I hoped that therapy would help me to change myself, but I lost hope after that interchange.

This report made strikingly clear to me the destructive effect of blaming a client for the failure of therapy. In doing so, one aims a crushing blow at his already diminished sense of hope, and unjustly adds to his burden of shame and guilt about his continued inability to help himself. The student's protest against this mistreatment—which she had dared voice only in writing—made me understand fully the meaning of Kaiser's (1955) statements about all responsibility for the outcome being the therapist's. To make the client feel blamed for what the therapist views as unconscious resistance is an effective way to undermine his hope and his trust.

The case just described made both of us aware of how important it is to inquire about the student's reaction to one's various interventions, not just at the end of the counseling period but all along the way. If the counselor had been in the habit of frequently asking for the student's response to the last session, or trying to pick up various loose ends, he might have been able to reverse the downhill direction that the therapeutic situation had taken. Another method the counselor can use to spot his mistakes, his dysfunctional comments, is to keep a record of his main interventions. Those whose interest is focused almost exclusively on the client's personal dynamics are not likely to use this method; nor are those who feel that their intuition insures the rightness of all their responses. I believe, however, that anyone who keeps a complete record finds it extremely useful when a review of the past course is needed. On several occasions, when faced with the fact that my communication with a client had worsened, I was able to identify from my notes the time when this deterioration had set in and the concomitant circumstances possibly responsible for it. These circumstances are not limited to the counselor's comments or the client's interpretation of them; students may have other weighty reasons for withholding information and resuming their initial reserve. In the center's early years, for example, I was first alerted to the existence of hidden loopholes in our confidentiality policies when some students unaccountably fell silent at certain stages of counseling.

In the case to be described next, my detailed notes have enabled me, in retrospect, to trace the events that made counseling take a turn for the worse, after a good beginning. Once I had gained some distance and perspective, my mistakes were not hard to spot, but by then it was too late to correct them, or so it seemed to me at the time. My dawning insight enabled me only to patch matters up to some small degree and was not of lasting benefit to the student.

Frank, a native of a southern state, came to the center at the beginning of his junior year. He was suffering from acute anxiety and plagued by obsessive thoughts about various dangers to his health and his life. As became obvious later, there had been some traumatic, confusion-fostering factors in his early and later childhood, and he was intent on getting the maximum possible "positive feedback" to balance the early negative one. He had been trying hard to please his parents and his teachers by "doing his best" and "doing what is right." Though indecisive and often mildly depressed, he had been fairly comfortable in the familiar surroundings of his southern home. Being admitted to Brandeis was a feather in his cap; but in the new environment—which he found cold and uncongenial—his anxiety level rose, and symptoms began to proliferate. Still feeling a stranger and a misfit here, he longed to return to his home state; in one of the early sessions he mentioned this possibility in passing. It did not, however, become clear to me at the time that he had already applied to his home university for the spring term and was likely to transfer if accepted. When I started working with Frank, I counted on being able to see him for the whole school year if necessary—and I believed that it would be necessary if more was to be achieved than the relief of acute symptoms. When a few weeks later the issue of transfer came to a head, it took me by surprise, and I handled it poorly.

Paradoxically, part of the trouble was that by that time Frank was further ahead than, given the intensity of his symptoms,

I had expected him to be. His initial panic quickly subsided, and we were able to move to a tentative identification of the personal attitudes that had contributed to it. Frank responded to my pointing out again and again how the tension generated by his desperate wish to succeed actually interfered with his functioning. He started wondering why he could not accept being just adequate in at least some of his pursuits and why he was finding it so difficult, almost impossible, to choose one course of study or one field of work. In looking for possible causes, he brought up some pertinent early memories and tackled the general issue of trust and mistrust. He then displayed increased trust by describing some tabooed activities and fantasies of his childhood.

These four or five weeks of productive work culminated in his reporting of a dream—a recurrent dream of long standing and a powerful representation of the noncommittal person's basic dilemma. Frank is imprisoned in a gloomy cave (which he later equated with his present existence—his depressions, compulsions, and panics). The only exit is a heavy trapdoor. He knows that it will open, but only once; he does not know when and for how long. When it lifts, he might be able to escape into fresh air and sunlight; but, in taking this once-in-a-lifetime chance to gain freedom, he might be crushed to death by the door's falling on him. If this unpredictable door was for Frank the prototype of all situations demanding decisions from him, small wonder that he could neither choose nor reject any course of action. Any course taken might be either his only chance to escape the "living-death" cave or his final undoing; there was no way to foretell.

In the session following the report of the dream, Frank was relaxed and cheerful and admitted improvements at which he had only hinted so far. He was now able to catch himself behaving with people in ways that made them reject him—and was sometimes able to change this behavior. He was enjoying his courses, getting interested in new fields, accepting B's with equanimity. He said humorously that he had given up being a superman right now, though he still had hopes for tomorrow. Everything seemed lighter, he said; perhaps we were making progress. To understand what followed, it is important to note that while this obvious improvement enabled Frank to hope that he had been "cured," it increased my wish to see him reach the stage where he could either go on by himself or be willing to seek further therapy.

Two weeks passed between this session and the next. A pleasant Thanksgiving spent with relatives stimulated Frank's reminiscences and self-observations; it also increased his wish for a supportive structured environment. As the time of decision about transferring drew near, Frank started questioning the promise and value of counseling. Lately he had enjoyed coming, he said, but didn't this mean that we were *not* making progress? Aren't upsets a condition of success in therapy? There may not be enough time for us to get results, and how can exploration of origins help anyway? All he needed was security, and this he could best get at home, in the South, if the state university would admit him.

Taken aback by the prospect of a termination I viewed as premature, I failed to be of use to Frank in the choice he was preparing to make. I should have tried to reduce his confusion by formulating clearly the conflict he was experiencing. That is, I should have acknowledged the reality factors that were making the choice difficult; and, at the same time, I should have related Frank's excessive anxiety to his fantasy that this was a life-and-death issue, with a terrible penalty to be paid for the "wrong" choice—his dream offered an excellent handle for that. In reducing Frank's confusion and anxiety, this wider perspective might have enabled him to abandon his either-or thinking in favor of an attempt at realistic problem solving. Since therapy, after all, could be obtained elsewhere, the benefits accruing from it might be combined with the advantages presented by a better environment. My failure to assist Frank by a sympathetic and impartial clarification of his conflict can only be explained by my not having been in truth impartial; my covert wish to get greater returns from my investment in his treatment prevented me from genuinely giving him the freedom of choice that I knew he should have. My resulting ambiguous behavior could only add to Frank's confusion and so endanger the very goals I was envisaging in wishing for more time with him. If the counselor stages a hidden fight with the client, all his statements, no matter how correct or how reasonable, turn into weapons of attack; the client's frantic search for some means to dispel his growing confusion disrupts communication still further.

That is what happened to Frank and me in the prevacation session devoted to sorting out the advantages and disadvantages of transferring. While pretending objectivity, I was acting as a "secret persuader." Frank's agitation grew; he desperately tried to get me to say something that would make the conflict disappear: that the improvement he had achieved would last, that a better environment was all that he needed. My failure to confirm these hopes threw him into a panic. He tried to put an end to the pain of uncertainty by "deciding" then and there that if accepted by the school he would go. This device failed to calm him; a decision against me must have made the misgivings I had earlier voiced turn into terrible threats. Frank was overcome with dread. On the day that followed this session and preceded his leaving for Christmas, he repeatedly appeared at my office, now insisting that I tell him whether he should immediately resume therapy at home or look for a better school environment; now imploring me to let him know just how long the improvement must last before he could be certain that he was "cured." My attempts to respond to his queries in terms other than the ones he was using proved very confusing to Frank; he felt that his quest for certainty was not being understood. But when I said that he acted as if getting something from me before leaving was his last chance to obtain help, he relaxed and reproached me, simply and directly, for the impatience I failed to suppress at his third reappearance in my office. I expressed regret about having forgotten for a moment how anxious he was and how anxiety feels. He replied that I too was human; he would try to spare me further questions and requests. This concluding interchange was open, different from all that preceded. The student did not reappear; and the next day he left for home.

During the vacation (which lasted for a month), Frank was accepted by a good school not too far from his home and decided to transfer. In the first of the two last sessions we had, he reported being at peace about this decision. His only problem now was the feeling that something was seriously wrong with him. By refusing to give him a clean bill of health, he said, I had confirmed him in this feeling, particularly since I had used the term *neurotic* when talking about the likely length of his therapy. Frank spoke on, tensely, seemingly intent on reopening these issues. But a glance at his face stopped me from getting involved in an argument about whether his problems were "the same as everybody's"; I asked him instead what he was feeling right then. He admitted feeling mistrustful of me—not of my intentions, he hastened to add, but of my competence; he doubted that I knew what was good for him, and he felt that this doubt would insult me.

For a moment I did feel insulted, but this very confirmation of the correctness of Frank's guess led to some dim recognition that I had indeed repeatedly failed to do what would have been good for him. Unable at the moment to put my finger on just what had been wrong, I told Frank that I was trying to think through how his prevacation upset could have been kept within limits and its bad effects avoided; I was sorry I had not made clear to him from the start that one could not expect to achieve too much in one term. After this admission of a possible mistake, I gave Frank my view of the good beginning we had made, summarizing his gains and their possible uses. I now discussed his possibly resuming therapy some-time, talking in a nonargumentative way which enabled him to take in what I was saying, though its content was no different from what had upset him earlier. In response, Frank described con-vincingly how he had become more self-reliant at home, better able to separate his own views from those of his parents. He had learned something about the circumstances that had early caused him to receive a great deal of "negative feedback" mixed with the positive one. He related the effects of these early experiences, the expectations resulting from them, to his present fears and doubts and his search for certainty and safety. In the last session (to which Frank came only because he did not have time to think about whether he wanted to come) he dwelt again on how badly he had been shaken by my reference to neurosis, though he realized now, he said, that he could not expect the counselor to say what he wanted to hear regardless of her own convictions. We discussed what Frank could do to apply his insights to his everyday life, to counteract anticipations of rejec-tion, to learn to act on probabilities instead of chasing after absolute certainty. In leaving, he thanked me for trying to be of use: "I guess you have done all you could to help me."

Within a year I had three communications from Frank. The first was a reply to my note of inquiry within a few weeks after his transfer. He felt well on the whole and hoped that the problems activated by the alien environment would soon submerge in the old familiar one. "The atmosphere here—the sunshine and the relaxed feeling—give the world a benevolence." In the questionnaire mailed to him a few months later, Frank did not check any of the categories provided, commenting that it was too early to say whether counseling had helped. He felt that he had obtained some understanding of the reasons for his mental habits and of how his thinking patterns got him into ruts. "Considering the brevity of the contact," he wrote, "the most helpful approach seemed to be when we discussed things to do, or orientations to seek which might make coping with problems easier." As to the negative aspects of counseling, it was difficult for him, he said, to separate them from his own disappointments. "I would only say that it is important that both parties understand—initially—how much time is available and how much can be done so that the proper approach can be taken." I last heard from Frank shortly after he had entered therapy.

Although this follow-up suggests some positive results, they were greatly outweighed, I feel, by the effects of my ambiguous behavior, which confirmed Frank in his basic uncertainty, his wavering between trust and mistrust. After having invited and gained a bit of his trust, I dealt with the issue of termination in a way that made me seem indifferent to his well-being and, worse still, looking down on him as sick and abnormal. No wonder he could not tell whether counseling was helpful. For reasons both realistic and fantastic, the client is greatly affected by all attitudes of the therapist, positive and negative, persistent and transitory. It is not enough for the counselor to avoid the repetitive patterns of inconsistency, evasions, defensiveness. A single error, a slip, if undetected and uncorrected, can become a serious obstacle to movement and can even undo what has already been achieved. It is not difficult to see why. If the counselor is caught lying, once is enough. He is proven a liar; his statements—past, present, and future—are not to be trusted; the encouragement one has received from him is null and void. This is a good example of how the past can be changed by later events—if they have changed the person's total perspective and made the past occurrence part of a different Gestalt. Fortunately, the change can take place in the opposite direction as

well: the harm done can be undone. If the counselor catches his
slip and admits it, he usually reaps rich rewards. It is a rare client
who does not feel great relief when his own uncertain perception
of an untoward interaction is validated by the counselor's admission of error. Not only are the bad effects canceled; the counselor
emerges as human, and a good human—trustworthy, if fallible.
Mistakes that can be caught and corrected need not be feared. A
counselor who has repeatedly experienced this sequence of events
becomes less worried about mistakes and, being more relaxed,
usually makes fewer of them. Had I been able, in time, to admit
my preference for Frank's continuing at Brandeis, as well as my
personal reasons for it, both of us would have benefited. My wish
to do a job I could be proud of, once admitted, would have taken
its proper subordinate place and would have been used to get
maximum therapeutic leverage from whatever opportunities our
situation offered: the process of decision, termination, review and
preview. I would have regained my awareness that the outcome of
no course of action can be predicted with certainty. Some choices
will prove good, some bad; but one can never know whether a
particular choice was the best possible one. Luckily, most choices
that have been thought through and found reasonable can be made
to work. From this perspective, I would have been able to promote
clarity instead of confusion.

Frank's case is a demonstration of the bad effects of emphasizing a disturbed client's illness, regardless of what has caused the
counselor to do so. This danger was brought home to me once again
by a student's letter, written after a session in which I had felt called
upon to do some "uncovering" and failed to counteract the fore-
seeable negative effects:

> Our talk of yesterday has been disturbing for me. Some
> things that you have said have confusing effects on me. Let me
> explain. You said I have a serious problem. I am miserable, so
> one could call that serious, and it may be true that my troubles
> and doubts stem from my past and can be resolved; we've been
> through all that before. I do understand it. Yet your words act
> in a strange way on me. I find myself saying—I have a serious
> problem—and then silently adding: and there is nothing I can
> do about it. This problem becomes a weight which I must carry

with me for the rest of my life. It becomes an excuse, in a way, for not being as happy as I can be. . . . When you warn me against believing that leaving for X will cure all my problems, it gets translated into, no matter what you do you will never be happy. But why shouldn't I believe that I can be happier in a different environment? . . . You seem to tell me that at bottom I am confused, while I have felt that at bottom I am really pretty integrated and that if I listen to that deepest part of me I will do what is best. I know I have doubts about Jim, but at bottom I have always believed that I love him and it is this feeling that I stake my actions on. Are you saying that there is no integrated part in me, that all is confusion, that I cannot think positively and must dwell in my misery? All I can say to this is that I have faith in my ability to get through the confusion and to live a full life. I know I am confused often, but I believe that part of me remains constant. Still, while I say all this I am crying. We can discuss this on Thursday.

During the intensely emotional session that followed, I was able to convey to this girl that behind her handicapping confusions I did indeed perceive and value her deepest feelings, her longing to trust and to love, to be whole, to live a full life. A shift of mood followed; she became aware of her pessimistic bias in decoding my earlier messages, and *then* some genetic insights came alive. The incident epitomized by this letter was part of a productive if slow-moving course of counseling. In such a context, a student who has good rapport with his counselor may see even a prolonged disturbance as temporary, as a price he is willing to pay for whatever gains he has made or expects to make: "Counseling may interfere for awhile with the person's daily life because of the struggle he is fighting within himself. Such is the case with me in the present state of my counseling." Students making such comments may express at the same time their reliance on the counselors who have tried to reduce and help manage the disturbance without discontinuing the counseling contact.

11

Persistent Failure of Communication

In the counseling courses discussed in this chapter, factors limiting or counteracting productiveness appeared not merely sporadically but seemed to be present throughout, although their presence did not always spell complete failure. The first example illustrates well a factor that can limit productiveness or even virtually destroy it. This example is contributed by Lawrence Bader (1974), who found with the help of student feedback that much of his success was due to his optimism, his respect for the feelings of others, and the relative ease of his communication with people. However:

> Students occasionally complained that my analysis of their troubles was not sufficiently penetrating, being limited to the outward manifestations of deeper problems. The meaning of this complaint was spelled out in vivid detail by a graduate student who came to counseling because of a mild depression

and a lack of involvement in her work. At the end of the school year, when our contact was terminated, the girl was involved in her studies, was less depressed and more self-confident than before; yet I had an uneasy feeling that these end results were not commensurate with the amount of time, involvement, and effort both of us had contributed. The student's questionnaire report is given below in its entirety.

I had a persistent feeling throughout the year that not enough communication was taking place, or that somehow I had to reshape my remarks, make them more civilized or easier to categorize, before they would actually be heard by the counselor. I felt—and I think this is a very valid point—that the counselor's personality type was radically different from my own, and that this (inevitably) engendered recurrent misunderstandings and verbal abbreviations of things I had felt should be explored in greater depth. I believe that my difficulties are not simple ones, and that too often rather futile simplifications were offered by the counselor. Example: my often profoundly violent impulses were interpreted as "angry thoughts"; the elaborate escapades from which I found it difficult to extricate myself, and my interpretations of them, were referred to as "nice stories." The difference between myself and the counselor was primarily one of depth, and I think in many instances this created a serious breach which the counselor did not appear to see. On the other hand, I think a more positive frame of reference *has* evolved out of these meetings with the counselor and that it definitely has helped. He was not overpassive, and participated in dialogue when necessary. If it were not for the fact that I felt I had to pickle and package an extremely nebulous and difficult psychic maze into the neat space of an hour's "lecture," to polish everything up and make it dainty and clean and palatable for the counselor's sober ear, greater progress might have occurred. As it is, however, I feel very much like a python or Jabberwock who is politely requested to attend a tea, not daring to refuse lest he be denied all congenial company, but obligated to shut up like a box lest his exotic savagery be detected.

On rereading my notes on the sessions with this student, I located several interchanges confirming her observations. She had indeed repeatedly hinted at ways of thinking and feeling which must have been more confusing, contradictory, and frightening than she was able to convey or than I was able to perceive empathically, since I shared neither her pessimism nor her involvement in complexities, a fact which she fully appreciated. This student's eloquent description of the resulting communication gap served to sensitize me to some of the ways of experiencing with which I had little first-hand acquaintance. I hope that I am less likely now to underestimate the intensity of some students' feelings, the strength of their rage or despair.

The situation so beautifully described by this student is not rare or atypical. It is often, however, more damaging to the outcome than it was in this case, where the counselor's genuine friendliness and optimistic outlook clearly outweighed the disadvantages resulting paradoxically from these very same assets. I mentioned in Chapter Nine some instances where disturbed students became discouraged from seeking help because overoptimistic counselors had pronounced them healthy and thriving. Failure to appreciate the depth of a client's disturbance is particularly likely to occur when a student with a strong obsessive-compulsive component in his character is paired with a counselor who lacks personal experience of this dimension of personality or neurosis but is quite at home with some aspects of the hysterical pattern. Some emotional attitudes have a very different meaning within these two contexts, so that, to start with, the counselor whose experience is limited cannot help but misinterpret them. If he views ambivalence, for example, merely as a person's naturally varying response to the mixed bag of good and bad experiences we all get from our parents and from others, without giving due weight to the factor of uncertainty and painful confusion, he will not be reflecting what his noncommittal client is experiencing, even if they are using the same words. He may not be able to deal adequately, for example, with the client's guilt feelings, the impact of which he cannot fathom. If he is reassuring, the client will not feel reassured for long, sensing that he is being reassured on a false basis: "He saw me as an adolescent rebelling against his parents and put himself entirely on my side against them; he did not understand that I myself was divided. There was not just fight but also guilt."

During the period when the low turnover of the center's staff enabled me to know several counselors quite well, I came across enough instances of this particular type of "mismatched counseling" to judge it a fairly frequent occurrence. Open discussion with the counselors involved turned out to be productive, and the student questionnaire comments also proved useful for conveying the message that the counselor's view was at times made faulty by a personal bias. Some counselors benefited from supervisory work focused on this particular issue; others learned to catch themselves at those moments when anxiety threatened to turn their personal assets into liabilities—by expanding their optimism far beyond realistic limits, for example, or making them promise the client, by implication at least, more than they could deliver.

The special case described here does not warrant the conclusion that psychological similarity between client and counselor is always a boon; one can easily visualize situations where similarities of certain kinds can lead to complications. It is up to each individual therapist to discover what client attitudes and what situations are difficult for him to deal with, and for what reason. Such difficult client traits will usually prove to be much more specific than the general patterns of neuroses, which can result in a great variety of behavior.

The disparity of the student's and the counselor's views on the proper conduct of their enterprise can also function as a persistent obstacle to communication and movement, as when students reject the counselors' inactivity or studied impersonality. Occasionally their differences are formulated in the questionnaire comments in theoretical or ideological terms. One older student, a foreigner, who had a none-too-successful experience at the center and who had talked at length to several friends in long-term therapies, arrived at the conclusion that "psychiatry often perpetuates or worsens the sickness it attempts to cure by reducing the 'patient' to the status of an object, making him see his own experience as an isolated phenomenon, which is to be explained by reference to a theoretical system which the psychiatrist but not the patient is in possession of." In his long postcounseling letter, this man noted that psychodynamic theory and therapy fail to give due weight to reality factors—in particular, to the multiple connections between the individual and his social environment, connections reflected in the therapeutic situation itself. In his view, the main obstacle to effective therapy is the "basically authoritarian" relationship between therapist and patient. Whenever he raised these issues in the sessions, however, he felt that his counselor became defensive:

> At least he always treated the questions as part of my psychological "problem," as examples of how I distort things (transfer, project, etc). He avoided treating them as realistic questions, not confined to my mind. On a trivial level this seems to me to typify the dehumanization of a "patient" in therapy: the validity of his ideas, perceptions, feelings, and so forth, is preempted, declared questionable, whereas the validity of the psychiatrist's assumptions is taken as absolute. The patient has to get his "wrong," "distorted" consciousness in line with that of the psychiatrist. His ideas and experience are only in his sick head, whereas those in the psychiatrist's head are universal human truths. This preemption of the patient's humanity is, to me, quite unacceptable, too high a price to pay for any "cure"!

This man has placed his experience within a well-worked-out framework of theory and ideology; in this he is unique among our respondents, most of whom remain close to the personal level. Yet the views he has expressed are not atypical, nor are they limited to the militants who are bent on fighting authority. I have read the letter to the members of a fieldwork course, interested and knowledgeable in the area of mental health work and in many respects quite similar to those students who seek counseling. They responded very strongly and positively to the sentiments expressed by the writer, obviously recognizing in his statements many of their own observations and views. Had these sentiments of the writer been fully expressed by him in the sessions and fully heard by his counselor, counseling might have been more productive than it proved to be in this case.

The next course of counseling demonstrates my own failure to modify my usual approach so as to meet the student's current needs. The causes of this persistent failure will be discussed in some detail because they involve some issues of general importance in the design of therapy.

During Cecily's first tentative visit to the center, she did not seem to me very different from many other freshmen struggling to adapt to their new situation, away from home. I was prepared to start working with her right away, but she chose to postpone counseling and did not come back that year. She reappeared in the fall, now definitely wanting counseling, and gradually disclosed the presence of an acute disturbance, with doubts and self-doubts, anxiety, indecision, and depression. The symptoms had recently become acute but had their roots in a distant past. Cecily proved to be an intelligent, perceptive, articulate girl who was quite accessible to psychological work, but only periodically. Whenever she was responsive and active in sessions, she not only gained insights but also experienced a shift of perspective and mood; she would then start feeling hopeful. After each such episode, however (an occasional one felt like a real breakthrough), she went back to the feeling: "All of this has gone on for so long that it cannot ever change." Except for brief periods, her misery would not subside.

Cecily was casting about for some way to achieve a more lasting improvement. Should she develop new interests, activities and friendships, change her major, change schools, return home, go to Israel, change to a male counselor, transfer to an outside therapist who—unlike myself—could give her all the time she needed, perhaps enter a hospital? I assisted her in exploring these alternatives. Some of the minor new projects paid off, but their good effects did not last; a chance contact with a male counselor did not lead to a transfer—Cecily found him not "firm" enough. Eventually I helped her to contact a well-recommended local psychiatrist, but she found him formal and cold and withdrew after two visits. This fiasco may have played a part in the decision that Cecily and her family reached soon after—namely, to disregard their initial reasons for wanting her to remain at Brandeis, where academically she was doing quite well. During the spring term, therefore, she returned to her midwestern home and entered a local college.

To the end of Cecily's counseling period, apathetic or struggling sessions alternated with reasonably productive ones, which elucidated the shape and the roots of her troubles. She realized that she was learning, but most of the time she was not happy with her counselor. Although I fulfilled as many of her requests as I could—for example, for additional time—she was often angry at me and at other would-be helpers for not doing enough, for not helping effectively. She felt that I was as half-hearted in my efforts as she was in hers. At times she tried, with desperation, to make me see how badly off she was, worse than any student she knew, as if hoping against hope that this realization would make me provide whatever I was withholding. I was puzzled by Cecily's reproaches and by the fact that the acute disturbance persisted. I was putting a great deal of time, thought, and active effort into working with her, and I could find no indication of any serious mistake I had made. Cecily's feeling about something missing was strong, but her complaints were vague. In her calmer moments she herself wondered why she so often felt that I was unconcerned and incompetent, in the face of sufficient evidence to the contrary. She noticed that while I was saying something that was helpful, that made her see more clearly or feel better, I seemed to her concerned and warm; but when my comments did not have such immediate good effects, she had the opposite impression of me, that of indifference and distance: "as if there was no person there, nothing constant underneath."

In the light of this observation of a lack of "object constancy," one might be tempted to assume that Cecily's difficulty in getting along with me was simply part of her own current emotional state and had little to do with my counseling performance. Still, all behavior results from an interrelation of inner and outer factors, even if one of them is more visible. In my experience, persisting difficulties between client and counselor usually have one of their roots in some aspects of their real interaction in the sessions. If the counselor understands the client's communications correctly, tries to meet those of his pressing needs that can be met, and also permits him to test the realities of the relationship, the client's trust gradually grows. Episodes of projecting on the counselor some fantasized roles, though they may occur frequently, do not under these conditions last long; they may function as stepping stones to insights, not only as obstacles.

Shortly before leaving, Cecily found a focus for her complaints: my behavior in our first contact. Two or three months after termination, in a letter she appended to the questionnaire (in which she said she had been helped to understand her problems), Cecily took up this complaint once more. Her letter and my reply follow:

Thank you for your note and interest. I am now seeing a therapist, a woman, Dr. Y, whom I saw once after my freshman year. I am extremely fond of her and feel she will help me very much. I am happy to be home and I am planning to attend a school about fifteen minutes from home to which I will commute. . . . This summer I will be working at the camp which I spoke about to you, and right now I am working as a salesgirl in the sportswear department of a nice store. I am not at all sorry I left Brandeis.

Again I want to thank you for all your time and effort, and at the same time I would like to again disagree with you on the moral responsibility of a therapist. I still feel that had you told me I had deep-rooted problems for which I needed help when I first saw you in my freshman year, you would have saved me a tremendous amount of agony—a year in which my neurotic habits and problems deepened. I went to you, a doctor, for help. I wouldn't have gone if I didn't want help, and instead of encouraging me to cure my illness or informing me of it, you sent me out as blind and unrealistic as I entered your office. You sent me out thinking things might be all right—the doctor I had consulted had given me that impression. And, as a result, the next time I walked into your office I was in much more pain and much less able to help myself than the first, or to be responsive to your help.

I am not intending to blame you for all my problems— believe me, I've learned a lot more about them. And I know you're quite sure I'm being ridiculous, but as my new therapist says, "I am not God. I try my best, but I make mistakes." I, in extending this viewpoint, just wanted to express my feelings and thoughts about this.

Dear Cecily,

Thank you for your letter; I am very glad to hear that you have made good arrangements for the present and good plans for the future, and that you have settled down to work with a therapist whom you like and trust.

I certainly do not think you "ridiculous" for trying to make sense of the events of the past year and to find out how your suffering could have been lessened. You are right on some points. I did underestimate the extent of your disturbance the first time I saw you. I realized it only gradually next year, when you told me more about your early troubles and let me glimpse the intensity of your current depressions and compulsions. I certainly missed the boat in my initial evaluation of your condition.

On the other hand, I am not as certain as you seem to be that if I had seen it more correctly I could have gotten you into therapy earlier and prevented the worst upsets of your freshman year. I say this because of what I repeatedly see happening here. I often do tell students who come to the center to explore their situation, that they do need help and should not waste time in getting it. But not many people act on this advice until they themselves reach this conclusion—usually after having lost hope that their suffering can be permanently assuaged by some other means, e.g., through a personal relationship. And if a person enters therapy on someone else's decision, the going is slow and difficult: you cannot do therapy *to* a patient. But of course I cannot know for sure that this most frequent course of events would have been true in your case, too. Like everybody I do make mistakes. And the responsibility for treatment is certainly the therapist's: though he can do nothing without the patient taking an active part, it is up to him to get the patient involved. If I have omitted doing something that might have been helpful to you I am sorry for that.

In my reply I said what I thought. I was glad that Cecily's specific grievance was attributable to an actual mistake of mine. It was easy to admit the inadequacy of my first view of her, though I could ascribe to this initial error neither the growth of her disturbance nor the difficulties we experienced in our work later. Rather, I felt that Cecily hit upon this particular episode as something more palpable than her other complaints, perhaps a demonstration that from the start something essential was lacking in my treatment of her.

What this something was became clear to Cecily—and convincing to me—through comparison with the approach of her new therapist, who proved better able than I to meet her current needs. Cecily convincingly supported her expression of trust and affection for her new therapist by describing this woman (in her questionnaire comments) as having warmth and intensity and a way of reaching her which she felt I had lacked. I had little doubt on reading this description that it reflected actual differences between the new therapist and me, but the precise cause of these differences was of some practical importance. If the behavior that put me at a disadvantage with Cecily was rooted exclusively in some of my personality traits, there was little to learn from the experience; it would be just another opaque case of counselor and client being somehow mismatched. The counselor's behavior, however, usually reflects also some ideological beliefs, some implicit assumptions about how it is proper, or therapeutic, for a counselor to behave. These assumptions are learned, often in an uncritical fashion; and they can be unlearned or modified when found to be dysfunctional. From this point of view, it was important to know just what attitude of mine had proved frustrating for Cecily and had obstructed communication between us. Cecily was ready with an answer: "I disliked the fact," she wrote, "that X took very little initiative in structuring my therapy, leaving my counseling time mostly to my discretion. I feel X is the doctor, and she could have helped me more if she had assumed this role more often, not only in the structuring of my therapy, but in all of its facets."

The message seems clear enough, but the reason for it was not clear to me at the time, nor did I know what specifically Cecily was missing. By the time of our contact, I had shed my original programmatic passivity, although I may still have been taking some conventions too seriously; I imagine, for instance, that I almost always left the first word to the client. But I was usually quite active in sessions in a variety of ways, and I was certainly active with Cecily. I asked questions, suggested topics, brought back things she had said earlier, offered descriptions and hypotheses. If I did not usually give advice on the choices she was facing, it was simply because of my inability to predict what course of action would be best for her. When I considered my opinions well founded, I did not withhold them, but this was rarely useful; in fact, her requests for specific advice were neither insistent nor frequent. Essentially, in working with Cecily I was trying to meet demands that I did not understand at the time. As a result, she must have felt that I did not understand what state she was in.

I did and did not understand. I thought of Cecily as being acutely disturbed, but not all characteristics of this state were vividly present in my mind. Its exceptional nature and its pervasiveness are not adequately expressed by the term *acute* (as contrasted with *chronic*), nor by a reference to a crisis situation and to specific symptoms. The fact that the person's total state is abnormal, not continuous with his usual experience, is connoted better by the term *nervous breakdown,* which is only used by laymen. Yet one's image may be determined by one's choice of the term. Kaiser, in a fictionalized biography, describes how his hero's life outside the work hours has become problematic, disorganized, and empty and has remained so for the better part of the year. Then a friend who had not seen him for a long time, on having spent part of an evening with him, remarked: "But you are in the midst of a depression, aren't you?"

> If his friend had said: "You have been depressed for quite a long time," he would probably have nodded, feeling that the friend no more than paraphrased what he himself had expressed. But the use of the noun "depression" took him aback. It seemed to throw a completely new light on the state of his mind. He had been tempted to answer immediately: "Oh, no, not at all!" but recognized at once that this was not what he thought. Somewhat sheepishly he had said: "Well, yes, I suppose you are right. I feel in an impasse. I do not see how this can go on and on, and I do not see how to jump out of it" [Kaiser, 1965, p. 17; the friend then suggested analysis].

As Kaiser's example shows, one can slide into an exceptional state gradually and even fail to realize for a long time the magnitude of the change. More typically, the person is only too well aware of the abnormal painful state he is in; he may have been aware of its incubation, sometimes even of the exact moment of the total shift. Yet this puzzling and terrifying experience is not easily revealed and shared. Acute anxiety and real depression are very different from the passing moods to which these terms are also applied.

People who have not experienced them, or who have not read vivid, detailed accounts by those who have, do not understand what the patient is talking about; this failure of communication may confirm his fear that he is losing his mind. The longer the abnormal state lasts, the greater its hold on the patient, who gradually loses hope that it will ever go away. The disturbance that might have been quickly dispelled by a timely discussion of its meaning and causes, and might have become a source of insights, becomes more and more of a trap.

What was missing in my offerings to Cecily was an *explicit acknowledgment* of her state of breakdown and an emphatic reassurance about its outcome. In retrospect, I can see some of the reasons for my failing to make the statement that I knew was needed in such situations. Although it was obvious almost from the start that the girl was disturbed, she revealed the extent of the disturbance only very gradually and in part indirectly. Cecily's initial tendency was to minimize her acute suffering and to try—with a degree of success—to cope with life on a day-to-day basis. She disclosed some of her most painful and handicapping symptoms only toward the end of the counseling period; at that time she also provided me with some information that helped explain her own ambivalence about admitting illness. In the absence of a weighty reason for me to take over, I resisted Cecily's desperate need to have me "do something" (that is, something different from what I was doing in sessions). In terms of the center's policies, "taking over" was reserved for those seriously disturbed students in whose situations their families and the administration had eventually to be involved. I had no difficulty in taking over and managing where it was clearly demanded by the student's situation and state, but Cecily's state did not seem to require any drastic action. Hers was not a psychotic breakdown; her depression seemed neither deep nor continuous. She was able to carry on transactions with her family and to work in courses and in sessions; in terms relevant to our policies she was not "abnormally" disturbed. I failed to consider that to an outside observer the presence of an exceptional state can be effectively disguised by the client's strenuous efforts at suppressing and coping and that the all-important subjective evidence can be withheld in part.

Only once (in a session that took place at an unusual time, in the evening) did Cecily let me glimpse the depth of her misery, her feeling of being utterly helpless and lost. On this occasion, to her great relief, I did feel impelled to take over; I told her "firmly" that she was not to return to her room but to go with me to the infirmary. She stayed there two or three days; the one session conducted in the infirmary was easily the most productive we had. Cecily told me that during this episode I seemed to her to be warm and caring; yet it made no difference for the further course of our interaction. I kept on working with Cecily without declaring a state of emergency, and I tried to meet some of the needs she was voicing in a way that could only add to her frustration. Whatever suggestions I made, I made very tentatively, leaving the decision and the initiation of action to her. This method, which has served me well with most students, saddled Cecily with precisely those functions which in her acute state of anxious indecision she was almost unable to perform. No wonder she was often exasperated about my not being more helpful. For example, she often wished for more time. I told her that she could ask me for additional sessions whenever she felt the need and that I would try to find the time if I could. To her this statement signaled a lack of appreciation of her needs. She told me at the end that she was sick and tired of having to ask, or having to decide whether to ask.

In most instances where the presence of an exceptional state is not made obvious right away, there soon comes a moment when the counselor adds two and two and says to himself "Oh, that is what it is!" and acts accordingly. In Cecily's case my all-too-gradual realization lacked such culmination; the moment of truth never arrived. I did not tell her emphatically that, although she was reluctant to admit it fully, she *was* in an abnormal state, a breakdown—a temporary state, *not* a beginning of insanity and *not* an indication of any dangerous illness or any basic flaw in herself, but very painful and frightening and to be gotten out of as quickly as possible. Let us review all available means. An integrated statement of this kind might not only have allayed Cecily's spiraling anxiety but also given her the much-needed proof of my competence and of my concern. With my more active sponsorship and support, her attempts at self-help would have turned into a common enterprise.

The final arrangements would probably have been the same as those eventually worked out, with Cecily deciding to transfer to a school in her home town and to resume therapy there. But had I not been hampered by remnants of preconceived notions about the value of nondirectiveness, I might have gained more clarity myself, and I might have been more explicit and direct in my dealings with Cecily, thus saving her some unnecessary anguish.

Cecily's case, particularly the feedback she provided, by helping me to overcome some of my either-or thinking in the matter of leaving the client his autonomy, made me more attentive to what was needed and what was feasible at a given time. A few years after my contact with Cecily, I was working with a girl who after a serious suicidal attempt was spending several weeks in the college infirmary. Jeanne was working hard in sessions and was gradually coming out of her state of depression, but she was still far from well, when another member of the center's staff consulted me about her. This counselor was black, as was the student; he visited her frequently and was clearly a constructive influence, but he was pushing Jeanne to be active on her own behalf and was troubled by my failure to do the same. Wasn't I acceding to the girl's neurotic dependency needs? Wouldn't we spoil and infantilize her by not insisting on mature behavior? I was able to make him see my reasons. My goal was the same as his, but in trying to encourage movement in the direction of greater self-reliance we had to observe and consult the person we were working with, to find out what was feasible for her at any given time. If the counselor confidently makes demands which the client cannot possibly fulfill, the outcome is not progress; it is humiliation and discouragement. When plans had to be made for Jeanne which required consulting her family, it became obvious that she could not face them even in writing—yet equally obvious that she had things to say to them. I offered to convey some of her thoughts and wishes in a letter to be written (and signed) by me and checked by her. Jeanne accepted this offer with alacrity; this was what at the time she could manage; she had the control over what was said, and she exercised it. The next letter she wrote herself. She invited first one family member to visit her, then another, and gradually resumed relations with the whole family. If the counselor, in partially taking over for the client, makes clear that this is a temporary device, does not act arbitrarily, and leaves the other as much activity and control as possible, he will be furthering progress by making it manageable, one step at a time.

The issue of dependence touched upon in the cases of Cecily and Jeanne is a common preoccupation of clients and counselors. Counselors most frequently explain and justify their inactivity by saying that they do not want to promote the client's dependence. In the report to be quoted next, the student views the commonly wished-for "personal concern" in a way that throws light on the often-neglected implications of the dependence-independence issue. As often happens, this girl has sharpened her perceptions by comparing her different experiences.

> My reasons for terminating counseling were twofold. One was fear and insecurity (which was also the reason why I had sought help). The fear was that of change, which I felt would have to be radical; it was a conservative reaction to having to accept or to reject some disclosures about myself. I left at the point when I could not "beat around the bush" any more. The other reason was the help I unexpectedly received from a psychology course taught by an excellent teacher where the topics of discussion were very close to my most crucial hang-ups. It was easier for me to accept the insights I gained there because the situation with this professor was more personal than with the center's counselor: I felt he cared particularly about me, or rather he cared about every person in the class in an individual way. Thus there was an element of love in his teaching us the theory of self and of personal growth, and it gave me an incentive for change which involved another, not just changing for my own sake alone. At the center this incentive was missing. My counselor was friendly, not too formal, he asked good questions, but the help was always to be self-help. I got some catharsis by unpacking my heart to a trained impartial listener, but nobody *demanded* anything from me. After the initial misery that brought me there passed, I lacked motivation and strength to go on: I could not be self-motivated because of the fear of change.
>
> The changes that I have noticed in myself—large changes—since my contact with this teacher were due in large part to the *demands he made* upon me. I don't mean he pro-

vided answers for me or told me what to do. It was my choice
to say yes or no to the situation; nobody forced me. But I
wanted to say yes, and my choosing to say yes was my response
to the teacher. At the center the professional objectivity I encountered made it difficult for me to respond; it did not offer
me the help I was seeking in overcoming my inability to make
effective contacts with other people.

This student's report is a good reply to all those counselors
who feel that the requisite "nonpossessive" and "nonjudgmental"
attitudes toward the client prohibit them from expressing their wish
for him to change. This girl has experienced her teacher's wishes
and expectations, his "demands" on her, not as a violation but as a
sign of his concern and his confidence. She is not unique in her perception. Even a demand made in a far from gentle way can at times
convey this positive message. I once lost patience with an acutely
disturbed girl who would not get beyond a complaining enumera-
tion of her troubles. I told her energetically to stop whining and
start talking, and she did, looking greatly relieved; I had broken
through her well-practiced routine of hectic complaints and demands. Months later this girl told me that this episode had led to
her acceptance of counseling: "Before I got to you I had seen three
doctors who were very sympathetic and wanted to take care of me
in a hospital. What you said was unexpected and refreshing and it
gave me some hope. I responded because I felt that you had expressed *confidence* in me."

The detailed student report given above should be equally
instructive to the many students who, afraid of "dependence" and
"weakness," insist on solving their problems all by themselves—
even if the problem is the difficulty of relating to others and the
hoped-for solution is actually expected to come from outside.

I was very unhappy, but I wanted, philosophically, to
solve my own problems because I frequently accused myself of
being weak and wanted to prove that I could take care of myself. This was my main motive for not going to the center, and
I was able to get through the next two years without developing
more serious problems. I am still unhappy, but I am confident
that someday it's got to be better (it couldn't get worse). You

know, when I meet a boy that I love and that loves me (hoping that he is strong), I'll be fine.

As a contrast, students who in their questionnaire comments manifest adequate self-reliance do not insist on independence. They do not feel violated by the other's divergent opinions, and they may even criticize counselors for anxiously abstaining from any semblance of giving advice: "Why not give advice if you have a good idea? Most of us are not so insecure or so suggestible that we would slavishly follow advice regardless of its merit." The tone of such comments makes them easily distinguishable from the requests for advice that are rooted in feelings of uncertainty or helplessness; in the context of a confident orientation, dependence is part of interdependence, an aspect of give and take.

Let us return to the counseling courses exemplifying persistent failure of communication between student and counselor. In the instances of such failure described so far, complaints made by students were quite specific and gave a clue to what the counselor had failed to understand or to provide. There are also cases in which, at the conclusion of a fairly long period of counseling, the student is able merely to express an uneasy feeling that something has been amiss. Some students have done this by checking the "cannot decide" category which was included in the early versions of the questionnaire (it was eliminated from the later versions because it proved ambiguous). After brief periods of counseling, doubt about the results appears natural and justified; sometimes it indicates the kind of confusion that precedes and invites clarification. But when a student expresses uncertainty after a long period of counseling, during which both the counselor and the student apparently assumed that nothing was amiss, it indicates a serious problem; the uncertainty might be indicative of "fake progress." Some students do improve without seeming to be aware of the change, but such inattention is not easily maintained when they are asked whether counseling has been useful; this invitation to self-examination is an important function of the questionnaire. If, on having asked this question of oneself, one cannot tell whether or not one is better off than before, chances are that one is not; changes of any real magnitude and stability are bound to be noticed. Those who disclaim all knowledge of their present status, or keep wavering between doubt and hope, reveal a degree of uncertainty tantamount to admission of failure. Yet they do not make this admission, and it is precisely its absence that makes the situation malignant, since it precludes a fresh start. How does counseling get into this blind alley? Since those who find themselves in it cannot give us a clear account of the matter, the following schematic description is a reconstruction from various bits of material in the questionnaires, guided by my personal knowledge of some counseling or therapy courses that have miscarried, seemingly without the participants' awareness.

For some students the initial period does not lead into that of counseling proper, perhaps because the tasks of "precounseling" have been left undone. If this situation is discovered at an early stage, no great harm is done; the realization may be the first step toward the removal of whatever obstacles exist, or counseling may be postponed to a more propitious time. But if the situation remains hidden, the student and the counselor may move from one unproductive session to another on the assumption that the student is "in" while in fact he is not. A great deal depends on whether, or how soon, his lack of involvement becomes obvious to the counselor. In this respect, I believe that the college setting has a decided advantage over long-term private therapy, which may foster long suffering in patient and therapist alike. Many an analysis has lasted years and years, precisely because little of therapeutic value was happening in the sessions. Yet "movement" so slow as to be indistinguishable from a standstill may be made tolerable to the therapist— and so to the patient—by his belief that analysis must take its course and will need to take a long time, so that what does not happen today may happen three years hence. It may, and the long time may be needed; but this assumption, in the absence of reliable knowledge of the conditions under which it is valid, can be easily used as an excuse. The patient may use it as an excuse for not moving; the therapist for not questioning his proceedings. When a student, faced with a problem that he considers "deep-seated," expresses his intention to tackle it at some future time when he thinks he will be in long-term therapy, I sometimes ask him: "Why not right now?" Usually, if I have a good idea how to help him tackle it, a beginning can be made in that session.

The college counselor, accustomed to the students' quick movement in therapy, usually notices without too much delay that something has gone awry or has altogether failed to happen. Once he communicates this discovery to the student, much can be learned by both. But in some instances even experienced counselors may take a long time to realize that all the talk has been empty, the emotional participation feigned, important facts and feelings withheld, unverifiable generalizations substituted for descriptive reports, insights parroted or used merely to please or impress, fantasies revealed but not discarded, and the hope never given up that disturbances will go away and problems solve themselves without being faced in earnest. When the counselor reads the signs correctly, he can start working on these unconscious or semiconscious falsifications. But if obstacles to movement have not been progressively tackled and overcome, the student and the counselor may be faced with the discouraging experience of having worked for nothing; they may strain to find some results, or else seek solace in the hope that such results will appear in the future. If, by the end of a prolonged counseling period, the student still does not feel that therapy has "taken hold," that "something happened," he may go on uneasily maintaining that he has been—somewhat at least—helped; but it will be difficult to persuade him to continue therapy elsewhere. And no wonder. Without clearly formulating his feeling, and without knowing why, he cannot help but suspect that the enterprise has been futile; he may have concluded that therapy is not for him, feeling perhaps that he is beyond help. Such outcomes should be avoided at all costs. A frank facing of failure by the patient and his counselor can open new paths and is preferable to the corroding, guilt-producing effects of hidden failure.

In certain cases of undiscovered "fake progress," the student's questionnaire report may be conspicuous by its inconsistency and disharmony. Expressions of satisfaction, even of enthusiasm, may alternate with signs of confusion; the student seems to be in the dark about what counseling has been all about. Occasionally such a report is an eye-opener for the unsuspecting counselor and leads, belatedly, to an attempt at correcting the situation. The following case demonstrates such a course.

A freshman girl, Hilda, who had a great wish to please and who defined her problems as difficulties in her relations with men, wished to continue at the center the therapy she had started privately a year earlier. The counselor, a man, was extremely pleased with the course their common effort was taking. When he presented a segment of it in a case seminar, everyone shared his enthusiasm about this ideal client. She talked relatively easily, bringing up vital material in her memories, dreams, and associations; she was responsive to the counselor's comments and felt understood and appreciated by him; she seemed to be getting an increasingly better and richer understanding of her problem. The counselor felt certain that even if practical results lagged behind insights, they would soon follow. He was puzzled when, in responding to the questionnaire at the end of the year, Hilda, after having noted that counseling had been "very helpful," wrote the following comments:

> You ask an extremely difficult thing; such an evaluation involves an objectivity that is close to impossible under the circumstances, but I *will* try.
>
> What confused me very much at first (and still does) was what exactly "counseling" was. I mean, is it a form of therapy, is it a type of analysis, is it just "talking over your problems"? Now to say that it is "whatever you make it" is avoiding the issue, for that is true of all kinds of therapy. Are the "counselors" hired as psychologists—it's not that it makes all that much difference. If you can meet with someone once a week with whom you can talk relatively freely and with whom you can work out problems, it hardly matters whether or not he has a degree of any specific nature, yet it would be a bit more reassuring to go into this new kind of experience with a bit more information.
>
> Most aspects about my experience in counseling were quite positive, not that so many problems were *solved* as much as worked on—new growth was sort of looked after, and though most of the old needs couldn't be torn up, at least no new ones grew. It took a while to adjust to my counselor; I had

seen a psychiatrist the year before and both personality and method were hard to get used to at first. Sometimes the long silences in which I had nothing to say got frustrating. But I don't suppose this is helping you much.

What was really wonderful about the set-up, besides the fact that my counselor was exceptionally sensitive and perceptive and wise (besides having an incredible memory), was the fact that because no fee existed, I didn't have to sit in the office trying to get "my money's worth." It's not that one would do this constantly were there a fee, but in addition to college expenses, one would almost feel guilty about spending so much more and not getting anywhere. I believe I made more progress in six months here than I did the preceding year in analysis. I'm just kind of sad it has to end, for it takes a great deal of time to click with a therapist, and once it's there, it's hard to give up.

The girl was saying, in effect, that though the counseling contact had been gratifying in some of its aspects, it did not get her anywhere. She did not exactly complain; she had, after all, no knowledge where—if anywhere—it was "supposed" to take her. What she had been concerned with was to learn what was wanted and expected of her—and that lesson she had learned quite well. The counselor realized that the girl's successful enacting of a "good patient's" role had made him lose all critical perspective. The next fall, after a review of what had taken place and why, the student and the counselor agreed on another short period of counseling meant to serve as a preparation for referral to an outside therapist. These sessions were in retrospect viewed by the student as a shared attempt "to get down to the nitty gritty: to the problem and cause and solution, not just variations on the theme of communication, recall, reminiscence."

12

Termination

Termination of therapy is a much discussed topic, and many valid observations have been made about the difficulties and the opportunities it presents. Unquestionably, the handling of termination can add to the therapy's success or, if done poorly, detract from it. Some of the discussions, however, seem to suggest that the end stage of therapy can be dealt with as a separate process, that its shaping does not depend on the total period of work, of which it is the completion. To make a "good" termination appear crucial for the therapy's success is to put the cart before the horse (unless "good termination" is used as a *pars pro toto,* as meaning a productive period of work well completed). Those who say that the therapist is responsible for a stagnating therapy because he failed to terminate it, and, instead, allowed the patient to cling to the gratifications of a dependent relationship, are disregarding the obvious: "The problem of weaning the patient is not the main issue in termination. The main issue is whether the goal of treatment has been achieved and a significant change has taken place. If it has, the patient will be

267

ready to leave or his reluctance will not last. . . . The patient may feel genuine grief at the parting, but if therapy has been successful the separation does not loom large" (Angyal, 1965, p. 311).

Responsibility for Failure

Sometimes the therapist, implicitly or explicitly, blames the failure of therapy on the client, or refuses altogether to acknowledge it. As a result, the client is left not merely without any gains but worse off than before. Either his confusion is increased, or his self-derogation, or both. He may sense at least dimly that the therapist, in blaming failure on the client's lack of motivation, or on his being "unanalyzable," is both illogical and unjust. These defects are, after all, part of the difficulties for which the person had sought help; if the therapist took him on and continued working with him in the absence of movement (or after it stopped), didn't he indicate thereby that he knew how to deal with these obstacles to progress? Yet the patient is able to reject any imputation of blame for failure only if his therapy has been successful in raising his faith in himself—in which case there would be no question of blame. But the patient who is "a failure," whose view of himself and the therapist reflects his neurotic assumptions, is extremely sensitive to any message, overt or covert, the therapist may convey at the end. Imputation of blame for the failure of an enterprise on which he had pinned all his hopes will greatly increase his burden of guilt, perhaps confirm with finality his assumed worthlessness. One unproductive long-term therapy I know of ended in an argument about whose failure it was. The therapist insisted that the patient share the blame with him. The patient, a student, maintained—correctly, I believe— that the kind of "uncovering" therapy he had been receiving only increased his despair; he was looking for a more optimistic faith, a more encouraging approach, which he knew existed elsewhere. He agreed to assume part of the blame only to end the distasteful wrangle; yet he did not resume his search for help until, a few months later, he made a suicidal attempt that almost succeeded. Even in less extreme cases, patients who have been made to feel blamed for failure are not likely to seek further therapy until they have had a chance to clarify their perception of what happened the first time. This is true also for patients whose therapist, at termination, did not blame them but, instead, implicitly denied a fairly obvious failure.

Why are therapists so frequently confused about the nature of outcomes and the responsibility for failures in therapy? At least part of the problem, I believe, has to do with our image of treatment. In the recent past, the predominance and prestige of psychoanalysis created a spurious agreement on what true therapy is and made it difficult for both therapists and patients to learn from their frustrations and failures. Instead, therapists had to explain these frustrations and failures without questioning the basic tenets of their creed. If "correct procedures" did not result in success, the therapist could either minimize the failure or view the patient as "untreatable," as incapable or unwilling to fit the "correct" method. For a long time, only exceptional people, such as Melitta Schmiedeberg (1958) and Hellmuth Kaiser (1955), among the analytically trained practitioners were able to note the indifferent or destructive effects of some procedures and attitudes fostered by the classical analytical approach, to state their observations without equivocation, and to start acting on them. Today no one familiar with the field will deny that therapists often fail, but not as many will concede that we often add insult to injury by letting the patient feel responsible for the failure. I have been astonished to discover how many therapists, both novices and old hands, find a blunt statement of the therapists' responsibility for the outcome unacceptable, shocking, and in fact absurd. Kaiser (1965, p. 2) must have had a similar experience with his colleagues to cause him to spell out the issue in detail:

> When the patient's illness is diagnosed as one which, in principle, can be cured with psychoanalysis, the failure of the treatment can be due only to the faultiness of its application, which means that the behavior of the analyst alone determines the success or failure. In this sense he has the whole responsibility for what happens. If, for instance, the patient is dishonest— or, in nonmoralistic language, he tells things which he knows to be untrue—that is just another symptom. To say that this

symptom sufficiently explains the analyst's failure would be as
devious as to say that an obsessional patient could not be cured
because he behaved obsessively.

Where does the patient's responsibility come in? The
correct answer is nowhere. The analyst's behavior should induce
in the patient a sense of responsibility for what he says and does
but this principle does not at all mean that the patient should
be held responsible to any extent for the outcome of treatment.

The difficulty many of us have with this statement is due
to more than our wish to minimize our own shortcomings; I believe
it testifies to some honest confusion, rooted in our conception of what
is effective in therapy but greatly augmented by the multiple meaning of the term *responsibility*. Calling someone "responsible" can
mean that he is trustworthy, or that he is the primary cause of an
event (as in "I am responsible for this last change of policy"), or
that he will be blamed or punished if anything should go wrong.
All references to responsibility have an aura of high morality, but
the anxiety that is at the basis of some of them can lead to irresponsible actions—those that aim at avoidance of blame by the one
"responsible," at the expense perhaps of the client's best interest.

The multiple meanings of *responsible* may lead us to confuse
causation with accountability. If being responsible is equivalent to
being a cause or even *the* cause of the outcome of treatment, how
can the therapist be said to be responsible? It is clear that what
happens in therapy is a function not only of the therapist's skill
but also of the kind and degree of the patient's disturbance. Seen
from another angle, we know that the therapist cannot make the
client well without the client's cooperation, that it is up to the person himself to make constructive changes in his own life. Responsibility for oneself is an axiom of personal existence, a correlate of
the individual's drive for self-determination. How can we convey
this axiom to the client if we ourselves assume responsibility for the
outcome of our contact? If it is a mistake for a therapist to claim
all credit for success, it is no more logical to charge him with all
responsibility for failure. The one who is always ready to say "mea
culpa" might well be a victim of his neurotic guilt feelings or be
expressing indirectly his grandiose expectations of unfailing success. Many theoretical formulations, old and new, can be used to

point out that the therapist can do just so much; the patient must at some point take over.

It is true, of course, that therapy is nothing if not a joint enterprise. The therapist's behavior is not the only factor that determines the course and the outcome of therapy, although it might prove to be the most important one. To determine the weight of "therapist variables" relative to selected "patient variables" is a task for research. But it is the therapist who is paid for his work and who, by his acceptance of the job, has signified that he has the requisite competence and is reasonably certain of his ability to carry out the therapeutic task. Not being infallible, he cannot claim absolute certainty, but his assumption of professional responsibility is equivalent to a pledge that he will do his utmost. He must adapt his offerings to the patient's state and needs, elicit his participation, keep track of what is happening and what may have gone wrong, seek effective consultation if he feels stuck, and transfer the patient if no progress is in sight. The therapist will interpret such guidelines according to what he knows, or believes, to be required for therapy's success. The concept of therapist responsibility, however, which such guidelines aim to implement, belongs in the framework of professional ethics, not that of empirical research on causes and effects. The therapist violates this code if he does not try to learn all he can from his failure, invoking instead some plausible and comforting cliché.

What is the best possible handling of termination after failure? The key to a productive termination of an unproductive counseling period is a shared insight into what has gone wrong. If the counselor, in reviewing the course of their work, can locate an error he made, or a point at which a misunderstanding arose, the client may at first be upset or angry, but he will leave counseling less confused than he would have been otherwise, perhaps also more hopeful and ready to envisage another attempt. In a favorable case, such a discovery communicated to the client can even revive and make retroactively effective some of the insights and gains he had made that fell victim to the subsequent confusions and disappointments. But even in the absence of articulate insight into the factors that have made counseling unproductive, the counselor can counteract confusion by squarely admitting failure and relieve the client of feelings of guilt by acknowledging his own responsibility, at least in principle. He can express his regret, his puzzlement, his tentative guesses about causes. He may have failed to understand the client or to make his own meaning clear; the focus for their work may have been chosen poorly, or they may have drifted away from it unaware. He can encourage the client to look for some clues in his own memories and feelings. A therapist who makes no effort at clarification may sometimes have to face former clients who have belatedly discovered the extent of their therapy's failure and their therapist's specific contribution to it. They can be extremely bitter about these discoveries. The counselor should accept whatever reproaches strike him as justified and, if possible, arrange for another try at counseling, with a different counselor if necessary.

Termination in Relation to School Failure

Termination after something of value has been clearly achieved is an altogether different matter. To handle it in optimal ways that would augment the client's gains, one has to take into account the relevant features of the given environmental framework. The features that make college counseling a time-limited enterprise bear most directly on the shaping of its end stage. These features include not only the all-important factor of the available staff time but also the duration and articulation of the school year and a student's total college career and the fact that his continuation in school depends on his academic performance. Let us first look at the cases where counseling is terminated by the student's forced or voluntary withdrawal from school, often a result of academic failure or near failure. The incidence of such cases varies from school to school and depends also on the nature of the counseling center. Services identified with academic advising or study counseling will register a larger proportion of complaints about difficulties in studying than services known to deal with a wide range of personal problems. At Brandeis the incidence of complaints centered on academic difficulties was quite low, particularly among girls, who in most years utilized the center much more extensively and actively than did men. The same sex difference has been reported by counseling services of other schools; it is plausible to assume that more men than women reject the idea of help and prefer to struggle on their own until failure threatens.

Male or female, many of the students threatened with academic failure enter counseling in an attempt to avert this outcome, thus presenting the counselor with their own deadline. Counseling of such students is often beset with complications. One of them is the initial hope of some students that the counselor will intercede with the administration or that the very fact of their having entered counseling will outweigh their poor grades when final decisions are made. If these unrealistic hopes are not quickly dispelled by a clarifying statement of the school's and the center's policies, counseling will have a very poor start; if undertaken for the purpose of influencing the dean, it is not likely to be optimally used by the student. To mention a more specific situation, we have found it signally difficult to work with those nonachievers whom the school administrators have actively referred to the center in deference to the wishes of their influential fathers. Eventually I succeeded in making the dean realize that under such conditions the counselor is viewed by the student as his father's agent and has little chance to be of use to him.

A different kind of complication arises when a student entering counseling minimizes the extent of his academic difficulties or conceals the present threat to his academic career. A student, for example, may mention poor grades as one of his problems initially, or in passing, and then focus on other topics, sometimes providing the counselor with fascinating memories, fantasies, and dreams— thus directing the discussion away from the immediate school issues. The counselor's efforts to outline his client's personality dynamics may then be rudely stopped by a sudden announcement of the student's imminent severance from school. He cannot even comfort himself with the hope that their work has been useful just the same; discoveries that have not been related to vital current issues are likely to remain "mere insights." It pays to inform oneself about the counseled student's academic status, even if the student has not mentioned study problems. The following episode shows that the timely discovery of the true state of affairs can precipitate important insights.

A girl began counseling by reporting, rather exaggeratedly,

that she was afraid she suffered from some sexual pathology. As if to qualify as a bona fide patient, she quickly aspired to an affair with the male counselor. Having thus committed herself to what she considered an advanced psychosexual level, she could not admit to less sophisticated feelings. After ten sessions the counselor was surprised to learn through official channels that this girl was on academic probation. In a subsequent session an offhand inquiry into her academic status brought an outburst of tears and then the information that she had just come from the dean's office, where her fears met such kindness that she "just bawled like a baby for the first time in front of someone." She then revealed previously suppressed feelings of being totally insignificant, and the sexual fantasies were approachable from this perspective.

I know of two students who concealed their academic failure from their counselors even after they were dropped from school; both kept coming to their appointments and discussing serious interpersonal problems not directly related to study or work. In one of these cases I found my counselee listed among the students who had been dropped from school at the end of the previous term. He was a seriously disturbed young man who had started working in counseling only after a long period of anxious stalling. Unable to find a safe alternative to the course the student had taken, I arranged to continue working with him to the end of the school year, when, having experienced some improvement, he made plans to transfer to an outpatient clinic.

Even in the absence of any unusual complications created by the imminence of failure, it is often more difficult to work with the nonachieving students than with those whose main initial complaints are formulated in terms of interpersonal relations or identity issues. The student's initial centering on one practical goal makes for a slow start, and the frequently present lifelong pattern of underachievement rarely permits quick success. Often one must be satisfied with the student's obtaining sufficient insight into the cause of his failure to make some realistic—even if temporary—decision: to modify his educational plans or to try to work out his problems in therapy before reentering college. Some students persistently deny the degree of their handicap, bolstering themselves with the knowledge of their high intelligence scores, for instance, and attributing their poor grades to a variety of external circumstances; for them the shock of severance, if well worked out in terminal sessions, can lead to productive results. Some students decide to leave school before catastrophe overtakes them, or for reasons other than a realistic threat of failure. In the latter case, particularly with academically successful students, some pressure against such a decision is often exercised by the school. The counselor must divorce himself from these influences and remain open to the student's feelings.

The student's decision to withdraw is often the result of a long internal struggle and may be the best solution for him at the time. For instance, the son of a successful father preoccupied with business and community affairs continually missed classes and read only books that were not assigned in courses; his progress toward failure was clearly directed against his father. Attempts at clarifying his motives did not lead to improvement but did result in a decision to withdraw voluntarily, in order to forestall failure, and to enter outside therapy. A few months later the student wrote the counselor of a dramatic discovery: he had been trying to test his father's love and to get some evidence of his interest, even if it were anger. A year later he entered another college.

While not opposing the student's decision to leave school, the counselor must insist within reason that it should be talked through, some realistic plans formulated, and the student's chances for reentering college protected. In the rare event of a student's withdrawing abruptly both from counseling and from school, the counselor's intervention may mitigate the self-destructive aspect of the step and the resulting sense of failure. One student, for example, felt inadequate and unworthy of being financed by a large fellowship, despite a brilliant academic record. She experienced severe depressions, and only with extensive therapeutic support was she able to remain in school. During Christmas vacation she became so fearful and blocked that she decided to remain at home and would not return to take her forthcoming examinations. Withdrawal at this time might have ended her college career on a note of failure. A series of letters and telephone calls from the counselor persuaded her to return to campus and to take some of the examinations. She passed them and was given a leave of absence from school, with permission to return when she felt ready. A year later she reentered school.

The Predetermined Time Limit

In many school settings there is a predetermined limit to the period of counseling, and the students are informed of this limit at the outset. Not all college setups manage their limited supply of staff time this way. If the aim is to provide counseling on a large scale, however, to all students "who need it and can use it," the time limit is a necessary consequence of the relation of available staff time to student demand and is acceptable to most students as insuring a fair chance to all. At Brandeis, where it was introduced at an early stage, the predetermined time limit to the counseling period proved advantageous, permitting a variety of uses. It makes all the difference, of course, whether the time limit is four, or twelve, or thirty sessions. Most of my experience with time-limited therapy was collected during the affluent years, when the time limit was defined as the equivalent of one school year of weekly sessions; that is, about twenty-five to thirty meetings.

When the allotment of time is generous, the advantages of the time limit seem to me to outweigh its disadvantages. In the first place, the counselor and the student tend to work in a more focused way and to try to further movement from the start; the attitude that what does not happen today will happen tomorrow (an attitude that often impedes progress in long-term therapy) does not arise, since each session counts. Working under these conditions, the counselor may discover that much more can be achieved in a short time than he had originally assumed, and his optimism is communicated to the student. There are also other advantages. The fixed time limit relieves the counselor of having to decide how to distribute his time among his counselees. Such decisions are usually difficult, often arbitrary; they may produce resentment in the student, guilt in the counselor, anxiety in both. The time limit, furthermore, vividly communicates to the student the transitional function of counseling and of his relationship to the counselor. This enterprise is not going to become a way of life, as the long-term therapy becomes for some patients. Like the adolescent stage as a whole, it must lead to something new: new relationships, greater self-reliance.

The deliberate use of a time limit as a therapeutic device stems from Otto Rank (1929, 1936). Viewing the traumatic separation from the mother at birth as the prototype of all future developments, Rank saw the forward-moving human life as a series of crises, a sequence of partial deaths and rebirths in which the familiar is painfully abandoned so that a new stage can come into being. This was the theoretical framework for his practice of setting a date for termination after a certain stage of therapy had been reached. Imposition of the time limit was for Rank one means of making the patient experience—and not merely recall or understand—the emotional struggles that accompany and further individuation. Some of his followers used the device of time limit to excellent advantage (Taft, 1962). That under certain conditions the setting of limits can speed up the course of therapy and improve its results has been proved in at least one well-controlled experiment (Shlien, Mosak, and Dreikurs, 1960). Given our present inability to accommodate all those seeking psychological help, this finding is of great practical importance. A recent brand of time-limited therapy has been developed by Mann (1961) in response to the needs of outpatient clinics that must serve large numbers of clients. In Mann's conception, the limited time represents reality; if well managed by the skilled therapist, the predetermined time limit can facilitate the patient's abandoning his regressive dream of a timeless, effortless Golden Age in favor of a more future-oriented, self-reliant outlook. At the start, Mann proposes a focus for this period of work, one that is vital and acceptable to the patient, suggesting directly and indirectly that the allotted time (usually twelve sessions) is sufficient for achieving this goal. He works with the patient very actively and promotes a positive, warm relationship; but, to keep reality intact, he adheres strictly to the date set for termination. He expects the awareness of its imminence to revive the patient's memories of earlier traumatic changes and losses, which then can be worked through and assimilated. Whether or not one agrees with the theoretical basis and with every detail of this design of short-term therapy, one can recognize certain effective factors: an arousal of hopeful expectations, a reliving of past traumas with a focus on the present, corrective experiences offered by the therapist's acceptance and concern. But my own experience with students—although it confirms that some can make substantial gains in a period of time as short as the one allotted by Mann—strongly contradicts his implicit assumption that a therapist, at least a skilled one, can confidently expect such progress from all or almost all his clients. Although Mann himself does emphasize the need for skill in conducting sessions, some discussions I have heard of time-limited therapy seemed to minimize this crucial factor, implying that success depends largely on the correct choice of patients and on the strict observance of the time limit. I cannot help wondering what happens when even a skillful therapist unwaveringly terminates a contact that has resulted in no gains for the client. The reality the latter is called upon to face can only confirm what he had assumed all along, that nothing is to be expected from people.

The way of handling termination that we developed at Brandeis was similar in some respects to the one suggested by Mann. The policy of a fixed time limit (conscientiously observed by the staff and well known to the student body) was discussed with each applicant in the first meeting and viewed in the light of his response and his personal history. Taking the attitude that something useful could surely be done, we did not turn students away just because they might need a longer period of work than the center could offer. If a student had a history of many traumatic losses, however, we discussed with him or her the feasibility of some alternative to college counseling, an outside referral or postponement of therapy. As the work got under way, counselors were advised to remind students, particularly in the second half of the counseling period, how much time remained. They would be watching for termination-related topics in whatever was brought up at that stage, and they would use such topics as ways of assessing the student's gains and discussing his plans. In cases where it seemed desirable to mitigate the arbitrariness of termination, one could arrange for it to take place at the end of the academic year, when most students leave the area to pursue their various summer plans. This timing permits the student to feel that he is the one who is leaving the counselor, rather than the other way around. In general, when both the student and the counselor remain on the campus, or plan to return to it next year, termination need not be abrupt. The student can return for a few additional sessions when the counselor has time available, or keep in touch through occasional visits. Some students who terminate counseling in the spring visit their counselors in the fall to tell of their summer experience and perhaps to discuss their further plans.

During the years when our allowance of time was generous, only a minority of the students counseled during the year used up their allotment. The existence of a time limit barely affects those students who complete counseling to their satisfaction (or terminate for other reasons) well in advance of the deadline. Termination after a brief, satisfying period of counseling can be simple and smooth, or it can be an enactment of a struggle for liberation from the old tie, an issue which is in the forefront for many students. This struggle may lead to an abrupt termination, but more often the dependence-independence dilemma is reflected in the uncertainty the students harbor about their readiness to leave counseling. Thus, a student, after having reached the satisfying decision to live away from home after graduation, may now demand reassurance from the counselor that he is ready to leave counseling; the next week he may decisively assert his independence and confidently stride out of the room.

The struggle for emancipation from counseling may also reveal to the student, sometimes in a dramatic fashion, the specific pattern involved in his or her dependence on parents. One girl who was very happy about what had been achieved in counseling spent several sessions inconclusively weighing the pros and cons of terminating. The counselor finally communicated to the student her impression that the student, though not sure of her reasons, really wanted to leave; and the counselor wondered why the girl could not just act on this wish, since she could always return if she wanted. The student, after a moment of silence, exclaimed with smiles and tears that she just realized that this was what she had always wanted her mother to say to her. She was then able to express the feelings that had been an obstacle to leaving the counselor: "We come here one after another with our problems and miseries, and when we leave happy—what reward do *you* get for the trouble you took? It isn't fair to you!" She left this last session with the feeling that her growing up would not leave her parents without any reward, nor herself without any affectionate ties to the family.

A standstill in counseling after a period of successful work is often an indication of conflict about the wish to leave, but this wish itself may stem from different sources. If it reflects the student's unwillingness to explore an emerging problem, he may leave on an impulse, avoiding a discussion of his reasons. Or he may leave abruptly in response to some false move or failure of understanding on the part of the counselor. Some exploration of the wish to leave is usually possible, however, and even students who leave abruptly will often accept an invitation to return for a concluding session. If the obstacles to continuation can be identified, they may be overcome in the process; if they prove too strong, the student may make a more conscious and responsible decision to leave counseling—at least for the time being.

Occasionally a girl who has made a good start in counseling slows down or stops working in sessions as soon as a relationship with a boy has been established or mended; yet she may show no wish to stop the counseling, since she has cast the counselor in the role of a confidante who must listen and sympathize. This behavior may reflect merely the girl's need for support, or pleasure in sharing, and may end (along with counseling) when her confidence in the new relationship has become secure. If, on the other hand, the affair is obviously unhappy and fraught with internal conflict, and yet every comment except reassurance is persistently denounced by the girl as devaluating her tie to the boy, the situation must not be permitted to drag. Its clarification, including a review of antecedents, will either remove the obstacles to movement or precipitate a decision to discontinue counseling. A student who makes this decision with some insight into her motives is likely to resume counseling if and when experience proves to her the futility of her hope that all her problems can be solved through a given relationship.

Sometimes, after a period of productive work, strong resistance to further movement sets in for reasons that are not transparent at the time. In one such case, when the student in question was spending her days in futile struggles to break through this inner wall, I first used our time limit as a means to get out of the impasse. I suggested to the girl that she stop struggling and save her allotment of sessions for later. She left with relief and returned in subsequent years for several brief but productive periods of work. Evoking the possibility of saving one's sessions for the future has proved a useful device for facilitating the termination of a stagnating counseling period and for initiating the method of distributing counseling over several years.

Students respond variously to the approach of the end of counseling, depending on how far they feel they have come and also on whether the summer vacation really signals termination or possibly only an interruption. Some of those who have moved rapidly in counseling continue to work with unabated energy to the end, the last sessions being as probing and exploratory as the earlier ones. The counselors need not feel uneasy about new areas being opened up even in the last session; after the summer vacations, these students often show not only consolidation of the gains previously made but also rapid movement toward a resolution of issues that have been barely if at all touched upon. Potential for growth at this age must not be underestimated, and the student is often right when he postpones until the fall the assessment of his gains and of his need for further therapy.

More often than not, a certain tapering off of self-exploration takes place toward the end of the counseling period, or of the school year, and the advent of the final examinations often leads to a decision to terminate. If the counselor has done his part, and particularly if the termination is "for real," its approach also precipitates conscious attempts by the student to evaluate the progress made and some less conscious testing of his readiness to leave. Some feelings about separation from the counselor are usually present, even if there has been no marked transference and the student is satisfied with his gains. His willingness to explore and acknowledge those feelings presages more readiness to be on one's own than does denial. One girl, in leaving counseling shortly before the time limit, though teary-eyed, strongly denied any regrets: "I don't feel guilty about leaving you, nor dependent, nor rejected. Maybe you want me to say I care for you and will miss you; besides," she smiled, "somehow I have the feeling that this isn't goodbye. I think I'll see

you around somewhere." And she did, in the counselor's office the
following year. An exploration of the student's feelings and fantasies
concerning separation brings him a step closer to an inner acceptance of termination. This process can sometimes be facilitated
by the questionnaire asking for an evaluation of counseling. A
questionnaire received by a student who is still in counseling, if it is
not pushed away and forgotten, may become connected with the
vital concerns of the terminal stage of counseling, facilitating their
expression and resolution. A graduate student who came to the
center because of difficulty in relating to people and apathy about
his work had by the end of the year made progress in both areas;
his depression had lifted, but some interpersonal problems remained.
In the last session he was relatively silent, looked sad, and devalued
what had been achieved. He left, promising to send in the questionnaire, which he had not yet found the time to answer. Two days
later, his counselor got the following letter.

> I want to apologize for the way I acted on Tuesday. I've
> been feeling miserable all week and just tonight I realized that
> it's because we won't be meeting anymore. It hit me very hard
> and I got very emotional about it and I just recovered. I think
> we accomplished quite a bit in our time together, mainly in
> terms of my ability to recognize my emotions, or lack of them.
> I think I know in which direction I want to go. It has to do with
> being able to make my feelings known to people who matter to
> me, and this is very clear to me at this moment because it is
> only through my loss that I was able to realize that I like you
> very much, not only as a therapist, but very much as a person,
> and I want you to like me. This is very hard for me to write
> even now, after I've rehearsed it in my head many times. Please
> accept this in lieu of the evaluation form. It's all I can write
> now. I would very much appreciate hearing from you, if only
> to know that you have received this. Thank you very much.

Without the stimulus of the unanswered questionnaire staring him in the face, this student might not have been able to make
the step forward that his letter represents. The request for feedback
served to legitimize his uneasy wish to express his feelings to the
counselor; it also offered a chance to do so from a distance and to

get a response, at a time when it still seemed too threatening to do it in the face-to-face situation.

To illustrate the handling of the issues of the end period, I shall here describe two cases of termination, both taking place after a productive and none-too-problematic period of work but resulting in very different degrees of completion.

In the first case, that of Amy, the lack of completion was due largely to a slow start and a shortage of time. Amy came to the center in the spring term of her senior year and was thus able to have fourteen sessions. She complained of interpersonal problems, stemming in part from overdependence on her mother, of being isolated and lonely and not too sure of her plans. It took some time before she was ready to disclose the aspects of her life which were making her feel angry at her parents and ashamed of herself. After the content of these disclosures had been discussed, Amy experienced a clear-cut shift of her perspective on herself and subsequently some slight improvement in her management of her current life. But the chance she now saw for a brighter future meant also that "changes are required, I must come to grips with so many things, so that joy is mixed with fear."

There was not much time left, however, for coming to grips with anything. As the school year was drawing to a close, Amy started assessing her years in college. She was uncertain about what she had gotten out of her college career and was in any case dissatisfied with it. She felt she had wasted time and not learned much in her courses. She particularly regretted that, on her mother's advice, she had switched from the study of Spanish to that of French. She was unsure of the grade the French teacher would give her, and, though she liked the language, the smattering of it that she had acquired could be of no practical use to her; nor would the mediocre grade she anticipated getting be of help if she applied to a graduate school.

I had discovered early that, in their discussions of academic matters, students often express their feelings about counseling, and I felt that Amy's deliberations contained several themes related to counseling and its termination: the change of her general orientation ("language"), with its pros and cons; insufficient gains; uncertainty about the counselor's attitude to her. So I asked her what grade she was expecting to get for the course she had taken with me. She responded by spelling out her feelings about the approaching end of our work. Most of what she said proved to correspond almost point by point to her complaints and uncertainties about her college past and her future course. She was aware of the center's policy forbidding counselors to take on counselees as private patients, and she anticipated with resentment that I would suggest her transferring to an outside therapist. She was afraid that this stranger's unfamiliar approach would require difficult readjustments. The venting of these feelings opened the way to a realistic review of her needs, wishes, and plans. Amy reaffirmed her strong wish to continue the work we had started, and I was soon able to transfer her to a therapist whose working "language" was similar to mine. They took up where we had left off, without any great delays or setbacks. A year later Amy called me up to tell me of the satisfactory completion of her therapy and of her plans for graduate study. In this case, as in many similar ones, the main practical achievement of a counseling course that led to a tentative shift of perspective was the student's decision to become seriously involved in therapy.

Another senior girl, Verna, entered counseling in the fall and worked intensively almost until her graduation, using all the time to which she was entitled. One of the traumatic events of her life was the death of her mother, which had occurred three years earlier, after a protracted incapacitating illness. Communication between mother and daughter had been disrupted during this period. Absorbed in the new experiences of her freshman year (which she could not share with her mother), Verna avoided visits at home as much as she could. She felt little grief at her mother's death, but in the subsequent years she was often depressed without cause and experienced many difficulties in her relations with family members and friends; feeling weak and worthless, she was unsure of her ability to survive in an indifferent world or to benefit from counseling. Yet it soon proved that she was able to work intensively, to acquire insights, and to make progress. A few weeks before graduation, after most of her difficulties had subsided and her mood greatly improved, Verna became clearly aware of the mixed feelings which her mother's long illness had evoked in her. Her image of her mother proved to be split into that of the earlier good, responsive

mother and the one whose survival as an invalid would have interfered with the daughter's enjoyment of life; this discovery led to
some belated grief for her mother.

As the school year was drawing to a close, Verna's thoughts
turned to her postgraduate plans. At that point she reported two
dreams that she had had on two succeeding nights, dreams that
reflected her feelings about termination. First she dreamed that she
was returning from a visit with a disliked aunt, whom she was leaving behind; she was waiting for further transportation on a plat-
form in the middle of a wide river with several other travelers,
whom she did not know and did not talk to. She was a bit
anxious—would a boat come or would she be stuck there?—yet
she was enjoying the fresh air and the wide horizons opening on all
sides. The next night Verna dreamed of a pleasant party with many
of her friends present. I, her counselor, was there, too, as well as
the nursery school teacher under whom Verna had worked that
year and by whom she felt liked and appreciated; the teacher put
her arm around her. Verna was glad that I had a chance to see her
in a real-life situation, but she also wanted to tell me her dream of
the night before. She knew that she could take me aside but decided
not to disturb what was going on; as people around me started
leaving, she used this moment to tell me the dream and was glad
she was able to do it before she too left. The second dream shows
Verna no longer anxious; she is among friends, at ease with her
two current "good mothers," certain of her place in their affection
and not reluctant to leave them. In our last meeting she stated
simply, with conviction, that she had gained a great deal from
counseling. By then she had found an interesting job, was developing her friendship with a boy, and was looking forward to her new
independent life with a confidence tinged with excitement. Neither
Verna nor I thought of raising the question of further therapy, and
I have not heard from her since.

For students whose problems are fairly severe, the issue of
discontinuing a promising therapeutic contact and accepting a referral can be a serious one; with such students termination, even if
well prepared, is potentially traumatic. Some students will "forget"
that a time limit exists, in spite of repeated reminders; others will
plead for continuation as private patients, with the parents joining

in the plea. Some students regard the time limit from the start as proof of the counselor's unconcern and an argument against getting personally involved in counseling. Others will make the issue of termination the focus of an open struggle with the counselor. Instead of the counselor, the administration may be viewed as the enforcer of the rule; and the student may propose to start a movement to effect a general extension of counseling periods. Some students will become acutely upset after termination and refuse to accept help from any but their former counselor. In most of these cases the counselor who remains uninvolved in the struggle has a good opportunity to clarify to himself and to the student the nature and the implications of the patterns being acted out. For some students the working through of the conflicts and struggles developing around the issue of termination and referral has at least as much therapeutic effect as the work done previously, or in the interval between such episodes.

A case showing some of these features in strong relief is that of a European-born freshman girl whose mother had early perished in a Nazi camp and who later experienced other losses as well as drastic changes of environment. On entering Brandeis, Ruth found herself unable to work; she was failing her courses and felt, in turn, depressed, guilty, and furious at everybody and everything; her obnoxious behavior made her an isolate on the campus. She did not seem to be a good candidate for time-limited work, but no source of help could be made available to her at the time except what the college provided. She was referred to me by her adviser, and we did establish some rapport even though, to start with, Ruth pronounced the enterprise hopeless and contested vehemently every single remark I made. For weeks our work was punctuated by frequent explosions, and the time limit soon became the main target of Ruth's attacks on our design of counseling. She felt that to offer her just one school year of sessions was both ridiculous and destructive; she would be left worse off than she was now and might just as soon kill herself; she *would* in fact kill herself if I were to carry out my intention to stop seeing her at the end of the school year; she would not transfer to another. Actually all the while we were making good progress in exploring Ruth's appalling past history and her present despondence born of anticipation of more disasters to come. Her desperate struggle to avert them by striking blindly against misperceived obstacles and "enemies" made some of the feared events (such as rejections by friends) come true, confirming her feelings of guilt and impending doom.

Yet these developing insights did not stop Ruth from trying, in almost every session, to intimidate me into removing the time limit. Even though I did not believe that she seriously intended to kill herself, I could not help but be affected by her threats, particularly since she had made suicidal attempts in the past. I decided to take up the matter with her. She was, of course, free, I told her, to give voice to all her thoughts and feelings in the sessions, the angry and the suicidal ones, too; but if her threats were more than just that, if she really meant what she was saying, then, given our time-limited setting, for me to continue working with her this winter meant setting her up for killing herself in the spring. Would she agree to stop threatening me with suicide? Ruth, who during my speech was gazing at the ceiling, promptly replied: "I would be a fool not to agree." She stopped talking about suicide and instead vented her anger about the time limit by saying now and then with great vehemence: "But if I ever catch you extending the time limit for someone else, you just wait and see." When counseling ended at the end of the year, nothing dramatic was enacted, although Ruth resolutely reaffirmed her decision not to have therapy with anyone else, ever. This issue, however, no longer seemed weighty or pressing. Ruth could look back at a satisfying, successful spring term and had exciting plans for the summer. She had also come to believe that I had no wish to get rid of her and was not preparing to disappear from her life; that, if she wished, she could keep in touch with me through occasional visits. She did so during the next school year, using the opportunity sparingly and to good advantage.

In retrospect, it seems to me that in this case the time limit provided a very useful focus both for reliving old traumas and for learning something new that could be used to erase their effects. My refusing to extend the time limit, while proving able and willing to give something of value, had undermined some of the assumptions held by Ruth in common with others in her situation: that she would be abandoned, her needs frustrated; that the great pressure of her needs indicated that they were tremendous, perhaps limitless;

that the only hope of having this neediness assuaged was to be given "more and more"; that the refusal of others to provide it was proof of their heartlessness, of their rejection of her; that the only way to get what she needed and to avoid being abandoned was to intimidate people into staying with her and into giving. It was clear to me, however, that the major factor in undermining this neurotic mythology was Ruth's relationship both to me and to several other people on campus who, without yielding to her angry demands, responded to her plight with sympathetic understanding. But time was needed for these relationships to develop and for their effects to take hold. If Ruth, who had reason to panic at the thought of any change, of any relationship's coming to an end, did not have ample time to review her present and her past, to test the counselor not once but again and again, and to experience some reliable improvement, the enforcing of the time limit might well have proved to be the destructive measure she expected it to be. If our allotment of time had been half of what it actually was, I doubt that I would have undertaken working with her.

The presence of a realistically determined time limit might well be one of the advantages of working and training in a college setting; it helps us learn to eliminate waste from our work and to utilize the termination itself therapeutically. But *adequate* time must be provided if we are to handle to the best advantage both the time limit and the other structural features of the college environment and to achieve the flexibility and versatility required to meet the special needs of each individual student. Contrary to some determined optimists, a shortage of staff time does not necessarily result in invention of effective short-cuts by the concerned mental health workers. For a counselor who is unable to meet the obvious needs of the students he is seeing, who is forced to terminate one promising contact after another before any gains have been made, self-deception or resignation is a more likely outcome.

13

Transfer
and Resumption

The issue of referral, of transferring students to outside therapists or clinics, arises when the period of work at the center proves insufficient or is not indicated from the start. The topic merits special attention, since to turn away or drop clients without providing another source of help can, under certain conditions, have very destructive effects. At Brandeis, a sizable proportion of those seeking counseling show chronic neurotic patterns which, to be reliably resolved, may require a longer period of work than the center could provide, or guarantee, even with the staff-student ratio at its highest. During the first decade of the service's existence, between 20 and 30 percent of all those seen during the school year were ultimately referred outside. Among the comments of those who feel that they received only limited help from the center, statements that counseling did no more than scratch the surface are balanced by others saying in effect: "a beginning but a good one." The student's ultimate judgment depends to a large degree on what happens after counseling ends, an instance of the future defining the past. Depending on the success of the subsequent referral, the modest achievement of the counseling period can be transformed—in *fact*, not just in the person's view—into a path to a hoped-for better life or a path to confirmed despair.

Whom to Refer

Who—if anyone—should be referred out from the start? This question presents itself to all college services that are not limited to diagnosis and referral but cannot accommodate all comers. Having to weed out applicants and wishing to do it rationally, one attempts to set up some criteria to determine who can or cannot be helped on campus. Psychotics, borderline cases, homosexuals, people with certain psychosomatic conditions may be regarded as unfit clients for a college service. Plausible as some of these generalizations may seem, they are invalid; the diagnostic label does not say too much about the individual case, particularly in late adolescence. Whether a student can move in counseling, and how fast, one can find only when one starts working with him; but one has no chance to find out if, from the start, one separates the presumed goats from the sheep and eliminates the former.

At Brandeis the first college psychiatrist tried to refer outside all applicants whose disturbance seemed severe, and all those judged to require long-term treatment who were able to pay for it. When it became obvious, however, that the large majority of those referred made no more than a token effort to obtain help outside, we resumed our earlier practice of working with all comers. We made some "amazing" discoveries. Some "borderline" students benefited substantially and durably from a short period of counseling—more than did some who had neurotic or "minor developmental problems." In some cases psychotic manifestations were eliminated or became less intense; elaborate obsessional systems bordering on delusional were weakened or completely dissolved. I recall one young man who was in good rapport with his counselor and was eventually persuaded by him to apply to a clinic for therapy. He was rejected as "borderline" and much too disturbed for outpatient treatment, and he reapplied to the center. His counselor, who did not consider him quite that disturbed, felt comfortable about working with him, and they did extremely well. Some confirmed neurotics were helped decisively by counseling distributed over three or four years, or else they became referrable very quickly. On the other hand, some of the students judged to have "normal adolescent problems" are now in their seventh or eighth year of intensive therapy. Some of these findings can be ascribed to false diagnoses, but others seem to me to bespeak our false assumptions about who is and is not treatable. For some of those who did not prove treatable, we were still able to be of use. In some cases the students' condition (for instance, that of extreme withdrawal) remained unchanged, but the contact they maintained with their counselors probably helped them to get through college without major breakdowns or upsets; some of them were scheduled to come once a month, and some would ask for an appointment when they felt the need. One girl, still essentially an autistic child at twenty and unresponsive to ordinary psychotherapy, was enabled to stay in school and do well in her studies by the strong, insightful support of her dormitory counselor, who had discovered that this girl was best treated as a five-year-old. The center's role in this case was to give encouragement to the resident counselor. In several other cases our service to an acutely disturbed student consisted of helping him or her survive in college while some promising alternative arrangement was being negotiated with the family. Having to meet the demands of atypical clients and of unusual situations served to develop versatility and to extend the counselors' competence. Willingness to vary offerings so as to meet the individual students' needs replaced uncritical reliance on formal diagnosis and the practice of selecting clients to fit one's standard methods.

In considering referrals outside, the nature and extent of *available resources* in the school and community are more important than diagnostic labels as such. If a larger number of local therapists specialized, successfully, in "psychotic" or "borderline" cases, we would be more justified and more effective than we have been in referring atypical cases outside. (As it is, when I tried, through the mediation of a knowledgeable analyst, to get an appropriate therapist for a well-to-do suicidal patient, he was turned down by no less than eight therapists, all of them choosing to remain anonymous so as to prevent possible future referrals.) Furthermore, if the outpatient clinics of our area had no waiting lists, we might handle our own admissions very selectively. We could then concentrate on the kinds of problems that individual staff members feel most capable of handling, referring out all others. Where staffs have little time for anything beyond emergencies, this type of personal selection actually takes place. However, the outside treatment resources are grossly insufficient, even in the Boston area; and a college mental health center worth the name should actually be a comprehensive community service, equipped to offer timely and adequate help to all—or almost all—students who need it. At the Brandeis center, through many years of its existence, we were able to accept all student comers for short periods of exploratory counseling and, subsequently, to offer longer periods of work to all those who were thought to need it.

Even in these nearly ideal circumstances, the existence of a time limit to school counseling makes this opportunity for therapy less than ideal for some. As discussed in Chapter Twelve, some students would benefit from a situation without externally predetermined limits. Then there are those given to distortion and to "acting out," who are easily tempted to strike back at the center whenever they feel let down by the counselor, for a real or fantasied reason, or to manipulate the staff for some purpose of their own. In one extreme case the center was deluged by telephone calls from friends, physicians, and faculty members, each of whom had received from the student a different but equally alarming version of what took place in the sessions. The counselor may be able to meet such challenges and turn them to therapeutic advantage; but in deciding whether "intramural" or "extramural" treatment would be best for a given student, one must take into account his potential for creating a disturbance on campus. Yet, for students with limited means, alternatives to college counseling are not easily available, and—all other considerations apart—the decision is not totally the counselor's. When the center is overcrowded, we naturally try to refer students out as speedily as possible, but no one can be referred successfully who is not ready for the move. It is well to consider all the pros and cons of a quick referral, but in the last analysis one selects for such referrals those whom one can refer without a lengthy preparation. To refer those who may say that they will go, but then do not go, is no more than pretense.

Prompt and Delayed Referrals

Factors facilitating quick referral are adequate finances, previous (favorable) experience with therapy on the part of the student or his family, and the person's own readiness, or near readiness, to commit himself to this project. The campus service can be approached by the student in a very tentative way; such an attitude is usually sufficient for entering the exploratory period, the period of "precounseling." A much more serious intention is needed for a student to commit himself to possibly prolonged outside therapy, with all the sacrifices it demands. Such readiness may result from an acute upset, from accumulated suffering, from giving up the prolonged struggle to solve one's problems on his own, or from a new-born hope for a better state of affairs. Most students, when they first approach the center, lack a combination of circumstances favorable to the initiation of therapy. Since their suffering is not extreme and their problems are not out of the ordinary, they would not think of seeking professional help were it not made easily available to them, requiring no changes or complications in their present design of life, or any great change in their self-image: "There are many people here like me who need professional help but who wouldn't go so far as to arrange and pay for private sessions." "So many students go to counseling, there is no stigma attached to it here; it is not like being in therapy." "I had money, but I was afraid to go to an unknown therapist, not knowing if I could trust him. I felt I could trust the center; the school would not employ incompetent people." "It was extremely valuable for me to have a therapist on campus, one I could go to without having to pay. My parents are quite ignorant about therapy, and it was a help to me to go independently, without having to involve them or get money from them. I had an opportunity to get to understand how therapy works." Occasionally one encounters students who justify their lack of involvement in sessions by their feeling that counseling is not, after all, "the real thing." When pressed, they may request a referral; in my experience, however, it is usually no more than a gesture at this stage.

When circumstances are exceptionally favorable, genuine readiness for an outside referral can be developed, with the counselor's participation, in the course of a few sessions. But in the absence of inner acceptance of this step, the prematurely referred student either will not go or will not stay or will not respond to the outside therapist's efforts to involve him. Furthermore, in referring a student before he knows him well, the counselor runs a greater risk of choosing a type of therapy, or a therapist, not suitable for him. In making a hasty referral, the counselor may forfeit his chance to be of any further use to the student: "I shall never again trust the counselor who referred me to X." A hasty denial by the counselor of the student's possible need for prolonged therapy may have a similar negative effect: "I felt worse and worse, but I did not return to the center to ask for a referral; X had told me that I had no serious problems, just a bit slow in developing." The demand that the student show cause why he should be sent into therapy does not work too well either: "My friend came to the center for a referral, but the counselor would not give her any names, asking for proof that she was really disturbed. So she got a name somewhere else." There is no substitute for a decision based on a possibly time-consuming, collaborative exploration.

Haste in making decisions may result from pressure of time or from some attitudes of the counselor; but, whatever the reasons, it is usually as wasteful in counseling as elsewhere. Below are reports of two students referred to outside therapists after brief consultations, one judiciously, the other hastily; both reports were written two years later.

The first student wrote: "After only two visits the counselor advised me to take an extended leave of absence and gave me the name of a very expensive psychiatrist. Like a fool I took his advice and started private treatment. Although I did settle a few minor problems while receiving help, I do not believe that this was worth the thousands it cost." The second student accepted the idea of outside therapy, after weighing its advantages and disadvantages during his one counseling session, and described, plausibly, the kind of person to whom he felt he would respond ("earthy, straightforward, even blunt"). He was referred to a man who matched the description, and he took to him: "I was advised after one session to enter private treatment with a psychiatrist whose name the center provided. I am extremely grateful for this, for I feel I would not have achieved as much in the time that would have been allowed me at the center."

One might assume that no preparation for referral is necessary if the student has already made up his mind to go into therapy and is merely asking for names. That is not necessarily true; to be of use, one often has to provide more than is requested explicitly. To send a student one knows nothing about to a therapist one knows next to nothing about is to engage in make-believe. A graduate student asked me to refer him to a private therapist. He had attended an outpatient clinic for a year and, having discovered during the next year that he was as miserable as ever, was persuaded by his girl friend to give therapy another try. He seemed unable to say anything about his experience with his first therapist: what he had disliked in his approach, what he had learned, what he wanted his new therapist to be like—except that he should be older than the first therapist. Finally, I told him that if he noticed nothing, felt nothing, would do whatever was suggested, his second therapy was fated to be as useless as the first—and I did not wish to contribute to such an outcome by providing him with a name. This jolted the student into talking to me "for real." He did have much to say about his experiences with the resident and, having said it, became involved in discussing with me various alternative plans for his therapy. His mood changed; he was no longer apathetic, but alert and hopeful. After taking some time to think matters over, he chose one alternative; later he let me know that the therapist he went to was working out very well.

An effective preparation for referral requires the client's participation. "Hasty" decisions leading to failure are often those that were made by the counselor unilaterally and never became the client's own, even if he acted on them. The situation here is similar to that of a person who goes into therapy merely to fulfill his family's wishes. Great readiness to accept such advice from any personal or professional counselor does not augur well for the success of the enterprise. Well-prepared referrals, on the other hand, can be extremely worthwhile.

Most of our successful referrals are made after a longer period of counseling. The task of transferring students at that time presents difficulties which are the obverse of the influences facilitating the entrance into counseling. What is involved is not only changing the therapist; the whole implication of the therapeutic endeavor may change when it is transplanted from the familiar school setting to an outside agency. Sacrifices demanded, in time and money, and the necessity to involve parents underline the importance of the undertaking; the student may feel that if such sacrifices are warranted he must be seriously ill. Separation of therapy from the semifamilial school environment may frighten and repel the student, making him feel that he is being pushed out into an unknown cold world. If these feelings are worked out well in counseling, the process of arriving at the decision to continue therapy may be accompanied by significant experiences and insights. Students who have been very resistant to the psychological approach may on this occasion acknowledge for the first time their serious need for help. Through acceptance of a referral, as well as of termination of counseling, dependence on the family may be brought a step closer to resolution.

A case in point is a student who hesitantly decided to go into therapy. When a therapist was found whom he immediately liked, his mother became worried and called the counselor to complain that her son was being sent to a stranger. After that the student became upset and tried to coax the counselor to see him for six more sessions, promising to transfer afterward. He was afraid to give up the security and comfort of the familiar relationship, just as he had been afraid to be away from home and mother. When the student was able to see the relationship between his past and present behavior, he grudgingly decided to transfer to the new therapist.

Parents may actively involve themselves in the issue of transfer in other ways as well. Their attitude to this plan, as well as the student's feelings about seeking their help, must be assessed in advance. If there is entrenched hostility toward the parents, or if the student for some other reason feels a strong need to make therapy his own unaided enterprise, he may decide against private therapy.

Students who apply to outpatient clinics, either for these reasons or because of the family's lack of funds, can do so without involving the parents. Most of the well-to-do students approach their parents eventually. The task of obtaining their support, or arriving at the decision to forgo it, usually arises during a late stage of the counseling period. This task presents pitfalls of its own.

If the parents have clear evidence of the student's progress in counseling, they are usually glad to support therapy if they can afford it. When such evidence is missing, or misperceived, or when the parents feel strongly about the stigma attached to psychiatric treatment or about the expenses involved, the student is faced with a difficult problem. In this situation he may once more feel in need of support and may want the counselor to plead his case with the parents. Justifiable as this wish appears, the insistence on it sometimes covers up the student's own unresolved conflicts about further therapy. If the counselor undertakes to convince the parents, he may find that once he succeeds the student himself loses interest in the plan. In most of our cases willingness to approach the parents on one's own is one of the criteria of the student's readiness for therapy. He may have fleeting fantasies about the counselor's doing the persuading but will not actually ask for assistance. He may feel relieved, however, if the counselor is willing to back him up in case of need.

Once the student is ready to face the parents in earnest, he often finds them much more receptive than he had expected, or than they had been before. If he has to go through a hard struggle to secure their help, or even fails to obtain it, he still gains insight and self-confidence in the process; the same is true if he arrives at a decision to forgo the parents' support, realizing that, in his particular circumstances, this support might make therapy less effective. For instance, the father of a girl who was much afraid of hurting and disillusioning her parents reluctantly agreed to pay for her therapy; when the first bill arrived, however, he explosively refused to pay it, maintaining that she had misunderstood him. The student returned to the counselor and, after facing her own suppressed fury, was able for the first time to confront her father with her disappointment and anger. Another student in a similar situation met the parents' challenge that he himself pay for the therapy by finding a job at school and borrowing a sum of money from a friend. In all such cases the counselor's well-intentioned intervention would have deprived the student of an opportunity for personal growth and for working out some of his problems with his parents. Intervention may be necessary, however, in cases of acute breakdown, in some atypical cases, or in cases when the parents themselves are severely disturbed.

To be handled successfully, the issue of referral, like that of termination, must be worked on *in advance*. It can be introduced, as an impersonal possibility, when the conditions of counseling, including the time limit that is currently in use, are first discussed; later it will be brought up, repeatedly if necessary, in relation to the student himself. Knowing that the period of work defined by the time limit is guaranteed in case of need, the counselor can feel free to consider and discuss the best time of termination and the possible advantages for the student of an early referral. Many good transfers are achieved long before the "deadline." But the timing of the suggestion is crucial. It has little chance to be considered by the student in earnest unless and until he has experienced some progress in counseling; this is true even of students who enter counseling for the express purpose of getting help in arranging for therapy. On the other hand, if continuation seems strongly indicated, the issue must be brought up early enough to permit the student to work out his misgivings before the end of the year. Impatient pushing of the plan by the counselor may lead to futile struggles or to a spurious acceptance by the student. An abrupt or authoritarian referral may be perceived as personal rejection and have very destructive effects. If the issue of referral has not been resolved when the time limit is reached, or by the end of the school year, the student may be invited to return for a few sessions in the fall for help in arriving at some decision. He may at that time ask for a referral; he may present convincing evidence that he can carry on on his own; or he may use the visit to review some of his doubts, perhaps getting a little closer to a real decision.

In some cases the process by which the decision is reached extends over months or even years following the termination of counseling; quite a bit of additional therapeutic work may be done during these sporadic contacts devoted to discussions of possible resumption of therapy. For instance, Ruth (the young woman whose story is given at the end of Chapter Twelve) from the start had protested termination and was dead set against accepting a transfer. She came in after the summer vacation to report substantial progress; she felt that she was now where she had wanted to be, or at least almost there. However, during her later occasional visits—devoted, on the face of it, to further progress reports—it gradually became obvious that old problems were reappearing in new guises. When the girl was finally confronted with this situation, she herself raised the issue of resuming therapy and was helped to make arrangements with a clinic, about a year after the official termination of counseling; soon after that she discontinued her contacts with the counselor. Most students, after having made contact with the new therapist, appreciate the opportunity to see their counselor a few more times, or at least once. The overlap makes the transition more comfortable and helps to resolve the problems involved in termination and transfer.

The testimony of students whom we have referred, and of the therapists to whom we have referred them, shows that it pays to put thought and effort into referrals. The well-referred students are well prepared to settle down to work. The questionnaire comments of those whose referrals "took" evaluate their period of campus counseling very positively, as having prepared them well for what was to follow: "Though we barely scratched the surface, the year of counseling was invaluable; it helped me to get started by making me aware of certain feelings and patterns which I had continuously denied; I finally recognized that problems existed and had to be dealt with." "The campus counseling mitigated many of the immediate dilemmas for which I sought help, provided me with a sense of support I needed so desperately for a time, but it was most successful in preparing me to enter a more intense therapy situation from which I benefited tremendously." Some students stress the importance of their own initiative, for which the campus setup or the handling of the transfer has provided a chance: "The year of counseling was my first experience in therapy and I went completely of my own accord. The first year was a period of 'opening up' and admitting things to myself." "At the time when I wanted to resume, my counselor was unavailable; he gave me the option of waiting for him but also suggested that I might need more time than I had left at the center and that it might be better for me to seek outside help. This proved the best alternative. Earlier I would not have been able to make constructive use of it, but now I did; and the fact that I assumed financial responsibility for private therapy made me take it more seriously." "As a preparation for intensive therapy outside, the informal setting of the center is invaluable."

Some Obstacles to Resumption

More instructive than successful referrals are cases in which attempts at reentering therapy fail, in spite of favorable circumstances and seemingly adequate preparation. I was shocked once by my failure to involve in therapy a graduate of Brandeis, Sharon, who, two years earlier, had had a good period of counseling with me, centered on a specific issue prominent in her life at the time. We both felt then that we had made very good use of the few weeks at our disposal, dealing successfully with all obstacles to movement. In her questionnaire Sharon evaluated her experience in a highly positive way; this was not just lip service. During the following summer she came to consult me about some important decision, and once more some general issues were brought up and clarified in this context. When, more than a year later, Sharon, no longer a student, decided to come to me as a private patient, I was confident that it would work out well, though I sensed the strength of her reservations. The situation was favorable; I knew this from my experience with therapies of several former students who had made good beginnings in counseling. Yet, when we started working, I found myself unable to initiate and maintain any genuine communication in sessions. Feeling that it should be possible to do so, I struggled hard for several weeks; finally Sharon unwillingly recalled an old dream that summarized the evidence I had been disregarding; namely, that at this point she wanted no intrusion into her privacy. She had pressured herself into therapy very much against her will, as some kind of a dreary obligation, and had tried to stick with it, feeling that she would never do it if she did not now. Once this realization was put into words, she acted on it immediately, abandoning the unwelcome project with great relief. (She returned to working with me a year later, greatly concerned now for the fate of a new and promising relationship, and eventually brought her therapy to a satisfying conclusion.)

Prominent among the factors that made the second try at therapy very different from the first were Sharon's definitions of two enterprises, counseling and therapy. Counseling (often organized around a specific problem) was nothing out of the ordinary for Brandeis students, but Sharon viewed the need for private therapy (possibly dealing with much wider personal issues) as a valid proof of some personal "wrongness," either illness or moral badness; given this premise, her refusal to enter the situation was indeed a positive act, one of safeguarding her self-respect. She was not unaware at this point of the need for some changes, and had also experienced some progress, but she wished to continue to work things out on her own.

The reservation about accepting help with one's problems is a familiar one. Most of those respondents who had decided against approaching the center felt that they should be able to help themselves; they felt that accepting help implied weakness and inferiority and led to dependence, to giving up one's own will. This particular apprehension concerning psychotherapy is so strong in our culture that the center's staff has tried to meet it in the general description of counseling given in the *Student Handbook*. But we still have to explain or demonstrate to many a student that, whatever assistance we may give, ultimately only he can help himself; most counseled students come to appreciate the role of the counselor as a facilitator, not an agent.

Conflict about receiving help is only one of the misgivings people have about therapy. In my first contacts with students approaching the center, I usually spend much time exploring their personal definitions of counseling or therapy, the hopes and particularly the fears, explicit or implicit, aroused by this unfamiliar enterprise. But in the instance described above, I neglected this task; I felt that our earlier shared experience guaranteed a shared definition of what to me was a natural continuation of the first period of work. Looking at a familiar face in the same office where we met before, I never suspected how different the situation looked to Sharon. Consequently, instead of listening as well as I did in our first contact and taking in her implicit refusal to participate, I tried much too actively to remove from our path what I thought were minor obstacles, some initial inertia that had to be overcome to get to the place where we had been before. Since my attitude implied the notion that this girl belonged in therapy (that is, was "sick" or "bad"), no wonder that she experienced none of the good feelings she had had during counseling; she felt the atmosphere to be solemn and oppressive, the time spent in sessions detracting from her life, rather than adding to it. Nor was she able as before to express her feelings about what was happening between us so that we could deal with them immediately.

Another student, in comparing her two periods of counseling (similar in some respects to the "counseling" and "therapy" in the case just discussed), explained the difference as follows:

> When I broke down on coming to Brandeis and started seeing you, I almost deliberately let myself remain in that state for a while and open up in counseling. I needed help and I got it; I learned a great deal and felt very good about it. There were no negative aspects; it was a complete success. But then I was only able to do it because I knew that if I did not get better soon I could go home any moment and get relief. Now [two years later] it is different; going home would not help. All I have now is my ability to study, stay in school, live from day to day. If I lost that by breaking down, there would be nothing left for me. That must be why this time I kept my feelings down; when they finally broke through, I was utterly miserable, unable to do anything at all. After a week of this hell, I just pushed it all back, and now I hope I can get involved in studies again; I could not risk going into therapy now. Yet I am glad to have seen what I have seen; maybe sometime it will make a difference. [At a later date this young woman entered outside therapy and completed it to her satisfaction.]

These cases demonstrate the extremes of the difficulties that may stand in the way of resuming therapy, of getting its "second installment," in school or outside. In long-term work with neurotic patients, resistance to changing one's way of life increases greatly as one moves from the periphery to the core of the neurotic pattern and the disturbances become more intense. Time and an established close contact with the therapist may be needed for the patient to engage in the struggle that leads to a "decision" to change. In a short-term contact we cannot afford prolonged deadlock; we must always be on the lookout for ways of bypassing obstacles, of saving time and pain. Perhaps for some of the center's clients repeated episodes of brief "crisis counseling" might prove the method of choice. If it was pursued productively in the initial contact, one might consider with the student the advisability of his using future minor crises as opportunities for doing some work at the center. This form of "distributed counseling" may serve as an alternative to transfer in some cases; in others, as a good preparation for it.

To Whom to Refer?

Once the student is ready for transfer, where or to whom should we refer him? In selecting a therapist for a given student, we must look for one whose style of working is likely to be acceptable to him. Some of these preferences are fairly general. Not many Brandeis students respond well to the authoritarian aspect of the "medical model," nor to an emphasis on "pathology," nor to a disregard of realities, nor to detachment and passivity in the therapist, by whatever theory these happen to be justified. As we have seen, complaints of this kind have been made also against the center's staff, relatively egalitarian on the whole; but if a student has been satisfied with his counselor, he tends to measure the new therapist against the standard set by the first, and he may find him wanting. Such rejection may prove transitory, but in other instances it has a sound basis and is likely to persist. "He did not *talk to me* like you do" is a rather frequent comment; "he just asked questions" or "he just sat there looking impassive." In trying to help students accept their new therapists, I used to share the general propensity to explain all difficulties by the "transference" to the old counselor, but I have found that this global explanation oversimplifies matters. The orientation of the center is indeed different from the one that students often meet "outside." Annie, after a period of counseling, dropped out of school and was seen for a year by a well-recommended psychiatrist with whom she made good progress; she then reentered school and later had another period of counseling with a different staff member. She wrote as follows:

> There are some special things about the center, I have found out. I worked with two counselors here, before and after I had a period of therapy with a private psychiatrist. With both counselors I felt that they saw not just my problems, but also, at all times, saw the health in me and were working to strengthen it; I was never made to feel that I am a hopeless neurotic. It felt good to be treated as just a human being who had some problem, not as a pathological case. With the outside psychiatrist I was first and foremost a patient.

Beyond considering the prospective therapist's general orientation and competence, one tries to determine how good he would be for a given patient. This is not an easy task. The referral practices of different counselors vary, but most of us welcome feedback from students and therapists and try to keep track of who has done well with whom. I feel, however, that these attempts have not been as active, systematic, and productive as they should have been. In the past my best successes were obtained with the following method: I consulted friends of mine who were working in training hospitals and clinics and had observed the performance of many beginning therapists. I then referred several students I had counseled to some of the young therapists whom my friends considered promising, and I also met the therapists. Then I would try to get feedback from both the student and the therapist. As a result, some therapists were eliminated, and some proved very successful—at least with a particular type of client; for a period of time they would function as my main resource for referrals. This method depends on having the right kind of friends working in the right kind of places, a condition that cannot be fulfilled at will.

In the case of therapists who are established, one of the obstacles to keeping track of referral outcomes is the belief subscribed to by many that, to be therapeutic, their relationship to their patients must not be shared with anyone, to any extent. Our adherence to the idea of "sacred privacy" of individual therapy obviously has many determinants, the valid assumptions being compounded by our natural reluctance to expose our weaknesses to an observer's

eyes. Frank interchanges with colleagues being as difficult as they
are, we lack reliable knowledge of the others' strengths and weaknesses in their actual day-to-day work and of the workings of the
"personal equation," of what makes for a "good fit" between patient and therapist. Most of our guesses about who might be good
for whom are no more than just that: conjectures based on little
or no evidence.

Lacking a sound basis for referrals, even after decades of
placing patients with therapists, I advocate shopping around. I give
a student the names of several people, known or reputed to be
generally competent, whom I tentatively believe to be "good prospects" for him or her; I tell students that they may have to consult
more than one candidate before they can make up their minds.
Many students resist this suggestion; they want the counselor to take
over, because they are embarrassed to shop around and regard the
decision as a great burden. One student, when she thought she had
to find a therapist without assistance from me, imagined herself,
panic-stricken, shouting in the streets of New York: "Help! I need
a psychiatrist!" Another former counselee, to whom I had explained
my policy, wrote asking for names of therapists "who you feel
would be most right for me. I reluctantly understand that I will
have to make a choice; you know of course that your preference
would be rejoiced at." Unless one has a candidate one is very certain of, one should try to overcome this reluctance. Some of the
young people we see tend to discount completely their personal
impressions and preferences in this unfamiliar and tense situation.
They may find the behavior of the prospective therapist puzzling or
disturbing; yet, thinking of people as roles, they assume that this
must be "just the way psychiatrists are." After consulting two or
three people, the prospective client realizes that—like any other
class of people—therapists vary, and that he likes and trusts some
much more than others. Choosing one's therapist contributes to
making therapy one's own enterprise; this is particularly important
if the student's family pressures him to go to someone of *their* choice,
a not infrequent occurrence.

Unfortunately, some practitioners seem to share and rein-
force the client's dislike of frank mutual inspection, as if the therapist
alone should make all decisions. I have even heard some maintain

that personal exploration is superfluous, since the therapist's training guarantees his competence with all types of people. This denial of the importance of personal traits is an obvious distortion of reality. Luckily, other therapists accept the need for a bilateral decision. Some few make this acceptance explicit; they invite prospective patients to ask them questions about points pertinent to their decision—in the case of Brandeis students these are often questions of theory—and try to answer them accurately, at length. I know one who does this customarily and does not charge for the exploratory sessions. Such an invitation may shock an "expert-oriented" client; if he accepts it, however, he can get a clearer idea of the person whom he might be hiring for this all-important job and of the approach to be used. I have good evidence that such exploration removes obstacles to communication between "partners in therapy" and eases the beginning of their work. The reaction of those few students who are frightened and repelled by being offered, from the start, their share of decisions about their therapy gives a clue to the kind of approach they would accept and may eventually facilitate a better referral.

If students can see their counselor while a referral is being worked out, they may use the sessions to sort out their positive or negative feelings about the prospective therapist. Which of them are irrationally exaggerated? Which have a basis in reality? Through such sorting they acquire a firmer basis for rejecting or accepting the prospect of this new relationship. In some cases a longer period of overlap is needed, as was the case with Lisa, the depressed young woman, described in Chapter Seven, who, after a fiasco with one therapist, had a period of counseling with me; only after several weeks of "overlap" did she decide to commit herself to working with the therapist to whom I had introduced her. In their questionnaire comments and in letters, many students express appreciation of having been referred to the right man: "I was very fortunate in that I had enjoyed contact with a psychologist at the counseling center for a year before going into therapy outside the school. He was able to recommend to me a person on the basis of accurate knowledge of both myself and the therapist." "The therapist has proved just right for me. We are told in social work school that a

good referral is one of the most valuable services you can render—
I see that now in my own case."

In addition to the normal difficulties of transferring from one
therapist to another and from inside the school to outside, we have
to contend at present with recent changes in attitudes, which make
many students reject traditional psychotherapy in favor of some new
method. Years ago this factor was not prominent. I was occasionally
charged with the task of locating a therapist well read in humanities
or sympathetic to existentialism, but there was no question of what
brand of therapy to select. "Therapy," in the Boston area at least,
meant psychoanalytically oriented therapy. Those students who
wanted the very best, or the most prestigeful, inquired about the
possibility of having a real analysis; today this is an infrequent occurrence, and the criticism of psychoanalysis is much more widespread: "This year I have had a chance to study psychotherapy in
various Boston settings. I have become thoroughly disillusioned in
the efficacy of any of the traditional analytic therapies. . . . I have
seen no evidence that there is any improvement resulting from them,
and their potential for harm is not to be underestimated either."

There is also the lure of the novel offerings. Most students
who are being referred by us to outside therapists do not specify
"therapy" as to kind, but some ask for referrals to groups or ask
the counselor's opinion of certain new techniques: motor therapy,
behavior modification, Gestalt, reality therapy, various relaxation
techniques. They do not usually seek the center's help in locating
settings that deviate too far from the traditional, to say nothing of
assistance in the therapeutically conceived use of drugs. They join
on their own the quasi-therapeutic, "consciousness-raising" groups
sponsored by various ideological movements, such as communes or
some of the women's liberation groups; they may want, however, to
discuss their experiences with their counselors. Of those who seek
no enduring contact with the center and no assistance in their
search for outside help, many turn to what is furthest from the
routine of the couch, being more willing to give a try to Zen or to
Yoga or to Transcendental Meditation. Still, the "new look" in
therapeutic devices faces the center's staff with the task of acquiring
information and forming an opinion about at least some of the new

methods and also about their practitioners. The last is more important than the first, since effectiveness does not inhere in isolated techniques as such. If we are to include the "new-look" therapists into our referral resources, we must locate the gifted among them who are reasonably and reliably effective, and we must make an effort to obtain feedback on their performance from those we refer.

14

The Uses of College Counseling: A Summary

I want to repeat and amplify here what I would most like to convey to counselors and therapists, particularly those who work with young people; to the college administrators concerned with providing counseling services to students; and also to the educated laymen at large. My observations, based on my work at Brandeis and on many other professional and personal experiences, fall under three headings, dealing with several interrelated topics: (1) the general issue of what makes therapy effective, (2) the role that psychological work with college students can and should play in promoting effective therapy, and (3) the organization needed for such promotion and for making assistance with a wide range of developmental problems readily available to students. If properly organized and conducted on a large scale, psychological work with the college group could raise the mental health level of the population—both directly, by assisting the emotional maturation of the college educated, and less directly, by being an excellent source of learning and a very promising method of training. At the time when, according to all available evidence, only a minority of therapists achieve reliable successes, the advantages of these training places are not to be neglected. There is an urgent need for a radical improvement in training.

What Makes Therapy Effective?

When, over fifteen years ago, I started using student questionnaires as a source of information on what furthers and what hinders progress in counseling, the bulk of the formal research on psychotherapy showed a very one-sided approach to the issue. One mostly studied "client variables" in an attempt to determine who were good or bad risks for psychotherapy; one mostly discovered that the less seriously disturbed the person, the better his chance to be helped. I did not want to use such findings to exclude many of those who needed help from the field of our interest and endeavor; I stopped looking at journals. When in recent years I started catching up on my reading, I was delighted to discover that the impetus given to research by Carl Rogers' early determination to subject his theory of therapy to a rigorous test has borne fruit. A great deal of research has become focused, at long last, on *therapist* variables. The results of these studies provide impressive evidence of how crucial for the outcome of the contact are the counselor's attitudes toward the client. Researchers most active in this field have defined the main "therapeutic ingredients" in terms close to those used at one time by Rogers, but no matter how these attitudes are labeled, the message is always the same. An accurately empathic, concerned, noncontrolling attitude toward the client, if genuinely held and consistently conveyed, is what distinguished the effective from the ineffective therapists, no matter to what school they belong.

I was delighted with these findings, but not actually surprised. I felt that formal research was catching up with the conclusions of those therapists who reflect on their experiences and ask questions of their patients. I myself have used the feedback from students to identify what they valued and what they rejected in their counselors. In reading the questionnaire comments of about four hundred students (seen by a total of ten counselors), I compared the responses of the 75 percent who found counseling helpful with the responses of the 25 percent who did not or were doubtful. While members of the second group had little good to say about their counselors, those who had benefited contributed both praise and criticism. Empathic understanding and comments stimulating the student's own thinking were greatly appreciated. Most of the positive comments, however, referred not to these skills but to the counselor's personal concern for the client—his readiness, as one student put it, "to take your problems to heart." The instances quoted to exemplify these concerns varied in kind. Some acutely disturbed students, who felt that the counselor was their strongest link with reality, stressed less his being able occasionally "to make some sense of the clutter in my mind" than simply his presence and his willingness to make himself available. Others emphasized the counselor's readiness to go beyond the call of duty in trying to meet their needs. Most frequently students simply referred to the value of talking, personally, to another human being and of being, in turn, treated like a person by him. The students' most frequent complaint was the counselors' insufficient activity. Student after student expressed annoyance with the "silent listener" or declared that they could more readily open up in a conversation than in "a speaker-audience" or "a press conference" situation. The notion that therapist inactivity is necessary and sufficient for promoting progress in therapy has emerged, via the student feedback, as the misconception most widely held by counselors in the 1960s.

There were other complaints in addition to inactivity. In trying to find the common denominator of those student complaints that occurred with some frequency, I soon discovered that what they basically objected to in a counselor was *detachment*. Distance and impersonality may be conveyed by silences; by a rigid adherence to rules or "contracts"; by stilted or technical language and an inexpressive face; by limiting one's comments to a few categories (such as questions and standard textbook interpretations); by consistently withholding information, opinions, and explanations; or by any other method of unaccountably rejecting the natural, flexible give and take that the interpersonal situation demands. Whatever the counselor's reasons for such behavior, students who are treated in this way do not feel merely discouraged from talking; they feel dehumanized, as if they were merely "specimens to be studied," and studied by someone who remains aloof and seems "not to care a hoot" about what happens to them.

Conversely, the common core of the students' specific wishes and the requests they make of the counselor is that he *be there,* be with them fully, not stay in a world apart. Just how his presence has to be manifested will differ with the clients and their momentary states, but there are some ways of acting with which such presence is incompatible. It excludes displaying superiority, disregarding the other's opinions, and exercising authority arbitrarily; it does *not* exclude the use of earned authority, one based on competence that has become manifest to the client, nor the use of a distribution of functions that is required by the task. Different from some ideologues of freedom and equality, most students in counseling naturally assume that the outcome of the enterprise is the responsibility of the counselor, who knows what it is all about and what he is doing. This assumption does not prevent them from taking a more and more active role in their therapy; it is indeed the therapist's responsibility to see that they do. "He talks to me" is what students say about a satisfactory counselor about as often as they say "He listens well." This means that he is willing to engage in the give and take of a genuinely communicative conversation. He does not "just sit there" or "just nod his head" or "just ask questions trying to figure me out"; nor does he "put words into my mouth" or "preach at me" or "know everything better." Rather, he is the one who "is willing to confront you and tell you what he thinks, take it or leave it," who "makes me think and does not hesitate to challenge me," who "is never dogmatic and bases his comments on the present behavior which we both can observe." As a result, "I never felt I was dealing with a magician but always with another human being." My personal experience as a therapist has also led me to realize the crucial importance of staying, undeviatingly, *with* the client, of focusing on his entire momentary state. My best successes have been achieved in those few cases where I found it easy to "be there" always, although what I actually *did* varied widely. But whenever some anxiety or some surfacing concern of my own—the wish to teach, to censure, to reassure, to prove a point, or simply "to get things done"—made me lose touch with the other person, there was trouble ahead. Issues would become clouded, doubts reawakened, progress stopped or slowed down. When I finally—with the help of my Brandeis clients—realized all of this, I started checking my messages for possible ambiguities, and I started following Angyal's advice to ask oneself every now and then: Am I satisfied with the human aspect of my interaction with this person, my client? Are things all right between us? If not, why not?

Is all this, research findings included, news or not news? Those who think not are not limited to therapists. If I were to tell a layman that people who have lost confidence in themselves and in others can be best helped to recover it by one who is understanding, genuinely concerned, and trustworthy, I doubt that he would be amazed. He might well be amazed to learn of the amount of elaborate research it took the professionals to discover this truth. The difficulty and the value of formal research are not to be minimized; respect for evidence needs constant fostering in a field of work where strong motives and beliefs make it extremely hard for us to be self-critical. But neither should we minimize the value and the findings of the informal research on how people function, in which all of us are engaged as long as we live. The assumptions resulting from our accumulated and sifted experiences, called "naive psychology" by Fritz Heider (1958), are the largest reservoir of our knowledge of "human nature." Talented observers and thinkers have extended this reservoir by depositing similar knowledge in their works: essays, novels, dramas, or discussions of philosophical issues. Heider has demonstrated that our everyday understanding of human affairs is based on implicit theories which more often than not meet the test of permitting valid predictions. Our analysis of interpersonal phenomena, though often distorted by our own preferences and needs, proceeds in a way analogous to experimental methods and leads to a veridical assessment of the important features of our social world. Since the quasi-scientific approach is already present in naive perception and judgment, the latter should not be devalued as sources of concepts and hypotheses to be elaborated and tested; they also provide guidelines to practical action. Anyone working with people, patients included, will find that a more precise and articulate awareness of the common logic of human interaction, which Heider has tried to promote, will sharpen his working tools and facilitate mutual understanding.

The fact that the research findings on therapist variables are consistent with the assumptions of common sense does not detract from their value; on the contrary, it adds to it. But can this research confirmation of what must be generally known be of practical significance for our field of work? I believe it can. Although almost all therapists acknowledge the importance of the relationship, of the "therapeutic alliance," not many give this factor the prominence it deserves. Some actually devalue all of it as "mere support," or as unprofessional "emotional involvement," simple-minded or sentimental. More typically, they view a good relationship as a necessary but not a sufficient condition of success; that is, as something that fosters the client's liking and trust for the therapist and thus predisposes him to respond favorably to the therapist's interventions, be they interpretations or suggestions. Therapeutic effects, they assume, are produced not by the "unspecific factor" of the counselor's attitudes but by his skilled "technical" interventions, the exclusive possession of a trained professional counselor. If proof of the actual neglect of the attitudinal factor be needed, it is provided by the students' complaints. My astonishment in reading the questionnaires was not at what students wished for but at the evidence of how often these wishes were not met—even at a center which, influenced by the ideas of Maslow and Angyal, emphasized growth and health, not pathology. Newcomers to the center's staff contributed more than their share of tactless questions, pessimistic prognoses, and stereotyped, unsubstantiated interpretations; but all staff members were occasionally guilty of employing alienating devices, many of them residues of techniques learned during their training.

It is true, of course, that the positive human approach is not a prerogative of counselors and that its efficacy is not limited to therapy. The "therapeutic ingredients" have favorable effects on well-functioning and disturbed people in a wide range of situations. Still, as the research findings strongly suggest, the attitudinal factor might well prove to be *the* therapeutic agent, the common component of all successful therapies, no matter how conducted and with what clients. Some gifted explorers of the workings of therapy arrived at this conclusion on their own; their accounts of their discoveries are most revealing. Hellmuth Kaiser (1965) has formulated his shift in orientation in a clear-cut radical way. His dictum that the therapist's task is "to be therapeutic" he spells out as follows. The therapist must be a person for whom establishing straightforward communication with another is an end in itself and who is not hampered in the pursuit of this crucial interest, either by his theoretical convictions or by any protective patterns of his own. If the therapist *is* this kind of person, he will not withdraw, psychologically, from the patient in the face of persisting obstacles to communication, and this is what matters; what he and the patient should *do* need not be legislated; it can be left fluid. "When . . . one has managed not to withdraw but to stick *with* the patient, and has in this way experienced how it feels to talk 'straight' with him, without being haunted by the obsession that one has to do the 'right thing'—well, one might stumble again later, but at least one has an image of what therapeutic communication could be" (Kaiser, 1965, p. 162). Angyal, who has developed his theory of therapy in much greater detail, also concludes that what the therapist *is* with the patient matters more than what he does: "Sincere sympathy and helpfulness are the minimum and the essence; without them there is no recovery" (Angyal, 1965, p. 305). This does not sound too difficult, since every therapist feels that he is a person of sympathy. Kaiser, however, states emphatically that his requirement for the therapist is much more radical than the words seem to convey. It is not easy to give up all props of fixed concepts and rules and to enter with the client "the unchartered field of undiluted humanity." The gains however are great: "The difference with regard to freedom of response between the one who is trained for a communicative attitude and the one who is not can be tremendous" (Kaiser, 1965, p. 168).

Before taking up the issue of attitude training, let us look at the circumstance so vividly conveyed by Kaiser: that a therapist's reliance on rules, theories, classifications, and strategies may impede his free communication with his client even if he conscientiously abstains from technical language and from theoretical discussions;

this very avoidance in fact is in obedience to a rule. What kind of counselor-held theories, one might ask, are most likely to hinder the requisite free interchange between him and the client? *Any* theory can have the effect of making the patient feel disregarded or violated if it is held by its proponent to be *the* truth, not just one profitable way to order the observable facts. But the hampering effect of an uncritically held theory will be the greater, the more specific its statements and the further its concepts from those of "naive psychology," from what the client, along with all of us, assumes about human perceiving, thinking, liking, wishing, striving. Holistic concepts, of the kind used by Angyal, do not abridge free exploration of the client's individual patterns; being quite general, they can accommodate a wide range of concrete content. They also counteract our predilection, demeaning and discouraging to the client, for comparing his state not with his own potentialities but with some external yardstick—for example, some unidimensional scale supposed to measure, unequivocally, the person's maturity or pathology. Such a scale does not make much sense if each person harbors a system of neurosis along with a system of health; though one is dominant, both can be strongly developed.

One advantage of Angyal's conceptualization of neurosis and treatment is precisely that of providing a clear explanation of the central importance of the relationship factor in therapy. His theory of "universal ambiguity" assigns a conceptual locus to the otherwise vague idea of the neurotic's "real" or "healthy" self. In his view, the "healthy" self is that individual patterning of personality which has taken place in an atmosphere free of threat, in the framework of confident self-acceptance. To discover this submerged nuclear pattern under the neurotic distortions and pretensions is a task even more important than outlining and discrediting the neurotic pattern, the residue of traumatic experiences, and at least as exacting. Angyal describes various possible approaches to the goal of reviving and developing the patient's healthy self, but he considers two of them of primary importance: (1) uncovering the healthy roots of the patient's unhealthy attitudes and (2) fostering a "communicative" relationship between therapist and patient. If the therapist, no matter what he discovers, continues to value the patient as a person and to show him sincere respect, the patient gradually becomes aware that the therapist sees in him, despite all his faults, a likable and worthwhile human being. Thus, it begins to dawn on him that there is something within him that is different from his neurosis, something that stands outside his neurotic way of life. The presence of the therapist as a real person, not just a screen for projection, is the most important point of anchorage outside the neurosis that the therapeutic situation offers the patient; it is up to the therapist to utilize it. Therapy cannot be effective unless it attends to both parts of its dual task: demolishing neurosis and fostering health.

But if the therapist influences the patient by his genuine attitudes, by what he in reality is, can he learn *to be* the kind of person he perhaps is not, one who will benefit rather than harm his patients? People differ greatly, it is true, in their ability to provide the "therapeutic ingredients," but this does not mean that this ability cannot be developed. What is required, of course, is a genuine change in one's way of viewing the other, not merely the adoption of some behavioral patterns commonly assumed to express positive attitudes. An attempt to cultivate "warmth" by adopting behavioral patterns may result in what one client described as her counselor's "very warm veneer." More to the point is to learn to keep in focus the other person's humanness, "otherness," and the potential for healthy functioning which is uniquely his. The therapist must be able to spot and drop those personal concerns that interfere with this focusing. Both Kaiser and Angyal leave no doubt that therapeutic, or "communicative," attitudes can be developed and are in fact being developed by therapists: "Though attitudes cannot be taught, they can be learned and developed. The therapist learns his in very personal ways as he gradually discovers that, apart from methods and techniques, he influences his patients by what he is and as he realizes the responsibility this places on him. One can grow as a therapist simply by reaching this conviction and by being constantly aware of the issues involved. There is no substitute for this experiential learning, but it can be facilitated by a discussion that sharpens awareness of these issues" (Angyal, 1965, p. 317).

The feasibility of attitude training has been confirmed experimentally by the same group of researchers who explored and confirmed the efficacy of the therapists' positive attitudes. Truax and Carkhuff (1967), in working with graduate students and lay counselors, demonstrated conclusively that a judicious combination of experiential learning with a discussion of relevant issues and theories does produce the desired results. Within a relatively short time, the beginners became able to function at levels of "therapeutic conditions" close to those provided by a comparison group made up of experienced effective therapists. One essential part of the program was participation in a quasi-therapy group in which training- and work-related personal issues were freely discussed. In functioning as leaders, the authors aimed to provide the group with the "therapeutic ingredients" in full measure. Another important part of the training was the study of different therapists' responses to clients' remarks and practice in distinguishing those that did convey understanding and genuine acceptance from those that did not, or in fact conveyed the opposite. A carefully constructed and exemplified five-step scale for scoring the level of the "therapeutic conditions" reflected in counselors' comments was used extensively as a tool in this practice. It was also used to measure the level of functioning that trained students achieved in their work, as it had been used in the studies that established the existence of a correlation between the therapists' attitudes and outcomes.

After this impressive confirmation of many therapists' observations, we can no longer disregard the evidence that a positive empathic focusing on the client is a precondition of success, that such focusing is far from common, and that it can be learned. One may wonder, in fact, why it has not been learned by more therapists in their posttraining experience, since it is certainly possible to discover the effects of one's practices on one's clients. The method most frequently used for discarding one important source of relevant information is the attribution of all client complaints to "transference fantasies" or other neurotic distortions. What is typically disregarded is, first of all, that the presence of such distortions must be demonstrated, not postulated, and, second, that even when clearly present they do not put out of commission the client's realistic perception; it is not an either-or or all-or-none business. When students talk about being reduced to the impersonal status of an object to be analyzed, or the humiliating and confusing experience of being proved "wrong" by faulty or unfair means, of being made to feel small and stupid in the face of the therapist's superior "secret knowledge," these feelings, regardless of their neurotic aspects and uses, usually have some of their roots in the counselor's actual behavior, if not usually in his intentions. Committed to what we consider aspects of our professional identity, we hold on tenaciously to attitudes and practices that increase the neurotic patient's feeling of "wrongness," isolation, and helplessness and thus confirm his assumption that he lacks personal worth and that his environment is hostile or indifferent.

Role of College Work in Promoting Effective Therapy

Given the current unsatisfactory state of therapy, no self-respecting program of counselor or therapist training can omit from its offerings work aimed at developing the requisite attitudes. What role can college work play in providing good training for young therapists (or for that matter retraining for older ones)? I am not thinking here of the role that graduate programs can play (and have played) in sponsoring experimentation in the training of counselors and a systematic evaluation of its results. I have in mind the actual counseling work done on campus insofar as it is conducted by therapists in training as part of their fieldwork for various clinical programs, or by staff members who are recent graduates of such programs.

For a learner the advantages of working in a student counseling center are great, although they can be fully realized only if its funding and staffing enables the center to fulfill its function as a comprehensive service for the student community. This means to welcome all comers, to see them without delay, and to provide at least a modicum of effective help to all. Such conditions make "triage" unnecessary; if no one is to be excluded, there is no need to raise barriers by decreeing that this or that condition cannot be dealt with on campus. The issue then is to discover in each individual case what might be useful to do and how it can best be done. In some settings the discovery may be relegated to a testing program expected to provide the answer, and the decision may be relegated to a senior staff member. If such routines are firmly established, the beginner will be deprived of essential opportunities for learning.

Fortunately, in most colleges this routine, if it exists, is sufficiently fluid to enable the counselor to discover for himself the pros and cons of an evaluation preceding counseling. At Brandeis, after the routine administration of some projective group tests to freshmen had been dropped as useless, the counselors were free to refer students outside for testing or to give them any relevant tests they themselves had found useful. After some experimenting all of them found that what they were able to learn from the "unprocessed" students in initial sessions was much more useful than testing and provided a much better introduction to counseling.

If nothing and nobody is interposed between the new client and the counselor, the counselor will come face to face with a fairly wide range of people and problems. If the service has lived up to its goal of being of use to students with *any* kind and degree of personal problems, some seriously disturbed clients are likely to appear, but the majority will consist of relatively well-functioning people. Those whom the beginner, after discussion, will decide to transfer to a more experienced counselor will be exceptions, though for a few of those he keeps he may have to seek consultation much more often than for the rest. What is important is that he will be faced with a variety of problems, situations, and requests, for which he has no ready-made solutions. He must sort matters out. How is this freshman's panic best dealt with? Will this senior be served best by a referral for vocational testing? Should this student be taken to the infirmary without delay or persuaded to telephone his family? Should the support of the dormitory counselor, or of a trusted teacher, or of some relevant support group be mobilized in the case of another? What should he tell a student who reports the suicidal talk of his roommate? Is this student ready to engage on the spot in a session of realistic problem solving? Is another asking, confusedly, for a clarification of the nature and promise of counseling? Should this "stray patient" be helped to return to his outside therapist, or, on the contrary, be helped to leave him? Solutions are rarely obvious, and decisions have to be made—fortunately, not all of them speedily. In an attempt to reach a plausible solution, a shared decision, the novice will be led to explore the situation with the student. If he decides unilaterally, he will soon discover that such decisions may be worse than useless; the student's acceptance of any plan must be more than a gesture. The more new clients he sees, the sooner he will learn to utilize the impetus that brought them there for speedily clarifying their needs and identifying possible solutions. Thus, already at this early stage of his contact with potential clients, an alert counselor will be led by the demands of his job to learn to make the task of the initial sessions a shared enterprise.

As the beginning counselor settles down to work with clients not preselected in advance for this or that kind of treatment— "support," short therapy, referral—he will keep trying to provide each with what seems needed and keep finding out what he is able to do in each case. He will discover in the process that some of the generalizations he has heard about the needs and potentialities of people with particular kinds of problems are faulty, and he may start replacing them with tentative generalizations based on his own observations, only to find out soon enough that these are not always valid either. His discoveries will be enhanced if he has a chance to work with a large number of clients, since many of them will prove similar in important respects. Richness of experience mediated by contact with large numbers can be easily obtained in college work. The counselor will increasingly draw on this experience as he explores again and again with each client what is required, what is feasible, what seems to work best.

The main value of training in a college setting results not from the size and range of the counselor's clientele but from its quality. At this stage of development many adolescents are introspective, critical, and self-critical; intent on coming to terms with themselves and their world; and more open and flexible than they are likely to be a few years later. Whatever the reasons, a sizable proportion of those who apply to an established, well-staffed campus service will make an uncommonly good use of the opportunity for pursuing self-knowledge and will move in counseling fast and far; quite a few will benefit strikingly within a relatively short time. Work with such clients is bound to make the counselor more optimistic about chances of success; his well-founded hopefulness communicates itself to the clients, promoting in turn good outcomes. The counselor will also become more discriminating in his appraisals of the results of his work. Knowing what really good outcomes look like, he will be less tempted to stretch his concept of success to outcomes that are far removed from this standard.

Whether they move fast or slowly, most students are able to observe their own and their counselors' reactions in sessions and are willing to discuss them. They can teach the therapist a great deal about the actual effects of his interventions and discredit some of his untested assumptions much better than a supervisor can. Being less in awe of the "expert" than are their elders, students will, with very little encouragement, give ample feedback to one who is willing to listen. As a result, the counselor's perceptions of the client's state will be more accurate and his method of conveying them more effective. By inviting and accepting client feedback, we remove an implicit taboo on the discussion of a vital area, the quality of our interactions, and clear the path to a two-way communication, which is likely to be transferred to other situations by the client. This, of course, can take place only if the student's comments are listened to with an open mind, not automatically "interpreted" nor merely "reflected." For the counselor, furthering client feedback implies a shift from the positions of a disciple, a believer, or an artist to that of a fellow explorer: one eager to have his discoveries or assumptions checked by empirical facts. This shift can motivate the counselor to start keeping records and collecting data on the course and outcome of his work.

As he listens to the students, the counselor will have many insights, developing gradually or suddenly. He will realize the value of straightforward communication and an egalitarian approach, the negative value of passivity and detachment, the destructiveness of some standard interpretations, and the invalidity of any rules formulated as absolutes. His growing insight into the workings of therapy and into himself as therapist will keep him excited about his work. His enthusiasm will grow rather than wane with time; instead of becoming complacent and routinized with experience, he will remain curious and become wiser. The counselor may even benefit as a person from becoming a better therapist. Although the attitudes demanded by his work will be easier to maintain in the relatively limited and protected counseling contact than elsewhere, their spread to other situations is possible; his interaction with others may improve. Professional and personal growth is obviously not the prerogative of college counselors; therapists from all walks of life—and not only they—will recognize themselves in this description of one who keeps learning. In pointing out the vivifying effects of working with today's college students, I speak as one who has experienced these effects very strongly and who subsequently has had the pleasure of observing and promoting similar shifts in others.

Optimal Organization of College Centers

A college service's potential as a training place can be fully realized only if conditions are met that are necessary for making students attend it year after year, in large numbers, with a wide range of complaints, a situation reflecting a high level of satisfaction with the service. They will be satisfied, and will believe that the center is for them, for *all* *students,* if all are welcomed and served quickly by competent, experienced counselors—not perhaps to the optimal extent, but providing something useful to all comers. What is required for this state of affairs is obvious: plenty of counselors (in my judgment, no less than one full-time counselor for about 400 students enrolled in school) and a low rate of turnover of staff, enabling the workers to capitalize on accumulating experience. Both require ample financing.

Another condition necessary for student satisfaction and trust is the maintenance of confidentiality—usually defined as the counselor's and the service's promise not to divulge to anyone the fact of the student's attendance and the content of his communications, except with his permission and/or in some special dangerous situation. This is the minimum guarantee a counseling service must provide to be accepted by the students as theirs. Actually, however, there is a much wider issue which determines whether such agreements can be reasonably formulated and reliably implemented: the basic issue of the function of the campus counseling or mental health service. The service is for the students, everyone will agree, but it will not be equally obvious to some that it cannot be the students' unless it is for *students alone.* Should not a service that is part of a school, one might ask, serve the institution as a whole, not just one of its segments? The answer is that it serves the institution only by serving that group for the sake of which the institution exists; it cannot serve it by assisting the administration in its dealings with students, because the unavoidable ambiguity of this position would undermine student trust. The clear realization that the client-counselor relationship is incompatible with the exercise of power requires the counseling service to refuse participation, overt or covert, in any administrative decisions about individual students, the actual or potential clients. The service must also have the right to define, in its statement of the confidentiality policy, the conditions that justify suspending this policy and also the right to determine in each given case whether these conditions have in fact been met. The counselor who knows the student is the one to decide (after consultation with his colleagues and if need be with others) whether his client's state requires notifying the family and/or the administration and justifies doing it without the client's permission. This degree of autonomy is necessary if students are to rely on the counselors' ability to make decisions that are in *their* best interests, not in the interests of the administration. To many all this will seem pedantic. Since the settings that place no restriction on their collaboration with the administration still have students applying for help, they can view the two tasks as compatible, even as complementary, as serving students directly and indirectly. But how many students apply to them, and in how great a distress? I can state on good evidence that a psychological service will not be accepted by the student body as a whole, will not be used freely and widely, unless it has established itself, by word and by deed, as being for the *students,* for *all* students, and for students *alone.*

Within the limits dictated by this position, counselors are free to explore, if they wish, activities outside their primary task, that of working with students. They may help spread pertinent information on campus: about symptoms of serious disturbance, about their service's work, about effective ways of referring students; they may decide in some cases to intercede with the school authorities for some students they know well. A counselor may be able occasionally to fulfill a faculty or a staff member's request for help with some interpersonal or personal problem by providing a non-authoritarian consultation, or by working out a referral for him or her. He may agree, or offer, to teach volunteers among faculty, staff, and students how to be of use to those coming to them with personal problems. If he is versed in group work, he may help set up and run groups of people with shared concerns and problems who can offer each other assistance and support. If he is an experimenting teacher, he can promote self-knowledge among his students by the methods he uses in his courses or set up a system for evaluating the counseling center's work. The slogan "for students only" is meant merely to assert the priority of the counselor's main and most promising task and to serve as a criterion of all other activities' admissibility and usefulness. Will a certain kind of consulting with administration or faculty endanger confidentiality or the students' trust in confidentiality? Will it cause confusion in their minds about the role and the power of the counselor and interfere with their free use of the center? Will certain instructional talks result merely in a greater demand for direct service, demands on the nonexistent staff time? Is some innovative activity likely to be useful enough to justify taking time away from direct work with most responsive, promising clients? What evidence does one need to decide this, and how can one get this evidence? These are the questions the director of counseling must raise and answer, in the course of deciding on policies, if the service is not to fall victim to conflicting pressures and demands.

The issue of provision of staff time is of paramount importance for the design of mental health work on campus and also the main determinant of its fates. Activities that aim to benefit students indirectly by sensitizing others in the school environment to their emotional needs are not a substitute for counseling proper, for a relatively long period of psychological work carried out by relatively skilled counselors. This becomes obvious if one considers that although not many students among those applying to a well-established college counseling service are severely or acutely disturbed, only 10–20 percent have very minor developmental or situational problems, requiring no skilled handling and no commitment of time. In view of the more extensive and pressing needs of the rest, activities other than counseling, even if potentially useful, should either be kept at a minimum or—in a situation of affluence—provided for separately, after the service's basic budgetary needs have been met. This is not how it works, however. The allowance of staff time required to provide some effective counseling or therapeutic help to all students who need it and can use it surpasses by far what is currently provided in most schools. Given this situation, the current emphasis on working through the environment, the introduction of social psychiatry to the campus, is to a great extent an effort to do something useful and not as time-consuming as counseling. The trained counselors' time is to be spent in supervision of those untrained or in other activities—consultative, instructional, political—in which, incidentally, most of the counselors have not been trained and are not too interested. To the extent that these activities can be proven useful to students, they are certainly better than nothing. I have found nothing, however, in my reading and my experience to justify the hopes of the would-be "agents of change" for achieving major reforms of the academic establishment. The policies and practices of universities, or their predominant social "atmospheres," are not likely to be decisively changed through the efforts of the campus mental health workers, even in the rare cases when the latter are able to offer well-founded practical advice to educational administrators. In some instances, the social psychiatrists' environmental slogans seem to be merely a dressing for their established practices of serving as administrators' advisers, practices that effectively prevent students from approaching these staff members as potential sources of help. Other proposals for changing the counselors' role are well meant but not well worked out; they strike one as vague or utopian.

The common ailment of the college mental health or counseling centers—insufficient funding, insufficient staff time—may or may not lead to a search for alternative ways of serving the cause of mental health in school. In either case, this lack invariably results in reduction and deterioration of direct service to students; that is, in the loss of a uniquely effective way of achieving substantial results on a large scale. This loss can be clearly perceived only in those uncommon settings that have known better times; there one can compare the earlier state of affairs with what happens when, through reduction of funding and/or the growth of the student body, time available for counseling gradually dwindles away. As the counselor-student ratio rolls down, the waiting lists, the almost arbitrary selection of clients, the hurried referrals, the rush, the premature and ill-prepared terminations, the counselors' mood of frustration—

all combine to impair the quality of the service's work and to under-mine its reputation on campus; fewer and fewer students apply. A counseling service that keeps reducing its allowance of time per student and/or sees a diminishing proportion of the student popula-tion forfeits its usefulness and its promise and may eventually be reduced to the functions of "evaluation and referral." These may be useful to a few, but the majority of applicants who might be in-duced into the counseling provided in school are not ready to enter outside therapy and are not likely to benefit from a dead-end evaluation.

To give an idea of what can be done if provision of time is maintained at the necessary high level by funding comparable to that of a large popular academic department, I shall extrapolate from what has been actually done under relatively favorable condi-tions—not too often, but in more places than one. If a well-funded psychological service has established itself on campus (preferably as a part of the educational system), if it is known to be autonomous, reliable, and prepared to serve all comers competently and without much delay, students will come in steadily growing numbers, with problems ranging from minor to major; "psych counseling" will be viewed as assisting personal growth—an opportunity, not a stigma. If one can maintain the competence level of the counselors by keeping the turnover of staff to a minimum, almost all those who come will receive something of value. For some it will be assistance in quickly getting out of a blind alley; if the counselor is skilled in consulting, this achievement may require only a few sessions—with luck, only one. Others will get assistance in managing an emergency, a major crisis or breakdown, in a way that may maximize their chances to benefit from the upset in the long run. The majority of applicants will be well served by a period of work varying between ten and thirty sessions if it is conducted by a counselor whose skills are governed by the personal attitudes needed for focusing on the client rather than by any rigid theoretical beliefs. Of advantage for a college counselor is also a readiness to pay attention to and to get therapeutic leverage from the various typical features of student life: teachers, courses, choices of major, current ideological issues, vacations, reunions with family, decisions to be made for the future, predetermined limits on counseling. With competent and unrushed handling of the initial sessions, fewer students would quickly drop out of counseling. With adequate time and close attention to each student's needs and progress in counseling, the number of those who terminate with the certainty of having been helped, not just of having obtained insights, would increase. Their percent would grow beyond what we have evidence for in the Brandeis questionnaire data: about 75 percent of that half of the students seen during the year who answer the questionnaire.

The group of those who feel that they have been helped includes two major subgroups (which do not represent any diagnostic categories): those who move vigorously, often under their own steam, and mature a great deal in a short time; and those who, handicapped by their rigid patterns or their circumstances, move slowly and usually require a great deal of activity from the counselor. On completion of counseling, members of the first group usually feel that they have obtained all the assistance they need and will keep moving on their own; some of them demonstrate and report spectacular gains. The typical achievement of the second group can be described as a shift of perspective; it results in a lessening of confusion, in a clearer and more hopeful view of themselves and of their chances in life; for some of these people this is indeed an impressive achievement, an astonishing change. The shift of perspective usually leads to the decision to continue therapy outside or to resume it later on; the counselor may be called upon to help work out a promising referral. There will always be some clients for whom the period of counseling results in no gains. In such instances a counselor who is willing to explore with the client what has been missing or what has gone wrong, and to admit any errors he discovers, can counteract the student's discouragement and self-blame, perhaps point the way to a better-prepared attempt. A college counseling service able to further effectively the emotional maturation, or emotional reeducation, of a large number of students, as many perhaps as 50–60 percent of each graduating class, can indeed view itself as contributing a great deal to the mental health of the population; it can also fulfill its potential as a uniquely effective training place for the counselors and the therapists of tomorrow.

In conclusion, a few words about what can be learned from the social and professional developments of the last decades. What bearing do changes in student attitudes and the emergence of new approaches to therapy have on the design of psychological work in colleges? Let us start with the students. During the 1960s, friends used to ask me whether my work was made difficult, or was greatly changed, by the students' revolutionary mood. For the bulk of my work this was clearly not the case. The most prominent earlier "revolutionaries" of the school, the leaders in any fight against the administration, were never likely to appear at the center, except in case of breakdown; their number may have grown during the 1960s. But the students who did come and did get involved in counseling continued to deal with the same basic issues: settling accounts with parents, finding one's own course, finding one's way to another person. Their ideals and their options were changing, to be sure; but what had proved effective—or ineffective—in my approach to their predecessors continued to be so with them. On the whole, I felt no call for a radical change of proceedings. This, however, is not to deny the existence of special cases, nor of the general problem. A striking disparity of values between the generations, created by fast-moving social and ideological changes, presents a college counseling center with problems which one must take into account in deciding on various policies and on staffing.

Over the years I heard many complaints from the students about the difficulty of working with the counselors who adhered to the traditional middle-class values which the students had rejected. There can be little doubt that trust is furthered and initial contact between student and counselor facilitated if they are aware of some shared opinions, or of some commonalities in their background and experience. In the absence of specific information about counselors, the students will, with good reason, assume that such similarities are more likely to be found in younger than older counselors; it is mandatory, therefore, for all college centers to have some young people on their staffs. On the other hand, not all students prefer to work with those whose age is closer to theirs; some factors favor a different choice. Many students come to the center because, while there is no shortage of age-equals in their world, their need for a personal relationship with a mature adult is not adequately satisfied by their few brief contacts with busy teachers. To quote one student's questionnaire comment: "It was good to talk for once to one who was clearly and unequivocally an adult!" Then there is also the factor of greatly wished-for competence based on experience, which is assumed to grow with age. Most students, in choosing between two counselors, will choose the one who shares their values only if all other things are equal—in particular, if he appears to be no less competent than the other. Some of our younger counselors shared the students' new values fully and made this known, but only those among them who proved highly gifted as therapists came to enjoy a lasting popularity. I myself have never felt greatly handicapped by the difference of my background and my opinions from those of the successive generations of college students. When special cultural similarities were present, as with some foreign students, I felt that they were an advantage, making for an easier start; but in cases of conspicuous differences, the need to find productive ways of dealing with them, to establish communication in the face of some obstacles, could be a stimulus to invention. With some clients whose beliefs were of great importance to them, I did feel at times that a counselor who spoke their language would have a better chance of success than I. If this feeling was shared by the student, I acted on it by arranging either an appropriate transfer or a periodic consultation. In general, however, after counseling Brandeis students through the years when their differences from the parental orientation grew to a peak and then diminished, I was left with the impression that only a few students truly wanted their counselors to share all their values.

I believe that the majority of students who worry about the difference of values are not so much intent on identity as on getting some assurance that the difference will not cause the counselor to fail on the job. Will he or she be able to understand them, to appreciate the personal importance of their beliefs, not try to convert them? These apprehensions have a realistic basis, but the threats need not materialize. The key to the situation lies in the counselor's own feeling about the difference and in his handling of the relevant situations. I have witnessed much soul searching by counselors as to the attitude they should take toward the students' new "deviant" values: the use of drugs, rejection of marriage or of the traditional roles of men and women, acceptance of homosexuality. For some it seemed to be a choice between two evils. Should they alienate students by contradicting their beliefs, or should they deceive them by abstaining from objections and perhaps even see them get into destructive situations without attempting to prevent such a course? Actually, these are false alternatives, a fact which the soul searching may help to discover. Differences of ideologies cause difficulties in counseling only if the counselor's views are so dogmatic that he cannot see what may be valid and valuable in a different approach. Most of us are only too ready to believe that what we teach and practice is not only the truth but the whole truth; anyone who advocates enlarged perspective may be accused of shallow eclecticism, if not of a refusal to stand up and be counted. Yet a larger and more differentiated view would enable a counselor to find a common language with his clients, without their having to agree on all points and without their feeling compelled to convert each other.

In thinking of human needs and values, we must distinguish the general trends that are common to all humans from the many expressions of these trends, which may vary from epoch to epoch, culture to culture, person to person. The appreciation of the relativity of these values and of the limited validity of all specific beliefs is furthered by acquaintance with anthropological studies and by personal experience of various cultures and culture changes. Such studies and experiences also demonstrate that, while values central to a given culture may be formulated in a very absolute fashion, the actual practices of a viable culture never follow the rigid guidelines resulting from such exclusive emphasis on one way of seeing or judging the world (Spiegel, 1971; Papajohn and Spiegel, 1975). Different emotions and moods, different ways of perceiving, thinking, valuing, and acting, are experienced by different people and by the same person in different situations or at different times, complementing each other and making for richness of life. They are not mutually exclusive or contradictory, unless someone creates conflict by making one or the other an absolute value and leaves no place to the others. An earmark of such an absolutistic belief is that it demands allegiance, a decision for or against it; it dispenses with the natural methods of testing the value of a given course of action— that is, by considering all the motives involved in choosing it, on the one hand, and the results that are most likely to evolve, on the other.

It is possible to answer yes or no to the question whether one believes in the divinity of Jesus Christ, but I never felt it possible to deal in the same way with the issues of "believing" in marriage, or in premarital intercourse, or in combining a "primary relationship" with several "secondary" ones; instead, I would try to demonstrate to the questioner that the question as asked was meaningless. Sometimes students come to the center for the express purpose of getting assistance in deciding what values or ideologies to make their own—in deciding, for example, whether sharing of sexual partners is permitted—or perhaps even demanded—by their concept of desirable human relationships. I would agree to try to be of use in this endeavor, but the ensuing circular or barren discussions would soon demonstrate that ideologies in the abstract are not a promising topic. The student would realize that, to be relevant to his life, a discussion of values would have to draw on his own wishes, thoughts, and experiences, both present and past; and the counseling would proceed along those personal lines.

Familiarity with the factual evidence available on some problematic issues (such as effects of various drugs, taken with different frequency, in different amounts and situations) helps the counselor respond in differentiated ways rather than in terms of moral absolutes, which only would make students avoid him. If the situation causes worry, the counselor can speak up, and speak strongly. Under other circumstances, one can work with the material of feelings and insights experienced during "trips" or from other stimuli favored by students; one can acknowledge their usefulness but also point out the advantages of some alternative sources of vital experiences. One can sympathize with the student's wish to get away from mere words as vehicles of interpersonal messages, yet demonstrate to some fanatic of nonverbal communication how slim his chances are to convey complex meanings through wordless staring.

The absence of reliable factual evidence on some hotly debated issues, or the presence of contradictory evidence, should help us realize that our theories and beliefs are not much more than tentative hypotheses or expressions of personal preferences. In fact, given the multiple determination of all human behavior, the participation in it of both personal and environmental factors, all explanations that acknowledge one factor only are suspect, whatever factor is chosen. I do not anticipate ever getting reliable proof that all or most cases of homosexuality are physiologically determined *or,* on the other hand, that sexual preference is always the result of learning, taking place early or late, under normal or under traumatic circumstances. The nature of a person's individual sexual preferences, their meaning for him, and his conflicts about them must be explored anew in each case; the decision about the course to take is the client's, but it should follow exploration, not precede it. The same holds for the choice of a life style.

It is important for the counselor to realize—and to convey to the student—that all beliefs can have different roots in different people and more than one root in the same person. They also have different functions, and constructive and destructive uses. If this differentiation is not made and clearly maintained, the student who is strongly invested in the values he subscribes to may try to keep them intact by seeking a like-minded counselor, or by declaring any discussion of his views to be out of bounds. Some students will quiz the prospective counselor or therapist on how he stands on this or that issue. Does he believe, for example, that radicalism, or feminism, is a symptom of neurosis, nothing more than a continued revolt against one's father, to be "cured" by therapy? In my reply I try to convey to the questioner two things: I do not assume of any belief that it is "nothing but" a neurotic symptom, but any belief can have some of its roots in traumatic experiences and/or be put to neurotic uses; radical beliefs are no exception. I respect people's right to varying beliefs, but I don't hold any of them sacred in the sense of being exempt from all examination. Most students accept this point of view as a general guideline, but it takes many instances of the counselor's actually making such differentiations for them to feel reassured that the baby will not be thrown out with the bath water. The use of ideologies to safeguard stabilized neurotic developments faces the counselors with a difficult task, one in which it is easy to fail if one gives in to one's own trend to dogmatism and the wish to convert the heretic. We do well to remind both ourselves and our clients that when the student's neurotic orientation loses dominance his beliefs are likely to lose their rigidity or immutability, but they will not necessarily change in content; transplanted into his new orientation, they may in fact become effective guidelines for a constructive reordering of his life.

What bearing do the new movements, theories, and techniques of therapy have on the psychological counseling in colleges? I believe there is an affinity between the two, or should be. Some of the early and the recent innovations have been developed with student-clients; college services are good places for experimenting, particularly when they have connections with the appropriate academic departments of the school. The graduate students, the interns, the younger counselors on the regular staff will be eager to try out the novel methods they have learned about in their training. The academic research orientation should support experimentation and foster respect for evidence; the feedback from the student-clients will be articulate and informative, whether one experiments with variations of the psychodynamic approach or with those based on rival theories and employing novel techniques, verbal or nonverbal.

Within the psychoanalytic orientation there has been a revival in the last decades of an interest in legitimizing some variants of short-term treatment, a challenge to the persisting belief that only full-scale analysis is fully efficacious. This interest was dormant for a long time. In analytic circles, the highly promising beginning made by Alexander and French (1946) "led to nothing but endless hostility and controversy . . . purely because it was presented as a modification of psychoanalytic technique, instead of being presented as a technique of brief psychotherapy based on that of psychoanalysis" (Malan, 1975, pp. 280–281). In the meantime, short-term therapy has become the stock-in-trade of clinically oriented student counseling centers. Its development there has been influenced both by the ideas borrowed from psychoanalysis and by their early rival, Rogers' client-centered approach; many other influences, however, facilitated the adaptation of the counseling methods to these particular clients' situations, abilities, and needs. It is to be hoped that the new analytically oriented approaches to short-term therapy (Mann, 1961; Sifneos, 1972) will help bridge the gap between those counselors on the staffs of college centers whose approach has been shaped by years of working with students and the newcomers to the field, graduates of clinical programs; in the past, the training some of them received made them too passive in their approach to clients and unable to find any viable alternatives to long-term treatment. The inclusion of the new short-term therapies in the training of psychiatrists would make them better prepared for work in colleges and facilitate their integration with the rest of the staff. For most counselors these newly formulated treatment variants can be a stimulus to thinking and experimenting, without making it necessary for them to come to grips with entirely new sets of assumptions about what is effective in therapy.

The situation seems to be different with those therapeutic offerings that are radically new. Some of them are connected with systems of beliefs that tend to demand complete allegiance from the practitioners—as if one could not focus on a client's behavior without having to subscribe to some brand of behaviorism. I believe, on the contrary, that the new therapeutic offerings are best viewed not as competing and mutually exclusive schools of theory and practice but as a variety of approaches, a multiplicity of methods that may help us do justice to the multiple human problems and the multiple aspects of human functioning. Today many practitioners and many researchers share this acceptance of multiplicity; Lazarus and his associates (1976) have explicitly formulated one design of a "multimodal" approach to treatment. Some hope that a rapprochement between the theories underlying different forms of therapy will be soon brought about by research on therapy and on therapy's outcomes. To my mind, the acknowledgment of multiplicity in humans and the acceptance of a multiple approach to treatment can be supported by a holistic theoretical framework much better than by any theory that gives primacy to some one segment or level of human functioning.

Apart from all issues of theory, the task that faces each of us is to evaluate the effectiveness of new methods and to try to discover the conditions that enhance or counteract their effects. In the absence of a body of well-conducted, mutually consistent evaluation studies, each of us will make his decisions on the basis of personal experiences and/or of reports that have happened to come our way. Over the years I have kept in touch with many former counselees who came to see our relationship as genuine, not as "merely professional." Among them were some quite disturbed young people who provided me with a record of their continued search for sources of help. One cannot generalize from the experience of twenty or twenty-five people; but, viewing their courses to date, I find that those who have experimented with a variety of approaches to the resolution of personal problems have fared better in the long run than those who merely changed therapists within the same traditional orientation. The alternative courses included approaches utilizing meditational techniques, work with fantasy and with movement, and various kinds of group work other than the customary group therapy: encounter groups, sensitivity training, Synanon games, Recovery self-help groups, religious retreats, and cocounseling (Jackins, 1964). One former counselee, as a result of a chance attendance at a lecture, got himself into the program of a Gestalt institute offering very intensive continuous work. At first he wrote that the going was hard: "I've felt very afraid to let go, to 'get into' anything; you've known that in me. Just those things that are hardest for me to do are those that the Gestalt groups are based on. At times I feel close to doing it, but only at times." Soon afterward he reported a breakthrough, a striking emotional experience that resulted in many changes. This was the beginning of my own interest in Gestalt therapy. I attended lectures, demonstrations, and workshops; made use of some of the methods myself; and subsequently referred several selected students, who had responded positively to my description of this method, to selected Gestalt therapists in the Boston area, most of them with good results. This group included some seriously disturbed students who had made several unsuccessful attempts to obtain help via traditional therapy. I also, with some success, referred selected students to therapists specializing in behavior modification—but only to those who, I knew, would relate well to clients and would use their knowledge of motivational dynamics both as a framework for their techniques and as a basis for discussions aimed at promoting insight. I can see no point in neglecting cognition when working with people of normal or superior intelligence, no matter what special methods one uses. Focusing on concrete issues is a strength of behavioral methods, but if one neglects the factors that promote integration—of which an awareness of connections and patterns is one—one will either fail to eliminate the symptoms or, eliminating them, will fail to affect the person's life very much.

The choice of new methods of approach need not be made blindly, but it can only be tentative. Rather than ask what kind of people would fit this or that method, we might experiment with how one can combine various approaches to serve a given person best. Different methods involve different capacities, which, though varying in prominence or degree, are present in all people; it should be more profitable to think in terms of combinations and sequences than in terms of alternatives. In one instance of severe neurotic malfunctioning, a school year of arduous counseling work resulted in a strongly felt shift of perspective, a crack in the neurotic structure; it was followed by a longer period of dynamically oriented behavior therapy in which fantasies embodying personal patterns of a wide bearing were used as material; clear-cut improvement resulted. The young man, not satisfied with having overcome his handicap, proceeded to work with a variety of novel approaches, including some meditational techniques. Subsequently, according to the testimony of the people who knew him at this stage and after, he displayed energy and vitality that were truly outstanding, not merely adequate. In another instance, a woman graduate student decided, at a certain point of her long-term therapy, to go through the two weekends' course of est; she hoped that this brief massive onslaught on neurosis would jolt her into entering the next, greatly feared, stage of her therapy; and, with her therapist's cooperation, it did. We may in time accumulate a large amount of material of this kind—reports of the experimentation pursued at present by many young people as well as by some therapeutic institutions that do not limit their work to any one method. I believe that college counseling services also should vary their offerings and attempt to evaluate the results systematically. I do hope, however, that we shall not be seduced by the promise of the new-look techniques into trying to solve the budgetary problem by substituting rap sessions or dramatic one-shot encounters for anything that requires more sustained effort from all concerned. The short duration of many of the recent endeavors to further personal growth places limits on their effectiveness. A reliably continuous relationship, a component of the old-style psychotherapy which a weekend workshop fails to provide, may be needed to assimilate and utilize the occasional dramatic experiences. Let me fall back on Kaiser's formulations. Having discarded all prescriptions for the therapist's specific activities, he maintains that "the purpose of therapy . . . demands no more nor less than that the patient spends sufficient time with a person of *certain personality characteristics* who is motivated to give his attention exclusively to the patient at the times they meet" (Kaiser, 1965, p. 158). "Certain personality characteristics" is what Kaiser underlines in this sentence, but in this context I would like to put emphasis on "sufficient time." The requisite characteristic is the therapist's genuine interest in establishing straightforward communication with people whose attitude, because of their neurosis, is uncommunicative and ambiguous. Time must be sufficient for him to convey this persistent intention in a varied, personal, and credible manner and for the patient to accept and explore this novel experience until its accumulated impact brings results by altering decisively the person's unspoken assumptions about himself and the world.

References

ALEXANDER, F., and FRENCH, T. M. *Psychoanalytic Therapy.* New York: Ronald Press, 1946.

ANGYAL, A. *Foundations for a Science of Personality.* New York: Commonwealth Fund, 1941. (Reprinted as a paperback; New York: Viking Press, 1972.)

ANGYAL, A. *Neurosis and Treatment: A Holistic Theory.* New York: Wiley, 1965. (Reprinted as a paperback; New York: Viking Press, 1973.)

BADER, L. J. "Feedback on Counseling: A Counselor's Use of a Questionnaire." *Professional Psychology,* 1974, *6,* 394–399.

BERGIN, A. E., and GARFIELD, S. L. (Eds.). *Handbook of Psychotherapy and Behavior Change.* New York: Wiley, 1971.

BLAINE, G. B., MCARTHUR, C. C., and OTHERS. *Emotional Problems of the Student.* New York: Appleton-Century-Crofts, 1961.

339

BORIS, H. "The *Seelsorger* in Rural Vermont." *International Journal of Group Psychotherapy,* 1971, *21,* 159–173.

BOY, A. V., and PINE, G. J. *The Counselor in the Schools: A Reconceptualization. Boston:* Houghton Mifflin, 1968.

BROWN, D. R. "Personality, College Environment, and Academic Productivity." In N. Sanford (Ed.), *The American College.* New York: Wiley, 1962.

CLARK, D. "Characteristics of Counseling Centers in Large Universities." *Personnel and Guidance Journal,* 1966, *44,* 817–823.

CONGDON, R. G., and LOTHROP, W. W. "Survey of College Counseling Practices in the United States." Unpublished manuscript, University of New Hampshire Library, 1961.

ERIKSON, E. H. *Childhood and Society.* New York: Norton, 1950.

FREUD, A. *The Ego and the Mechanisms of Defense.* London: Hogarth, 1942.

GLASSCOTE, R. M., FISHMAN, M. E., and OTHERS. *Mental Health on the Campus: A Field Study.* Washington, D.C.: American Psychiatric Association, 1973.

GORDON, T. *P.E.T.: Parent Effectiveness Training.* New York: Wyden, 1970.

GORDON, T. *T.E.T.: Teacher Effectiveness Training.* New York: Wyden, 1974.

HANFMANN, E. "Life at an Innovative College." Unpublished report to the Committee on Student Life, New College, Sarasota, Florida, 1970.

HANFMANN, E., JONES, R. M., BAKER, E., and KOVAR, L. *Psychological Counseling in a Small College.* Cambridge, Mass.: Schenkman, 1963.

HEIDER, F. *The Psychology of Interpersonal Relations.* New York: Wiley, 1958.

JACKINS, H. *The Human Side of Human Beings.* Seattle: Rational Island Press, 1964.

JONES, R. M. (Ed.) *Contemporary Educational Psychology.* New York: Harper & Row, 1966.

JONES, R. M. *Fantasy and Feeling in Education.* New York: Harper & Row, 1968.

JONES, R. M. *The Dream Poet*. Cambridge, Mass.: Schenkman, 1978.

KAHNE, M., and SCHWARTZ, C. "The College as a Psychiatric Workplace: A Sociological Perspective." *Psychiatry*, 1975, *38*, 107–123.

KAISER, H. "The Problem of Responsibility in Psychotherapy." *Psychiatry*, 1955, *18*, 205–211.

KAISER, H. *Effective Psychotherapy*. New York: Free Press, 1965.

KUBIE, L. S. "The Forgotten Man of Education." *Harvard Alumni Bulletin*, 1954, *56*, 349–353.

LAMB, D. W., SUTTER, E. L., and PARRISH, J. H. "A Survey of College and University Counseling Centers." Unpublished manuscript, Memphis State University, 1969.

LAZARUS, A. A., and OTHERS. *Multi-Modal Behavior Therapy*. New York: Springer, 1976.

LOW, A. *Mental Health Through Will Training*. Boston: Christopher, 1950.

MALAN, D. H. *A Study of Brief Psychotherapy*. New York: Plenum, 1975.

MANN, J. *Time-Limited Psychotherapy*. Cambridge, Mass.: Harvard University Press, 1961.

NIXON, R. E. *The Art of Growing: A Guide to Psychological Maturity*. New York: Random House, 1962.

OETTING, E. R., IVEY, A. E., and WEIGEL, R. G. *The College and University Counseling Center*. Washington, D.C.: American Personnel and Guidance Association, 1970.

PAPAJOHN, J., and SPIEGEL, J. P. *Transactions in Families: A Modern Approach for Resolving Cultural and Generational Conflicts*. San Francisco: Jossey-Bass, 1975.

PERRY, W. *Forms of Intellectual and Ethical Development in the College Years*. New York: Holt, Rinehart and Winston, 1968.

PIAGET, J. *The Psychology of Intelligence*. New York: Harcourt, 1950.

RANK, O. *The Trauma of Birth*. New York: Harcourt, 1929.

RANK, O. *Will Therapy: An Analysis of the Therapeutic Process in Terms of Relationship*. New York: Knopf, 1936.

SHLIEN, J. M., MOSAK, H. H., and DREIKURS, R. "Effects of Time Limits: A Comparison of Client-Centered and Adlerian Psychotherapy." *American Psychologist,* 1960, *15,* 415.

SCHMIEDEBERG, M. "Values and Goals in Psychotherapy." *Psychiatric Quarterly,* 1958, *32,* 233–265.

SIFNEOS, P. E. *Short-Term Psychotherapy and Emotional Crisis.* Cambridge, Mass.: Harvard University Press, 1972.

SPIEGEL, J. P. *Transactions: Interplay Between Individual, Family, and Society.* New York: Aronson, 1971.

STEWART, L. H., and WARNATH, C. F. *The Counselor and Society: A Cultural Approach.* Boston: Houghton Mifflin, 1965.

SZASZ, T. S. "The Psychiatrist as Double Agent." *Transaction,* October 1967, *4,* 18–24.

TAFT, J. *The Dynamics of Therapy in a Controlled Relationship.* New York: Dover, 1962.

TRUAX, C. B., and CARKHUFF, R. R. *Toward Effective Counseling and Psychotherapy.* Chicago: Aldine, 1967.

VYGOTSKY, L. S. *Thought and Language.* Cambridge, Mass.: M.I.T. Press, 1962.

WARNATH, C. F. "Therapy for All." *Contemporary Psychology,* 1964, *9,* 399–400.

WARNATH, C. F., and ASSOCIATES. *New Directions for College Counselors: A Handbook for Redesigning Professional Roles.* San Francisco: Jossey-Bass, 1973.

YABLONSKY, L. *Synanon: The Tunnel Back.* Baltimore: Penguin Books, 1967.

Index

DATE DUE